Playing Chess with the Devil

Zhang Yawen

Published by
ACA Publishing Ltd.
University House
11-13 Lower Grosvenor Place
London SW1W 0EX, UK
Tel: +44 (0)20 7834 7676
Fax: +44 (0)20 7973 0076
Email: info@alaincharlesasia.com
Web: www.alaincharlesasia.com
Beijing Office
Tel: +86(0)10 8472 1250
Fax: +86(0)10 5885 0639

Author: Zhang Yawen
Translator: Robert Kapp
Editor: Matthew Keeler
Cover art: Daniel Li

Published by ACA Publishing Ltd in association
with the China Translation and Publishing House

© 2016, by China Translation and Publishing House, Beijing, China
ALL RIGHTS RESERVED. NO PART OF THIS
PUBLICATION MAY BE REPRODUCED IN MATERIAL FORM,
BY ANY MEANS, WHETHER GRAPHIC,
ELECTRONIC, MECHANICAL OR OTHER, INCLUDING
PHOTOCOPYING OR INFORMATION STORAGE, IN WHOLE OR IN PART, AND
MAY NOT BE USED TO PREPARE
OTHER PUBLICATIONS WITHOUT WRITTEN
PERMISSION FROM THE PUBLISHER.

The greatest care has been taken to ensure accuracy but the
publisher can accept no responsibility for errors or omissions, or
for any liability occasioned by relying on its content.

ISBN 978-1-910760-30-7

A catalogue record for *Playing Chess with the Devil* is available from the National
Bibliographic Service of the British Library.

Zhang Yawen was born in a poverty-stricken remote mountain region of Liaoning province, northeast China in 1944. She had to walk for 10 kilometres each day to get to school, and the Cultural Revolution prevented her from going to college. Her writing career began in 1979 with a 3,000-word story that was published in a newspaper. Since then, she has travelled around 10 countries and written more than eight million words, including her autobiography Cry For Life.

Her dramatisation of the life of Qian Xiuling, a Chinese woman who saved more than a hundred citizens of Belgium with the help of the country's German military governor, was adapted for television and won the China Writers Association's Ordos Prize for Literary Excellence. The film rights for this book, A Chinese Woman at Gestapo Gunpoint, were purchased in October 2017 for 2,400,000 CNY.

FOREWORD

To Express the Reverence in My Heart

(1)

I recall the words of Bernhard Sindberg the Sailor, in the autumn of his years, writing about his lifetime wandering the blue ocean amid swaying palms. By then, the ship of his life was moored at a retirement home. But his eyes still gleamed with the old gaze into the far distance, and his heart still burned with the desire to go to sea. His arms ached to do battle with the ocean's billows, as a pilot dreams of the blue skies or an athlete longs to be back on the race track.

I am not a sailor, and my old and flickering eyes do not gaze afar. But I do have questions about life itself, even now, long after the years when I pursued my dreams, rather like the sailor's dream of going to sea, or a fine horse's dream of racing across the grasslands. For me, now, my life's boat is also moored in the quiet cove of old age. Still, my heart is filled with reverence for that which is noble. We do not live in an era of reverence and awe, but, for me, that feeling of awe is like a religious disciple's devout reverence for the Holy Spirit. Perhaps this is because, for people of my generation, education had too deep an influence. Or maybe I just have the personality of a feeble-minded old athlete.

In any case, I love the lofty, and I love the written word. To find the materials I need, I will pay any price. Playing the wheeler-dealer,

I went into Russia many times. I have been to Korea and Hong Kong, to Chechnya, to Ukraine and to other countries in Europe.

I remember my first trip to Belgium in November 1999. Clutching my little purse, I flew alone to Brussels with no money, no language and no interpreter. I could not stay in a regular hotel or eat a regular meal. In my pocket, I carried Chinese-English and Chinese-French illustrated dictionaries. I stayed at an Overseas Chinese home that had no heat, no mattress and not even a pillow – only a thin cotton bedcover. I cried my eyes out and felt sorry for myself. But my only reason for being there was to visit a lady whom the Belgians had named as their country's 'Chinese mother'. With all my heart, I wanted to introduce this woman to the whole world so that people would take note of her. I wanted to be sure that her brilliance would radiate forever across a world filled with killing and plundering.

At the time, I also hoped to visit the former home of a Nazi general. But in those days, China was not so close to the rest of the world. The threshold at Europe's gate was nowhere near as low as it is today, and I had to leave empty-handed.

Now, 15 long years have passed. Time has filtered out much dross and many materials of little value. But the old desire to interview the Nazi general stayed with me under the surface, and I never let it go. As the years passed, my thirst only grew more urgent.

In the spring of 2014, I heard a voice from afar calling to me: "Go! Go and dig up those materials. Do not wait any longer. Go and write about them – about Qian Xiuling who saved so many lives, and about von Falkenhausen, and Rabe, and Sindberg, and Günther. Use the story of their nobler natures to wash away the foulness and arouse the better nature that has never been completely extinguished."

Indeed, back in those years, when the world was swept by insane aggression and fawning hypocrisy, and naked slaughter lay exposed, certain giant figures appeared, disregarding their individual safety and igniting their own lives in order to fire the blaze of justice and illuminate a piece of the blood-drenched night sky, leaving behind for all mankind a priceless treasure – the luminous rays of human nature.

This sense of reverence for the noble was worth writing about, and worth researching. That powerful call overcame all my heart's hesitations. It filled my ageing existence with a new and irresistible strength. It called me to go and realise my long-unfulfilled yearning. But in the end, what finally impelled me to make the trip to Europe were several political figures with whom, previously, I had had absolutely nothing to do.

In April 2014, the newspapers reported that Queen Margrethe of Denmark had visited the Nanjing Massacre Memorial. I was reminded of German Chancellor Willy Brandt's act of contrition as he knelt before a monument to slain Jews in Warsaw. I thought of the rightist forces of Japan's Prime Minister Abe, worshipping time and again at the Yasukuni Shrine while never acknowledging the Nanjing Massacre, never acknowledging the 'comfort women', calling over and over again for 'constitutional revision'. I thought of their systematic attempts to claim China's Diaoyu Islands as sovereign Japanese territory.

I am from northeast China. My father's generation underwent the tribulations of 14 years of slavery in their lost nation. They bear in their hearts an insatiable hatred for Japan's militarism.

I pondered this question: Japan and Germany both had people who were guilty of historical crimes, so why do their approaches to history differ so completely? Is it a question of racial and cultural contrasts? Maybe it is that Japan's 'culture of shame' and the western 'culture of guilt' are so different. Or perhaps there are factors more deeply embedded in the international background.

Being a northeastern Chinese writer of good heart, an old person who has seen a great deal of human suffering, I came to hear a new sense of mission and responsibility calling to me and driving me to take on this project, whatever the costs might be. With that, I started excitedly to make my preparations before embarking on my journey.

(2)

I knew that this topic was vast, and that no matter how many people I interviewed or how many books I read it would be a huge challenge. For a long time now, I have known the challenges that old age brings, but I still love to take them on. My life as a writer has been a constant process of meeting challenges, overcoming them and moving forward.

Nevertheless, I knew well that this project of going to Europe in search of so many people long dead, and tracking down their descendants, visiting their old places of residence and looking for materials would be more than one person alone could fulfil. I would need to make use of the power of our embassies in various countries.

I therefore made a report to the Ministry of Culture, laying out my visit plans and my hopes of gaining help from Chinese embassies in a number of European countries. I didn't imagine that the ministry would view my project so favourably and provide such support to me. Mr Zheng Hao, chief of the Northern Europe Bureau at the ministry's Department of Foreign Liaison, put me in contact with the cultural sections of China's embassies in Germany, Denmark, Austria and Belgium. Various comrades in cultural affairs sections of their embassies worked hard to provide assistance with my travel and interview plans, helping me to meet John Rabe's grandson and Bernhard Sindberg's niece, as well as locating General von Falkenhausen's former residence, and setting up a schedule of interviews. Miss Li Wen, of the cultural affairs section at the Chinese embassy in Germany, gave me particularly great assistance.

I decided to bring my granddaughter, Zhang Runqiao, with me on the trip to Europe. She had studied for years in the US and spoke beautiful English, so she could be my interpreter.

But on the morning of 1 August 2014, just a day before we were to board our plane, Runqiao came down with a temperature of 39C, and fainted. She continued to vomit and showed all the signs of acute gastric distress. I was struck dumb: what to do? I couldn't change my visa, and Li Wen in Germany had already made an appointment for me with John Rabe's grandson. She had scheduled that interview for the morning of 3 August in Heidelberg, and had confirmed a visit with three former mayors of Nassau, where General von Falkenhausen had lived, for the following day. There was nothing for it; I had to go by myself the next day, still worried about Runqiao. So, on 2 August, I flew to Frankfurt.

I urgently asked Li Wen to help me find a Chinese student in Heidelberg who could be my interpreter during my interviews with Rabe's family. The embassy in Berlin contacted Deng Wei, of the Chinese consulate general in Frankfurt, and he hurried to Heidelberg by car to be my interpreter in the meeting with the three former mayors of Nassau.

Little did I know that, on the evening of 5 August, Runqiao would fly to Berlin. My young partner was afraid that I would be without an interpreter and my whole visit would be affected. She hurried to join me, even though she was just starting to recover from serious illness. With Runqiao along as my interpreter, my interviews went much, much more smoothly.

Over 20 days, we travelled to Germany, Denmark, Austria and France. We interviewed John Rabe's grandson Thomas Rabe, visited the John Rabe Communication Centre, interviewed three former mayors of Nassau who had been friends with General von Falkenhausen when he lived there, and listened to their accounts of the general's later years in their town. They gave me a precious, privately-printed autobiography of the general. I visited Bernhard Sindberg's niece Marianne and other family members, and heard their tales of Sindberg's youth. At 22 Johannstrasse in Vienna, I was able to view the stone tablet commemorating Dr He Fengshan, who saved the lives of many Jews by providing them with visas. I visited the Berlin Wall, Nazi concentration camps and the monument to Jews slaughtered by the Nazis. I went to the Jewish Museum and to the suburban cemetery, where I stood before the inscribed stone erected in memory of Chancellor Willy Brandt's kneeling expression of atonement before the monument to Jews killed in Warsaw. I visited Shi Mingde, China's ambassador to Germany, and met with many German people.

My trip to Europe brought into my hands a great deal of first-hand, personal material. After my return to China, I spent time with Wang Taiping, a high-ranking diplomat who had done a great deal of research on Japan. I also interviewed Jiang Yuchun, who had been Thomas Rabe's Chinese secretary.

Prior to this, I had twice travelled to Nanjing to examine and read materials at the Nanjing Massacre Commemorative Hall and to visit the home that John Rabe had occupied in the city. Twice I had interviewed aged employees of the Jiangnan Cement Works in Nanjing, and I had read materials on the company and the plant.

In Beijing and Shanghai, I interviewed Chen Kekuan and Chen Kejian, who are descendants of Jiangnan Cement's general manager Chen Fanyou, as well as their friends Xu Erxin and Xu Zuzhe.

Over and above all this, I read several million words' worth of written material.

(3)

Throughout the time that I was immersed in writing, I communed every day with the souls of my book's subjects, feeling their pulses and searching for the true meaning of their lives.

What I discovered, though, were completely different essential natures – human, bestial and sheep-like – as is true with all humanity.

The deeds of several of my subjects left me both shaken and encouraged. The lofty heights that they reached, through their selfless rescuing of others, purified my own soul time after time, and forced me to examine the good and evil within my own nature. Meanwhile, those satanic fascist elements displayed their utter lack of humanity and revealed the ugly face of bestiality.

In writing, I often lost track of myself, and discarded my own defensive armour, escaping from the discipline that authorship imposes. It was like riding a horse without holding the reins, unburdening myself to my heart's content, telling myself that I was doing fine. What was there to fear? The era of the Chinese people's 'calcium deficiency' – that time when we always had to worry about angering the wolf or the tiger, and when others deceived us or we deceived ourselves – is in the past now, and our true selves can come forth.

To tell the truth, my emotions have never before felt as free and unconstrained as they do today. My mood has never been as open and candid as it is now. I feel like a wild horse, galloping freely to its heart's content.

But I have also, on many occasions, reined myself in, telling myself to be rational and not to get too emotional. Only by being rational, I told myself, could I go deeply into my topic and ultimately be objective about it. Yet the keyboard under my fingers would often not listen to my heart's instructions. Rationality was incinerated. Words became more than just words; they became a cudgel, laced with thorns, for smashing away at people's intentional or unintentional forgetfulness.

In creating this, I have used materials to analyse and corroborate both the historical roots of the Japanese extreme right's fanaticism and the reasons for its manifestations today. I did so as to awaken my people's understanding of the fundamental aggressiveness of Japanese militarism, and to call on my people to reflect upon themselves, discipline themselves and strengthen themselves. Only by strengthening ourselves will we be able to prevent others from bullying us and taking advantage of us.

I offer this work, the product of long years of thinking, to my beloved readers.

I offer my most sincere thanks to all those who assisted me in my work, including the Ministry of Culture, which helped so greatly, and the cultural affairs sections of Chinese embassies in several countries. My thanks as well to all those who allowed me to interview them; to my French language interpreter Fan Xiu and my English language interpreter Zhang Runqiao. Thank you for all your warm-hearted help! It was only because of your enormous support that I was able to complete this laboriously created work.

Here, let me also extend my heartfelt thanks to the Chongqing Publishing House for their heroic labours in editing my book.

Thank you!

8 April 2015

PART 1

Chess with the Devil

For the Power of Life

What is war?

War is a meat grinder, operated by a small group of people. Numberless innocent lives, and numberless warm and beautiful families are all thrown into the maw of the grinder. Those who save others from the machine, risking their lives without regard for their own danger, are angels among humanity.

The father of Écaussines Mayor Jean Dutrieux was one of the 96 hostages saved by Qian Xiuling.

(1)

A flyer announcing a hanging broadcast the smashed hopes of an entire village. A young and tender Chinese girl had knelt and opened the gate of a great Nazi general. A great German general, decorated by Hitler himself, was thrown into a concentration camp by the Gestapo. Why would a Belgian resistance hero – a woman – fall wildly in love with the top-ranked war criminal in Belgium? Why would the Belgian government bestow a medal for heroism on a Chinese woman?

What could all this mean?

This is a once-in-a-hundred-years story. The unconstrained flow of its plot reveals much about the magnificence of human nature. Its treasures glow more brilliantly than any fiction, because they emerge from historical truth. For 15 years, I followed the trails of the people in this story, and with my heart filled with reverence, I here begin this true tale.

Let me begin in a time that is now so distant yet still excites my heart.

Half a world away from China, Belgium celebrated its first national holiday following the end of the war in Europe on 21 July 1945.

On that morning, in the heroic little town of Écaussines, on the central square where three members of the Gestapo had been killed, a crowd assembled to cherish the memories of those who were gone, and to recognise and commemorate the heroes who contributed so valiantly to the anti-German resistance. As flags fluttered over a sea of heads, all eyes turned to gaze at the arrival of a most important person.

Following the sound of an approaching car, the sedan provided by the mayor entered the square. The only people visible inside the car, a delicate and elegant Oriental woman and her husband, alighted, and the crowd began to boil with excitement.

Flowers, applause and tears. People surged forward to embrace her, their arms waving without tiring, their faces drenched with tears, clustering around her, showering her with emotional praise, calling her 'Holy Mary' and 'Belgium's mother', the pride of the Chinese and the Belgian people, the spirit of Écaussines' renewal, calling for her name to be placed on a boulevard and for her to receive Belgium's highest honours for heroism.

She only smiled a little, saying over and over again: "No, no. Please do not do this! I only did what I ought to have done. All of this was the result of the help General von Falkenhausen gave me."

At that moment, no one knew in what dark and damp cell the man she spoke of was imprisoned, awaiting the victorious authorities' verdict on whether he would live or die.

In those days, when yellow-skinned people often faced discrimination in Europe, why would one Chinese woman receive all these gifts of such veneration? What judgment would this towering Nazi general face?

And what soul-rending tale had transpired between the two of them?

To answer these questions, we must begin our story on a terrifying morning in 1943 in a remote little Belgian village called Herbeumont.

I have been to that village, in the south of Belgium. Its population is tiny – fewer than a thousand – and it is secluded and peaceful, surrounded by dense forest. A clear brook winds its way around the edge of Herbeumont and disappears. Farther away, the ruined rooftops on the ancient walls of a 13th century village could barely be made out.

The morning of 12 March dawned amid heavy haze.

Until that time, the village of Herbeumont had lived peacefully. While four German soldiers were billeted there, there had been no bloodshed. Food was scarce, and people were sometimes forced to forage for mushrooms in the forest to stave off their hunger. But the days passed peacefully.

At dawn on 12 March, though, a burst of agonised wailing rose from the village square, smashing the little village's peace. Everyone in the village – men and women, young and old – ran towards the square. They found a middle-aged husband and wife collapsed on the ground before a posted announcement, in unbearable pain. It was an execution notice, and this is what it said:

> The execution by hanging of the resistance fighter Gérard Roger will take place in this square three days hence. Every inhabitant of the village must attend.

12 March 1943

A bolt from the blue cast a village's tranquillity into the cauldron.

All at once, every person's spirit was filled with despair, dread, lamentation and confusion. Herbeumont crashed into hopelessness and panic.

Gérard Roger was a fine young man, with striking grey-blue eyes, and of graceful bearing. He was well regarded in the village, and was his parents' only child. His father was a policeman. His fiancée was a charming primary school teacher. This young couple, deeply in love, had decided to marry, and were planning to wed in the village church only a few days later.

But like a demon from the King of Hell, this execution notice tore their hopes to shreds in an instant; what now awaited the young man was not his wedding, but the scaffold. And God had only granted him three days to live.

In three days' time, he would be hanged by the Gestapo in front of the gaping public.

Gérard Roger, a full-blooded youth, had secretly joined a resistance unit.

In the first world war, Belgium had been ravaged by the German army. In the second world war, they invaded Belgium again. Independence was impossible for this proud little country. Like other invaded nations, Belgium's people became destitute. Starving mobs swarmed over the land. Hatred of the Nazis penetrated the marrow of the Belgians' bones, and they set up all sorts of resistance organisations, secretly attacking German army installations, bombing rail lines, demolishing mining operations and secretly putting out more than forty resistance publications. Furthermore, because of its location, Brussels became a centre of European espionage, and the headquarters of a 'red band' that infuriated Hitler and Himmler.

Once the Nazis had occupied Belgium, the Netherlands, Luxembourg and northern France in May 1940, Belgian resistance activities did not let up. One night, Gérard Roger was secretly mining a rail line in order to bomb a Nazi train when he was discovered by the Gestapo. The Gestapo's policy towards resistance fighters was simple: kill them, without any discussion. Once a resistance fighter was taken, all thought of living was ended; only the scaffold or a firing squad lay ahead.

Once his son was captured, Gérard Roger's father sought help everywhere; he even managed to contact the King of the Belgians. The king and his wife pleaded with the head of the Gestapo in Brussels on Gérard Roger's behalf, but to no avail. In their grief, Gérard Roger's mother and father knew that only death lay before their son.

The villagers swarmed to Gérard Roger's home, surrounding his family and weeping, but they were powerless and could only make the sign of the cross and pray to God.

But where was God?

Now, just at the moment when the people were appealing to heaven and earth in their grief, a person of unusual appearance, a small and delicately framed Asian woman, appeared in front of them.

As soon as she arrived, she said: "Please, everyone, do not suffer so. I think I have a way of saving Gérard Roger."

Playing Chess with the Devil

Hearing these words, the people stood in silence, staring at her with doubt in their eyes: "The King and Queen of the Belgians could do nothing. How could you – a Chinese woman without position or power – save Gérard Roger?"

The villagers found it strange: who was this Mme de Perlinghi, so modest of speech, apparently well-educated and well regarded by the people? And why, at this terrible time, would she make such a horrible joke? What was going on with her this day?

Gérard Roger's parents shook their heads, and thanked the Chinese woman. Deep down, they didn't believe her. They knew their son was doomed, and that no one could turn the situation around.

Who, in the end, was this Chinese woman?

Why did she dare to say such bold words at this terrible moment? What connections did she have in the upper Nazi echelons?

(2)

This takes us back even further in time, and begins with an even more important figure.

April 1934. A foggy dawn in China. Amid the screams of seagulls and the clamour of men's voices, one of Chiang Kai-shek's secretaries and a few other officials welcomed a highly esteemed guest from far away. The man was Alexander von Falkenhausen, invited by Chiang as his senior military adviser and leader of a military advisory group.

A thin and upright man of about sixty, with a cold visage, arm in arm with an elegant wife, and leading three dogs with one hand, striding with military steps, disembarked from the passenger ship Duisberg.

The elderly couple were childless. Their three dogs were their children, by their sides from morning to night. They were inseparable. When General von Falkenhausen decided to take up his duties in China, he had no thought to leave the dogs behind, but took them

General von Falkenhausen in his middle years.

with him aboard ship, spending weeks with them on the seas, before arriving all together in China.

During my interviews, I discovered how deeply he loved his dogs, and I saw many photographs of him hugging them. Riding in a convertible car, a German shepherd could be seen on the seat next to him.

The invitation to General von Falkenhausen to come to China as head of a military advisory group had its roots in the period of military exchanges between China and Germany in the 1920s and early 1930s.

At that time, Chiang Kai-shek could see the speed of Germany's military and industrial development. He dreamed of bringing Germany's advanced militarisation skills, war strategies and fighting expertise, and especially the 'German spirit' to China's military forces. He sought to create in China a powerful national defence force, to play a vital role in defending China's sovereignty and withstanding external aggression. And so, for a fee of US$2,000 per month, he brought to China a senior retired German army general to be his military adviser.

In November 1928, Colonel Max Bauer brought to China a 25-person German military advisory group, consisting of 10 military trainers, six military logistics specialists, four military police experts, and five people with expertise in economics, railway management, medicine and chemicals. Upon arrival in Nanjing, they became the first group of German military advisers. Over the next 10 years, a total of 135 German military advisers arrived to assist China, eight of whom died in the line of duty.

Serving in succession as heads of the German military advisory groups were Max Bauer, Hermann Kleber, George Weser, Hans von Seeckt and Alexander von Falkenhausen. These five illustrious military men, each of stern German bearing and the highest calibre of military nature, brought reorganisation, guidance and training, with the aim of raising the warrior spirit and effectiveness of the Chinese military and modernising its equipment; they each played a significant role.

With the start of Japanese aggression against China in the 1932 Song-Hu Shanghai War and conflicts such as the defence of Shanghai and later the Taierzhuang battle, the lasting influence of the German advisers could be clearly seen, and they themselves took part in the fighting. Needless to say, they also played indispensable roles in Chiang Kai-shek's five 'extermination campaigns' against the Chinese Red Army of peasants and workers.

In that period, Sino-German trade also grew at an unprecedented rate. China became a major market for German industrial products and armaments; it was Germany's greatest trade partner in the far east. And China's rich deposits of strategic minerals such as tungsten, manganese and antimony were indispensable for Germany's arms manufacturers.

In March 1934, General Hans von Seeckt, known as the 'Father of Germany's National Defence', asked Chiang Kai-shek for permission to step down from the position of chief of the military advisory group for reasons of health. Alexander von Falkenhausen succeeded von Seeckt as Chiang's military adviser and head of the group. Von Seeckt had worked closely with von Falkenhausen, and had a high regard for his military skills and personal character. Chiang accepted von Seeckt's recommendation, and agreed to invite von Falkenhausen to China to succeed von Seeckt.

And so, von Falkenhausen, who had already retired, set out for China in the late days of March 1934, with his wife Paula von Wedderkop and his three beloved dogs. They sailed from Hamburg aboard the passenger ship Duisberg.

With so much talent to be found in the German army, what led von Seeckt to recommend von Falkenhausen to succeed him in China? What sort of man was this von Falkenhausen?

(3)

Alexander von Falkenhausen was born on 29 October 1878 in a grand mansion in Silesia, which is now part of Poland. The second of nine children, this tiny new life bore the inheritance of two illustrious families.

Alexander's great grandfather was the Margrave of Brandenburg-Ansbach, and master of two vast tracts of land. He fought in the Napoleonic wars. His grandfather took up the inherited profession and was also a great landowner.

His maternal grandfather was a renowned German military officer who had fought in the Franco-German war of 1870 and had been rewarded for his leadership. Alexander's father, prominent in Catholic Church affairs, was a fine horseman, but of sickly disposition.

Born to such a noble family, the young von Falkenhausen lived an aristocratic life, free of care and much the envy of others, his days filled with fishing, swimming, horseback riding and hunting. But, like so many over-privileged boys, he and his elder brother brought little glory to the family. Their school grades were poor and they were held back. Their bad behaviour caused their parents much shame in front of their teachers.

As a boy, von Falkenhausen's heart was not in his school books, but he was absorbed in tales of the heroes of ancient Greece, just as Chinese youths today bury themselves in the martial arts books of Jin Yong. Today, online games based on ancient Greek literature such as Homer's epics or the Peloponnesian Wars are popular with young people. Buried in these tales of warfare, they imagine themselves grown to maturity and embodying the spirit of ancient Greek heroes such as Orpheus, Odysseus or Aeneas, smiting their enemies and rescuing their fellow citizens.

This life of young von Falkenhausen was dominated by this hero complex.

The tales of the Greek heroes told him that to be a man was to be courageous, righteous and filled with a spirit of daring, and that one must never retreat. This hero complex imbued him with many admirable qualities, and gradually became the core narrative of his life.

Silesia, where von Falkenhausen was born, was a region of ethnic and national diversity. Poles, Germans, Czechs, Moravians and Jews all lived there, and many languages, including German, French and Slovak, could be heard. Against that background, von Falkenhausen learned several languages from childhood and was exposed to multiple cultural influences. When Hitler began his campaign against the Jews, von Falkenhausen reasoned to himself that Jews had made vast contributions to Germany – in food, animal husbandry, science, technology and business. Jews had the right to live, he felt, and should not be turned into enemies of the state.

His parents grew vexed at their disappointing boys. Hoping to cure them of their wildness and set them to rights, the elder von Falkenhausen bought a large residence in the more culturally civilised town of Brig, Switzerland. Perhaps placing them in this new environment would make more serious scholars of them, he reasoned. But shortly after placing the boys in one of the town's new schools, their father received a letter from the school's headmaster, asking that the boys be taken back to their home because the school could do nothing with them.

Thus, the two boys were pulled out of school.

The older boy was an even weaker student than his younger sibling, and as a result he was held back over and over, until he was actually in the same class as his younger brother. But the elder brother was the family's oldest son; no matter how weak a student he might be, he would inherit the family's assets. According to German law at that time, only the eldest son could inherit in this way, and the other offspring were only entitled to a portion of the estate.

Seeing that his boys were poor students, the elder von Falkenhausen could only send them off to a military academy attended by the sons of the von Falkenhausen clan in Wahlstatt. The elder boy entered as a fourth-year student, and young Alexander joined as a fifth-year student.

For a boy already enamoured of fantasy, this move was like unlocking the door to a whole new realm. Military academy gave young von Falkenhausen a key to open a rusty lock. What opened the lock was not the rigid rules of the military school, but a young man's arrival at self-awareness.

Life at the military academy was mostly bitter and harsh. Each day, five or six hours of class, plus drill and combat skills training. The academy required students to eat their meals in a common mess hall – a far cry from their earlier home experiences. The day's three meals were not only simple; they were inadequate. Cadets frequently came to blows over something as small as a crust of bread.

For most 12-year-old boys from aristocratic families, life in the military academy was grim and abhorrent. But for this boy, obsessed with the lore of ancient heroes, it was something else entirely.

Young von Falkenhausen at that time had absolutely no inkling that the ancient Chinese philosopher Mencius had said long ago: "Thus, when Heaven is about to confer a great office on any man, it first exercises his mind with suffering, and his sinews and bones with toil. It exposes his body to hunger, and subjects him to extreme poverty. It confounds his undertakings. By all these means it stimulates his mind, hardens his nature and supplies his incompetencies."[1]

But he understood that the rigorous conditions of the academy were, for him, an enormous personal test – the refinery that would determine whether he himself would become a hero.

He came to the realisation that he would lead a military life. He subscribed to Napoleon's idea that "the soldier who doesn't aspire to be a general is not a good soldier". Naturally, he aimed to be a general – the greatest general of all!

And so, he began not only to apply himself to his studies, and to the rigorous drills of his academy, but also to read poetry in German, English and French. Reciting aloud the works of Goethe and Tennyson, he could shed his loneliness, experience deep pleasure and find encouragement and inspiration. He loved to read history, for history offered wisdom. He read with gusto the works of Socrates, Plato and Aristotle. One line from Socrates stayed with him forever: "To die for the truth."

His readings not only gave him knowledge and encouragement; they also broadened his thinking. He regularly pondered national and global affairs. As a boy, he spent his time thinking about questions that older youths never considered: Why is Europe so unstable, with each nation's politics in turmoil, ready to burst into warfare at any given moment? As a young cadet, what should he prepare to do in service to his country?

His learning matured him ahead of his years, and opened up chasms between him and his contemporaries.

On 18 March 1894, von Falkenhausen left Silesia and entered a higher military academy. Assigned to the Eighth Army Group, he was now a fully-fledged soldier, with a helmet upon his head and a firearm on his belt. From the moment he entered this senior military school, he became even more self-aware and worked even harder.

He pondered problems far graver than usually considered by people his age, such as which monarchical system was most suited to the spirit of the age and whether people were leaning more towards a republic. With respect to Germany itself, the monarchy at hand was still most appropriate to the nation's structure. It was only natural that a young officer like von Falkenhausen thought most of all about what ought to be done for his own country.

By 1896, the 18-year-old von Falkenhausen was already a brilliant and dashing young man. He took first place in his all-school examination, earning the respect of his peers, and becoming an outstanding student in his higher-level military academy. The opportunity to serve as an army officer came a full year earlier than it did for the other cadets of his age. He became a member of the Kaiser's Guards, charged with protecting the monarch at his birthday celebrations. The following year he became a second lieutenant in the Oldenburg Infantry.

Thus, it happened that this young man, whose teachers had expelled him and whose parents had despaired of him as a student, transformed himself into one of Germany's most renowned military students and the pride of his illustrious family.

His father wept for joy when he learned that his son had acquired a brilliant reputation, affirming that he had always believed in him, and that he surely had a great future ahead of him.

On 24 September 1904, von Falkenhausen and his bride, the beautiful and intelligent Paula von Wedderkop, became husband and wife in a grand wedding. The bride was born to an aristocratic family in the north German city of Oldenburg. Her father was a photographer. When her mother heard that her daughter was in love with a military officer, she said: "Ah, my daughter, you and von Falkenhausen are certainly going to have an exciting life." Prophetic words indeed!

Paula von Wedderkop loved her husband passionately, and remained at his side without complaint as his duties took them to multiple locations throughout their lives.

Von Falkenhausen's innate talents carved for him an illustrious and distinguished military career.

In 1900, as a lieutenant, von Falkenhausen accompanied the German contingent of the Eight Nation Allied Army that invaded Beijing. Soon after that, he entered the staff college for further study, and then took up studies at the Oriental Institute of the University of Berlin. After graduation, he was assigned in 1909 to the German staff headquarters as an intelligence officer. In 1912, he became military attaché at the German embassy in Tokyo. In 1914, as a company commander, he took part in the first world war. His wartime service earned him several awards. After the war, he served as a military training supervisor, and rose to the rank of infantry regimental commander. In 1927, he became commandant of the Dresden Infantry Academy, and in April 1928 he rose to the rank of major general. In October 1929, he reached the rank of lieutenant general, but on 31 January 1931, he resigned from the service. To that point, his life and his military career shared a common brilliance.

But no man's destiny can escape its karma.

(4)

Von Falkenhausen could not have imagined that he would return to China. The first time he went there, he was an invader. The second time, he went at the invitation of Chiang Kai-shek to serve as leader of a German military advisory group.

He was a professional military man. Over his long military career, he followed his commanders' orders, fought many battles for his nation, and saw more than his share of brutality and bloodshed. But his first experience in China had a deep impression on him. So, he boarded ship to return to a country where the brutal memories of his mission decades before remained very much alive.

The north China weather in March was bitterly cold, and the icy wind was penetrating, especially on board the ship carrying von Falkenhausen there.

But every windless evening, von Falkenhausen would pace alone on the top deck, in a heavy overcoat, until late at night when his wife would call him back to their first-class cabin to rest.

His wife could see that his visage, always cold and stern, was growing ever more profound and grave. She said to him: "Dear husband, it seems that something is bothering you. Is it that you don't wish to go to China?"

Von Falkenhausen did not offer a reply.

Back in August 1900, von Falkenhausen, then a 22-year-old lieutenant, followed his orders and joined the Eight Nation Allied Army, made up of tens of thousands of soldiers, that invaded Beijing in the name of repressing the Boxer uprising, forcing the imperial family to flee westward from the capital. The 150,000 imperial troops and the 300,000 Boxer rebels had little military skill, and in the space of only five hours the allied army succeeded in occupying Beijing. The events that followed burned deeply into von Falkenhausen's memory, leaving him with vivid recollections for the rest of his life.

The German General Alfred von Waldersee sent out his order to his officers and men: "Now hear this: you all loot at will for the next three days. If you run into any Chinese, your orders are to kill them – men, women, old or young. You are authorised to kill on the spot."

And so, the thousand-year capital was plundered day after day, night after night. Several hundred thousand Chinese were slain.

According to an English account: "Beijing became a necropolis. The dead lay in all directions. No one tried to cover the corpses. Wild dogs ran about, feasting on the bodies."

Another foreigner said of Beijing: "Other than ruins, ruins, ruins, nothing else remained."

The great imperial palace, and all the smaller halls, were looted of absolutely everything. The Summer Palace was reduced to ruins, with only a few fragments of shattered walls left standing.

It is said that in the Oriental collection of the British Museum lie twenty thousand rare Chinese historical artefacts, most of them acquired through the plunder of 1900. A Hall of China within the Palace of Fontainebleau in France displays treasures violently stolen from China. In both Japan and Germany, museums focused on the Eight Nation Allied Army display many cultural artefacts collected during the plundering of 1900.

The Qing imperial rulers of the time were most certainly too weak to be able to do anything about this.

The emperor and the empress dowager fled. One hundred and fifty thousand Qing troops could not resist the force of a few tens of thousands of foreigners armed with foreign weapons and ammunition. In five hours, they, too, all fled the city.

A year later, the dynasty signed the Boxer Protocol, forced upon them by the foreigners. Germany, Japan, Great Britain, France, the US, Russia, Italy and Austria-Hungary, whose forces had comprised the Eight Nation Allied Army, plus Belgium, Spain, the Netherlands,

Portugal, Sweden and Norway, joined in demanding vast war reparations to cover the costs of their military invasion of China.

In the words of more than a thousand unequal treaty provisions are inscribed the humiliation of China and the story of the strong devouring the flesh of the weak.

According to the terms of one single reparation provision in the Boxer Protocol, a payment of 450 million taels of silver was to be made to the Great Powers – one tael per person based on China's population at that time. Payment was to be made over a period of 39 years, at an interest rate of four per cent, so the principal and interest together amounted to 982 million taels. In addition, the provinces were expected to pay 20 million taels, bringing the total Boxer reparation to a billion taels of silver bullion.

This gigantic sum amounted to twelve times the annual revenue of the Qing dynasty. Broken down by recipient country, the numbers were these:

Russia: 130,371,120 taels

Germany: 90,070,505 taels

France: 70,878,240 taels

Great Britain: 50,620,545 taels

Japan: 34,793,100 taels

United States: 32,939,055 taels

Italy: 32,939,055 taels

Belgium: 8,484,345 taels

Austria-Hungary: 4,003,920 taels

The Netherlands: 782,100 taels

The remaining 430,000 taels of silver bullion were to be shared among Spain, Portugal, Norway and Sweden.

Between 1901 and 1937, China paid a total of 653,200,000 taels of silver bullion to the Great Powers.

Typing these Boxer indemnity figures on my keyboard was, for me, like opening up an old and yellowing account book. In my heart, I felt as if I were picking my way along a mountain pathway overgrown with thorns. Staring at these strings of numbers was like seeing the blood-stained footprints our ancestors had left behind on that mountain track – a blood debt owed to the Chinese people by their plunderers!

After 1925, the US, the USSR, France, Great Britain, Belgium and Italy decided to lift the indemnities, which placed an intolerable burden on every man, woman and child in China, and most of these countries used the indemnity obligations to recruit and educate Chinese students.

But not Japan. Not until the full-scale invasion of China in 1937 did Japan stop collecting its Boxer indemnity share. Japan was the only state not to withdraw its Boxer claim, and it used the major sums it drew from that claim to advance its own military industries.

As his ship tossed on the seas, the memories of the advance on Beijing arose more than once in von Falkenhausen's mind.

The wind blew up, and heavy waves buffeted the upper deck of von Falkenhausen's ship with a thunderous roar. On that freezing night, amid the howling and icy winds, his thoughts were complex and wide-ranging. He said quietly to himself: "When I reach China, I will exert myself to the fullest to assist its supreme leader Chiang Kai-shek and his people, who have suffered so many disasters and misfortunes."

Von Falkenhausen's sea voyage to China was anything but smooth. The Duisberg departed from Hamburg and made its way to the North Sea on its way to the Orient. But after running into an English steamer, the ship had to put into port for two weeks of repairs.

Finally, at the end of April, after many weeks at sea, the Duisberg made port at Shanghai.

(5)

In 1934, when General von Falkenhausen arrived in China, the world was again on the eve of war; as the expression has it: "The mansion is filled with the wind, as the mountain rains approach." A great war of all mankind was taking form in the hearts of a few major figures in Japan and Germany.

Adolf Hitler rose to the chancellorship of Germany on 1 April 1933, through subterfuge. In August the following year, he took the position of president as well, gathering into his hands supreme power in Germany. Von Falkenhausen had a low opinion of the Austrian tramp with the little moustache. He knew that Hitler had been jailed after his failed Beer Hall Putsch, and that while incarcerated he had written his little pamphlet *Mein Kampf* to bewitch people's minds; that he used his snarling speeches to whip up the masses; and that he exploited the anger of the German people, amid the country's economic collapse, to drive his Nazi Party to overthrow the German government and thus realise his savage dream of supreme political power. Von Falkenhausen considered Hitler wildly ambitious, and on the many occasions when he was pressed to join the Nazi Party he refused.

At that moment, the situation in China was even more wretched.

In 1931, the Japanese Imperial Army set off the 18 September Incident, and occupied China's three northeastern provinces. On 1 March 1932, Japan established 'Manchukuo', its puppet state, in Changchun, the major city in Jilin province. In March 1934, the Japanese installed Pu Yi, the last Qing dynasty emperor who had been overthrown in the Republican Revolution of 1911, as their puppet emperor in Manchukuo. The Japanese army advanced into eastern Hebei in March 1933, and established a three-sided encirclement of Beiping, as present-day Beijing was then known. By 30 May, they had compelled the Chinese government to sign the humiliating Tanggu Agreement.

These were the ugly and complex circumstances in which Chiang Kai-shek invited General von Falkenhausen to come to China as chief of the military advisory group.

From his arrival in China in April 1934 until his removal from his responsibilities in July 1938, von Falkenhausen served for four years and three months. During that period, the people of China saw the Lugouqiao Incident in Beiping, the launch of full-scale Japanese war against China, the bitter and debilitating Songjiang-Shanghai campaign, the bloodletting of the Nanjing Massacre and the rousing battle of Taierzhuang. Von Falkenhausen and his German advisers saw all of this at close range.

At the ceremony welcoming him to Nanjing, General von Falkenhausen laid eyes on Chiang Kai-shek for the first time. He formed a favourable impression. Chiang was tall and lean, his face stern, his eyes deep and penetrating, his speaking poised. Everything about him suggested strength and resoluteness. Von Falkenhausen reached the conclusion that Chiang was the one national leader who could govern China, the world's most populous nation which was suffering from ceaseless armed conflict.

He quickly discovered, however, that this Chinese leader was deficient in his understanding and judgment about contemporary world conditions and modern warfare.

For his part, Chiang Kai-shek placed huge hopes in von Falkenhausen, expecting that the German military advisory group would be able to help China build a modern army.

Von Falkenhausen and his team were billeted in a small building in central Nanjing. In front of von Falkenhausen's residence was a lovely garden with doves and pheasants. Mandarin ducks splashed in the waters of a formal pond. His working and living spaces were separated only by a wall, and he could enter his office simply by passing through a fan-shaped entryway. Von Falkenhausen loved this environment, especially the garden with its fragrant flowers, its doves and its mandarin ducks. Often, of an evening, he would stroll in the garden with his wife and beloved dogs.

Von Falkenhausen and his military adviser team quickly set to work. They travelled widely, inspecting the Kuomintang forces, accompanied by military officers assigned to them by Chiang. From these inspections, von Falkenhausen formed some preliminary impressions of the Chinese forces.

As he saw China's beloved rivers and mountains, he discovered that in the 40 years since he had first entered Beijing, the men had cut off their queues and discarded the ways of the imperial court. But he also found that China had long suffered from continuous warfare; that the people were unable to provide for themselves; that Chiang Kai-shek's government was ridden with internal turmoil; and that his military forces were feeble. The army desperately needed better training and modern weapons from abroad. It would be essential to form a military force whose weapons were the best available and whose levels of training were superior.

Von Falkenhausen also found, however, that discipline within the Kuomintang army was loose, and that family relations played a strong role within the forces. He said of the rampant corruption: "Personal links between officers and men were deeply entrenched. Senior officers abused their positions, and their subordinates depended on their officers to protect their livelihoods." He concluded that, with the army in this condition, rigorous training would be impossible; creating conditions of ironclad discipline would be even more difficult. An army without that strong discipline had no soul; it would have no war-fighting ability. It would be necessary, he concluded, to carry out a strict reorganisation of the army.

So, von Falkenhausen reported to Chiang Kai-shek that if they were to reorganise the army, they would have to equip it with superior armaments; if they were to retrain the troops with old-fashioned weapons, they would not be able to contend with enemy forces using advanced arms. On von Falkenhausen's advice, the national government then purchased large quantities of arms and military supplies from Germany.

Von Falkenhausen further discovered that the Chinese government under Chiang Kai-shek did not have a clear understanding of who its primary enemy was. Under the policy that 'resisting foreign aggression first requires internal pacification', the government was turning its guns on its own countrymen. To von Falkenhausen, it seemed that Chiang Kai-shek had failed to open his eyes and see the true nature of the island nation to the east.

Von Falkenhausen had served as a German intelligence officer and as military attaché at Germany's embassy in Japan. He had been studying Japan for a long time, and had developed a deep understanding of the island nation. He realised that, for a century, Japan's leaders had had one overriding goal – to occupy and plunder China.

(6)

Of course, if we look at Japan's modern history, what we see is a history of aggression against China, full of great and small events, one after another; unequal treaties, one after another. We might as well have a simple look at it here:

1874 – after the Meiji Restoration, Japan sent forces to attack Taiwan and forcibly occupied the island of Liuqiu, which belonged to China, renaming it Okinawa.

1894 – Japan launched the Sino-Japanese war, in which China was defeated.

1895 – China was forced to sign the Treaty of Shimonoseki, and in the same year Japanese forces occupied Taiwan.

1900 – Japan was the only Asian participant in the Eight Nation Allied Army invasion of China, and its forces were the most numerous.

1901 – Japan claimed an indemnity of 34,793,100 taels of silver bullion in the Boxer Protocol.

1915 – the Chinese government of Yuan Shikai secretly agreed to Japan's '21 Demands', which slashed at China's national sovereignty.

1926 – the Japanese navy bombarded Chinese forces at the Dagu Forts near Tianjin, in a premeditated attack.

1927 – Japanese Prime Minister Tanaka sent a memorial to the emperor, entitled: 'An active policy for our empire with regard to Manchuria and Mongolia.' It included this line: "If we want to conquer China, we must first conquer Manchuria and Mongolia. If we want to conquer the world, we must first conquer China."

1928 – the Japanese military attacked Jinan, in Shandong province, killing a number of Chinese diplomats and killing or wounding several thousand Chinese soldiers and civilians in the so-called Jinan Incident.

1931 – Japanese forces staged the Mukden Incident and proceeded to occupy China's three northeastern provinces.

1932 – the Japanese military launched the 28 January Incident and attacked Shanghai.

1933 – the Japanese army manufactured the so-called Rehe Incident, attacking Shanhaiguan and the area known as Jehol, inside the Great Wall northeast of Beiping.

1935 – in the so-called North China Incident, Japanese forces sought to create five independent provinces in north China.

Playing Chess with the Devil

From the time of the Meiji Restoration, Japan proceeded with a policy of capitalist transformation called 'shedding Asia and entering Europe', with the aim of building a permanent, modern, industrialised and powerful military state. Its ideology of militarist expansion penetrated deeply into the minds of the populace. Thus, the 'Bushi spirit' served as a powerful ideological weapon in support of Japan's militarism. In 1878, Japan issued the 'Admonition to the Army', calling for complete loyalty to the emperor, and proclaiming that the worthiest act was to die for him. In 1882, the imperial edict called on all military personnel to follow the values of loyalty, valour, faithfulness and ceremonial propriety as the central standards of the Bushidō code. The spirit of Bushidō – the Way of the Samurai – had already emerged as the standard of conduct for the Japanese people, having permeated their hearts and their culture. Strengthening the militarisation of the populace, paying highest homage to Bushidō and promoting the idea, as summed up in a familiar four-character phrase: "All the world is ours, all the world belongs to the emperor."

The idea of expanding Japan's territorial grasp by armed force took root early among the populace. Adults taught boys as young as five or six to kill chickens as a way of building their courage. Students in schools and novices in Buddhist temples all underwent military training. The poetry of Japan's *rōnin* – armed warriors with no masters – often adopted the theme of invading China as a way of stimulating martial spirit: "My soaring ambitions cramped inside my schoolbooks, I draw my precious blade and practise my attack. When will I whip my iron-hoofed steed and press against the icy Yalu river line?"[2]

Thus read the published Japanese nursery rhymes sung by children every day, with the aim of stimulating popular determination to invade China.

In the early stages of its mission to invade China, Japan used *rōnin*, military attachés, opium dens, brothels and even restaurants as covers to send into China many spies and agents bent on developing long-term schemes that might take decades to execute. These concealed agents numbered not in the thousands or even the tens of thousands, but rather more than a hundred thousand. They penetrated all parts of China, at all levels of society. They corrupted the Chinese people by peddling opium and organising prostitution. They used money, beautiful women, corrupt high officials and secret societies to purchase the souls of Chinese people, all as part of their preparations for invasion.

Precious few Chinese people could see clearly all that Japan was doing.

And so, when at last Japan opened its bloody jaws after a century of preparation, expecting to swallow China and eradicate the Chinese race, Chiang Kai-shek, the leader of China's national government, not only failed to stand in resistance to Japan, but instead turned vast numbers of his troops against the Chinese Red Army of workers, peasants and soldiers in a series of five extermination campaigns. Chiang issued a series of ringing commands to his generals:

> Resistance to Japan first requires extermination of the bandits. Until the bandits are eliminated, we will be unable to fight Japan. Anyone who violates this command will suffer the most severe punishment!

> Foreign aggressors are not the key concern. The bandits within are a disease of the heart and belly. If we fail to destroy the domestic bandits, we most certainly will be unable to control those who affront us from without.

> We must concentrate all our energies on bandit suppression. If we want to realise the great goal of our long-term peaceful governance, and place our revolution on solid foundations, we cannot fail to eradicate this disease of our internal organs. If we are overly ambitious, and prattle on extravagantly about Japan, failing to see reality for what it is and failing to uproot this domestic cancer, that will only be a way of trying to succeed by

trickery... No matter how much we are slandered by foreigners, we must first of all eliminate the domestic bandits – that is our only task. If we fail to do that, everything will be back to front, everything will be upside down.

Those who wildly call for resistance to Japan shall be killed without mercy!

In September 1934, paying no attention to the fall of China's three northeastern provinces, instead of turning to face the Japanese empire, Chiang assigned nearly a million of his troops to carry out the fifth extermination campaign, forcing the Red Army to set off on its more than seven-thousand-mile Long March.

In 1935, Japan set off a series of new incidents, in its customary manner. Leaving aside countless small events, the major incidents were these:

- In January, the Japanese army fabricated the so-called Eastern Chahar Incident.

- In early May, the Japanese compelled the national government to sign the infamous Ho-Umezu Agreement.

- In June, the national government again buckled under Japanese pressure and signed the Chahar Agreement (also known as the Qin-Doihara Agreement), under which China ceded sovereignty over most of the provinces of Hebei and Chahar, and Japan made a giant step forward in its campaign to swallow up and incorporate China.

Japan's Foreign Minister Hirota Kōki addressed the Diet at this time, putting emphasis on the 'close friendship' between China and Japan, and pressing Chiang Kai-shek and Wang Jingwei to espouse a viewpoint of 'close and friendly relations' between the two nations.

In response, Chiang and Wang issued an order: "All activities aimed at resisting or opposing Japan are strictly forbidden."

And so, relations between China and Japan were raised from the level of ministers to the ambassadorial level.

(7)

From his understanding of the Japanese state and the nature of the Japanese people, von Falkenhausen believed that aggression and expansionism were at the core of the Japanese imperial state. To him, Japan's ambitions would not stop with China's three northeastern provinces, but only with all of China! Throughout the Japanese islands, swords were being sharpened for the all-out war of aggression into China. But he realised that Chiang Kai-shek's government still had not clearly discerned Japan's ambitions, no matter how long they had been brewing, and that Chiang lacked the resolve to face the Japanese. After each Japanese provocation, the Chinese government not only failed to resist; it submitted to compromise, signing the Qin-Doihara Agreement and the Ho-Umezu Agreement which both sacrificed China's territorial sovereignty.

As von Falkenhausen saw it, these Japanese advances into China were not merely minor disputes; instead they amounted to a war between aggression and counter-aggression, a war in defence of the sovereignty of the Chinese people. Such a war would not be resolved by 'close and friendly' relations or 'co-prosperity'; the difference between a reactionary, aggressive war and a war to protect national sovereignty in the interests of the people was the difference between heaven and earth.

In von Falkenhausen's view, the supreme leader of a nation, facing a powerful enemy, had to have a clear understanding of the nature of the war and take the lead to unite all the people in bitter hatred of the enemy and a common commitment to fight. The attitude of the supreme leader determined the attitude of the people. The goals of the leader would become the goals of the people.

Years of military life had bred in von Falkenhausen the qualities of bluntness and resoluteness. But he also inherited his mother's irascibility and ill temper. Procedures often left him impatient, and when he learned of the Qin-Doihara Agreement between the Chinese government and Japan, he immediately called Chiang Kai-shek's secretary and asked for a meeting with Chiang.

On the 31 July 1935, in a grand hall of the presidential palace in Nanjing, Chiang Kai-shek received von Falkenhausen with smiles and personal warmth. He made small talk, and enquired about von Falkenhausen's life in Nanjing. Nanjing summers are much hotter than summers in Berlin, Chiang observed; were General von Falkenhausen and his wife managing to adjust?

Von Falkenhausen responded: "Nanjing is fine, and my wife and I are adjusted to it. It is your nation's current situation that does not admit of optimism, however. Please allow me to speak frankly..."

Von Falkenhausen then delivered his views on present conditions to Chiang. He observed sharply that Chiang's attitude of passive resistance to the Japanese army would not be helpful to China's situation. Instead, he pointed out, such an attitude would only encourage the Japanese to act more and more boldly, and to continue to press against China, one step at a time. If the leader himself lacked a commitment to resisting Japan, this could seriously affect the people's resolve to resist! Von Falkenhausen asserted that in both the North China Incident and the Zhangbei Incident that led to the Qin-Doihara Agreement, the Japanese side used diplomatic ultimatums to force China to step back from conflict. If the Japanese had seen that China was really prepared to resist, the outcomes of these two incidents would have been very different.

He warned Chiang: "If we don't bend every ounce of our strength to fight a struggle for survival, China will lose all of north China, including Shandong province."

He said vigorously to Chiang: "I hope that Chairman Chiang will abandon his illusions and execute a plan of firm resistance!"

The pity of all this was that this German general's clear-eyed perception, and the advice he offered from the bottom of his heart, failed to dent the determination of the leader of the Chinese national government to stick with his policy of 'internal pacification first, then resistance'.

Faced with Chiang Kai-shek's smiles, von Falkenhausen could read the Chinese leader's thoughts. He knew the real nature of the Oriental: true feelings are only obscurely expressed, while the innermost thoughts of the heart remain hidden.

But the nature of the Germanic peoples is just the opposite.

For the next several days, von Falkenhausen scribbled furiously, bent over his desk. He produced a long report entitled 'Recommendations of the German Adviser von Falkenhausen on Policies to Respond to the Current Situation'.

On 20 August 1935, von Falkenhausen had his report delivered directly to Chiang Kai-shek by a military liaison officer, hoping that it would bring about a change in Chiang's thinking on how best to deal with the Japanese army.

In the 'Recommendations', he wrote:

> My humble views on how to deal with the current situation are contained in the memorial that I respectfully presented to Your Excellency on 31 July, and will be summed up below. But I must first declare that, having served for five years in Japan and having thereby conducted extensive study and gained deep familiarity with the Japanese military world, I have a credible understanding of the Japanese military's thinking on both strategy and war-fighting skills, and of the psychology of the Japanese land army...
>
> The most urgent and severe threats facing China today come from Japan. I am fully familiar with Japanese thinking regarding China. Japan's interests are diametrically opposed to China's,

and Japan will use every means to undermine China's internal unity and China's plans for increased strength. At the very least, Japan will seek to retard those efforts. In my humble opinion, popular sentiment is a hundred per cent in favour of resistance to the Japanese – this should not be taken lightly. If you, as Leader, do not share this popular sentiment, the people will not commit themselves to that resistance. The goal of resistance must be backed by military strength if it is to have any kind of strong foundation. Today's Chinese armies have no way of undertaking modern warfare...

Once military conflict begins, all of China will be threatened. If China does not fight to liberate north China, the Longhai railway, running from the east coast to Shaanxi province, and all the cities along its route will fall into an active and unprecedented war zone. If that happens, it is not hard to imagine that the Yellow river line, including Shandong province, could be rolled up by the Japanese...

At present the main Chinese army forces are in south China and west China. All forces that can be spared must be moved to the areas where they will be needed for combat. These forces should be concentrated in the areas of Xuzhou, Zhengzhou, Wuhan, Nanchang and Nanjing. The north must serve as a protective screen for the Longhai railway and critical equipment and supplies. Therefore, the first military effort must be to advance to the north. The line from Cangxian to Baoding must be defended. The ultimate line of defence is the Yellow river, and plans must be made to cause extensive flooding in order to strengthen the defences there...

In the east, two matters are of greatest gravity. One is to close the Yangtze, and the other is to defend Nanjing, the capital. The two tasks are intertwined. Secondary points such as Wuhan and Nanchang can serve as support bases, and must be fully defended, in order to protect vital links to Guangzhou. Finally, Sichuan must become the final defended position.[3]

Falkenhausen's 'Recommendations' were very long, and there is no need to go through them item by item.

Von Falkenhausen's statement that the primary threat to China was coming from Japan marked the first time since the formation of the German military advisory group that its leader had expressed this view. This document, which brought together von Falkenhausen's military skills, wisdom and his deep sense of responsibility, contained invaluable recommendations, not only with regard to the military dangers China was facing, but also the condition of the Chinese armies and the strategies the Chinese national government needed to adopt to meet the crises it faced.

Regrettably, however, von Falkenhausen's 'Recommendations', written from the heart and based on his vast knowledge, made no dent in Chiang Kai-shek's determined policy of 'domestic pacification before resistance to external aggression'.

Chiang's mind was completely focused on annihilating the Red Army, and devoted no thought to the Japanese militarism that was hammering at the gates of the nation, bent on exterminating China.

At this time, under the pressure of Chiang's fifth extermination campaign, the Red Army was compelled to set out on its Long March. Departing in October 1934 from Ruijin in Jiangxi and Changting in Fujian, the Long Marchers passed through twelve provinces over a period of two years on their trek of more than seven thousand miles – Fujian, Jiangxi, Guangdong, Guangxi, Hunan, Guizhou, Yunnan, Sichuan, Xikang, Gansu, Ningxia, and Shaanxi – before ending their journey in northern Shaanxi.

The heroic Long March infuriated Chiang Kai-shek, but it earned high praise from General von Falkenhausen, who later wrote:

> Only someone who knows the geography of the Long March and the means the marchers adopted to make their way can understand the greatness of the march and the magnitude of the

march's achievement. This group of people, accompanied by their wives, their children and all their equipment and machinery and household goods, crossed high mountains and deep valleys, battled their way through raging torrents, and advanced across vast distances. Anyone familiar with the terrain knows that this was a victorious choice, and that no one would be able to stop them.

Von Falkenhausen perceived in the Red Army a spirit that the government's armed forces simply did not possess.

(8)

The China that von Falkenhausen inherited was still operating according to Chiang Kai-shek's principles of 'pacification first, then resistance' and 'friendship' or 'fraternal relations' with Japan.

On 23 November 1936, the national government threw the leaders of the National Salvation Association of All Sectors – Shen Junru, Zhang Naiqi, Zou Taofen, Li Gongpu Sha Qianli, Shi Liang and Wang Zaoshi – in jail, on the charge of 'endangering the Republic', thus creating the horrifying Seven Gentlemen Incident.

On 12 December 1936, the Xian Incident shocked China and the world; Generals Zhang Xueliang and Yang Hucheng seized Chiang Kai-shek in an effort to compel him to call off the civil war and turn to resisting Japan. On the eve of the uprising, the northeastern general Zhang Xueliang, who bore the title of Bandit Extermination Chief for the Northwest, determined to smash through the stalemate, and tearfully appealed to Chiang:

> The Japanese invaders are steadily advancing into our country. Once the northeast was lost, north China fell to them in all but name. Now Suiyuan is under threat. The very survival of our people has reached the ultimate moment of crisis. Failing to resist Japan will not save the nation. Failing to end the civil

war and forge our nation's unity will not suffice to resist Japan. Continuing the campaign to exterminate the bandits is a complete and utter dead end!

Chiang was furious. He accused Zhang Xueliang of not knowing the difference between right and wrong, being unwilling to fight the communists, talking too casually about resisting Japan, blocking the achievement of the nation's great plans and being hopelessly ignorant because of his young age.

Their appeal unsuccessful, Zhang Xueliang and Yang Hucheng had no alternative but to issue the order to "seize Chiang" and compel him, by force, to turn to the fight against Japan.

In their draft message to the nation regarding the Xian uprising, Zhang and Yang wrote as follows:

> Five years have passed since the northeast was lost. Pressure on our territory has grown without cease. Starting with the Song Hu Agreement and then with the Tanggu Agreement and the Ho-Umezu Agreement, every person in our nation feels our bitter pain.
>
> Members of the Kuomintang who maintained their spirit have finally roared, shaking the entire world. Two military leaders have seized Chiang Kai-shek by force, in order to end the policy of non-resistance to Japan that has persisted for the past five years, start the process of joining the Kuomintang and the Chinese Communist Party in common resistance to Japan, and put an end to the days of Japan's crimes on China's soil.
>
> In the past, the national government has repeatedly sought compromise, trying to arrange terms in exchange for non-existent 'fraternal feelings' or East Asian Co-Prosperity. These sweet-sounding terms were nothing more than disguises, making the hideous jaws of the wolf appear like the face of a grandmother. Once the mask is ripped off, the full hideous savagery will be clear for all to see.

The critical danger to the nation, to which von Falkenhausen had tried to alert Chiang Kai-shek in July 1935, had finally come to pass.

On 7 July 1937, at the Lugou Bridge near Beiping, the Japanese armed forces ignited their full-scale war of aggression against China. Once the war had broken out, von Falkenhausen and the German military advisory group stood with the Chinese forces in many battles, including the great Battle of Songjiang and Shanghai.

In a short memo describing the state of affairs on 5 December 1937, von Falkenhausen wrote:

> Broadly speaking, we can confidently say that we will successfully fight a resistance war over a prolonged period. At the present time, opportunities to inflict heavy losses on the enemy are arising everywhere. But there is one prerequisite: all in the military, officers and soldiers alike, and everyone in the populace itself, must turn every ounce of their strength to the resistance battle.

In the battle against the Japanese, Chiang Kai-shek paid great attention to von Falkenhausen's ideas, and many of his policy decisions reflected the recommendations of von Falkenhausen and his military advisory group. But in the heat of battle, von Falkenhausen's and Chiang's leadership concepts often came into conflict.

After Shanghai fell to the Japanese, von Falkenhausen opposed the plan to move the national government inland to Chongqing. He reasoned that, because west China was too far from the Chinese coast and from vital communication routes, the national government would be unable to perform its critical functions. Furthermore, he reasoned, once Japan had seized the richest and most populous regions of the country, the war would likely go on indefinitely. His recommendation was for the national government's forces to evacuate to an area south of Nanjing, making use of the resources found in the Yangtze cities of Wuhan and Nanchang, in order to protect the capital at Nanjing. But von Falkenhausen was only the military advisory group leader, and all he could do was offer recommendations; final decisions were not in his hands.

The Battle of Taierzhuang, which ran from March to April 1938, has come to be called the Great Taierzhuang Victory. Chinese forces surrounded and annihilated twenty thousand Japanese soldiers and smashed at the arrogance of the Japanese forces. The battle gave a huge boost to the morale of the Chinese officers and soldiers fighting the enemy. In the early days following the victory, von Falkenhausen wrote to Chiang Kai-shek: "We must order the troops to advance; we must energise their aggressive attacks and pursue the fleeing enemy. If we don't do that, the Japanese will be able to send eight to ten divisions along the line to Xuzhou, and by then it will be too late."

Von Falkenhausen sent his message, but the Chinese army did not press the attack as he had advised, and did not take advantage of their victory to pursue the enemy. He was thunderously furious. He tore at his own hair, shouting: "How could this be happening?"

(9)

The Battle of Taierzhuang caused serious concern in Japanese military circles.

The Japanese discovered that the Chinese forces were not only using modern German weapons, but that German military experts were joining them in battle and even providing direction. The Japanese government quickly sent a telegram to the German government demanding the immediate dissolution of the German military advisory group, the return of all its personnel to Germany and the complete cessation of arms trade between China and Germany.

As early as November 1936, Germany and Japan had joined in signing the Anti-Comintern Pact. Nazi Germany naturally would not permit one of its own German-trained generals to run off to China to join in military planning, and to help China in its war with Japan.

The German embassy in China cabled von Falkenhausen: "The German government does not support your assistance to China in fighting against Japan."

Von Falkenhausen responded: "I retired long ago, and am not now a professional military man. I have freely made the personal decision to help the Chinese people and take responsibility for it."

On 21 June 1938, von Falkenhausen received a sternly worded message from the German embassy ordering all advisory personnel in China: "Leave China at once. Violators will be regarded as traitors, and their citizenship will be cancelled and their assets seized."

Von Falkenhausen spent a sleepless night.

He did not want to leave. He hoped to fulfil the mission and the responsibilities of the German military advisory group. He dreamed that the Chinese army would rise up to fight the War of Resistance and achieve final victory.

But the German government gave the Chinese government an ultimatum in the form of a telegram from its foreign office: "Whether Sino-German relations shall be maintained, or whether the German government will unilaterally break relations depends on the outcome of the current military advisory group matter."

Chiang Kai-shek had no choice, under those circumstances, but to agree to send the German military advisory group home. In July 1938, with fighting between China and Japan at its peak, General von Falkenhausen had no alternative but to lead his military advisory group out of China and back to Germany.

On the night before the group departed, 4 July 1938, Chiang Kai-shek held a farewell party for the members of the group in Wuhan. Chiang's wife Song Meiling and more than a hundred military figures attended. At the banquet, the sadness on both sides at the moment of parting was expressed in both word and gesture.

Chiang Kai-shek made a speech, praising the German military advisory group for its many contributions to China during its tenure, and expressing his personal thanks to the entire team. He thanked them for devoting all their efforts to helping the Chinese people fight against Japan and for their participation in the Songjiang-Shanghai and Xuzhou battles. The military advisory group had contributed in all ways to the Chinese military: in strategic planning, battlefield planning, developing military industries, training troops, army reorganisation and in assisting individuals on a personal level. The 87th and 88th Divisions, directly trained by the Germans, had become the model for the entire army. Chiang concluded by expressing wholehearted thanks to the German military advisory group under its leader, General von Falkenhausen.

But amid the festivities, traces of anxiety welled up on the faces of the Chinese officers in attendance. What worried them was not only that the military advisory group's departure would leave China without the German participation in the highest military councils. Far worse, the Germans had become privy to China's most important military secrets. If members of the military advisory group leaked those secrets to the Japanese, the effects on China would be unforeseeable.

But as von Falkenhausen and members of his group offered their solemn pledges, the Chinese officers' fears soon gave way to feelings of deep emotion and respect.

Von Falkenhausen rose to his feet, his face grave, and offered a military salute to all in attendance. He spoke soberly: "As leader of the German military advisory group and as a German general, I offer this pledge to Chairman Chiang Kai-shek and all the Chinese officers assembled here. The members of our military advisory group, for China's sake, will protect all military secrets, and will offer absolutely no information about China to the Japanese."

With that, the great hall was filled with prolonged applause.

The members of the military advisory group then took an oath never to reveal Chinese military secrets to the Japanese.

General von Falkenhausen had not only personal integrity, but also the noble qualities that German people display in the seriousness of their work and the scrupulousness with which they perform their duties. Von Falkenhausen's view was that he had been sent to China and thus would, in his work, be loyal to China. He could absolutely not betray China's interests. In the arms trade between China and Germany that he had encouraged, he made every effort to take China's interests into account and to foster fairness in the commerce. As he said: "In my work in service to China, it was only by introducing to China items that China genuinely needed that I could prove myself competent." Because of this, he had been warned repeatedly by the German Foreign Ministry.

On the 5 July 1938, at the Yangtze river mooring in Hankow, General von Falkenhausen and the members of the German military advisory group took their leave of more than a hundred Chinese military representatives, including the leading figures – He Yaozu, He Yingqin and Yu Feipeng – whom Chiang Kai-shek had dispatched for the occasion. They boarded a gunboat headed for Guangzhou.

One of the last people to bid von Falkenhausen farewell was a general named Qian Zhuolun. Four years earlier, Qian Zhuolun had had a liaison assignment with von Falkenhausen, and they had become good friends. Von Falkenhausen said to him: "General Qian, if in the future you need anything in Germany, please contact me directly, and I'll do everything I can to help."

General Qian replied: "Many thanks. And if there's anything you need in China, please contact me directly as well. I'll do all I can to be of assistance." The two men agreed to continue to correspond.

Who would have thought, hearing these two generals exchange pleasantries, that in the days to come this would become a stepping stone to the saving of other people's lives.

On the evening of 15 July 1938, General von Falkenhausen and his team boarded a passenger steamer in Hong Kong and left China. They arrived in Venice on 10 August.

(10)

At the end of August, General von Falkenhausen and his wife returned to the city they had left four years before, Berlin. By now, having spent so much of his life in the military amid turmoil in so many places, his main aim was to return to the countryside, take care of his health, and live out his later years in peace. But a person's fate is never in his own hands, and cannot be isolated from the destiny of either his country or the entire world. Military generals in particular cannot take personal control over their own fates.

By now, Germany had fallen under Hitler's power, just as Japan had fallen under the power of the militarists. All of Germany lurched into a frenzy. The opening acts of a world war were unfolding under Hitler's vicious direction.

On 14 March 1938, Germany absorbed Austria. Czechoslovakia was invaded in March 1939. Everyone wondered what country would be devoured next.

As was mentioned earlier, von Falkenhausen had a very poor impression of Hitler – especially after Kristallnacht on 9 November 1938 when the Germans violently assaulted Jews and their properties in an orgy of murder and destruction. Von Falkenhausen and a number of other generals said to themselves: "Annihilating people in this manner is conduct forbidden by God and is the great shame of the German people." They had no idea where Hitler would lead Germany.

But Hitler was well aware of von Falkenhausen's military abilities. Indeed, this was the period in which the Nazis' need for such expertise was at its peak.

On 25 May 1939, nine years into his retirement and well past his 60th birthday, von Falkenhausen received orders to return to active duty with the rank of general.

On 28 May 1940, the Nazis seized three independent countries: the Netherlands, Luxembourg and Belgium.

Already, on 17 May, von Falkenhausen had received new orders, and was assigned to be the Nazi military governor in the Netherlands. He went to The Hague on 18 May. On the 26 May, yet another assignment arrived, making him the military governor of Belgium and northern France, and ordering him to proceed immediately to Brussels. The man who replaced him in the Netherlands as Reich commissar, a tough Nazi official and loyal follower of Hitler named Arthur Seyss-Inquart, was convicted at the Nuremberg Trials at the end of the war, and hanged.

On 30 May 1940, von Falkenhausen took his leave of The Hague and moved to Brussels.

(11)

Now, we must return to that terrifying morning of 12 March 1943.

With the citizens of the village of Herbeumont sunk in despair and terror, a young Chinese woman stepped forth and said to the crowd: "Please! Do not suffer so. I think I have a way of saving Gérard Roger."

The young woman was Qian Xiuling, a doctoral graduate in chemistry from the University of Leuven and the cousin of General Qian Zhuolun.

In December 1999, I travelled to Brussels to visit her, and was warmly received not only by Qian Xiuling herself, but also by her elder son and his family, as well as her nephew Qian Xianren and his wife. The warmth of their reception made my visit a great success.

The elder Mme Qian is no longer with us, but her voice, her face and her smile remain vivid before my eyes. When I first met her, she was an elderly lady of 86, wearing a gauzy red dress and only the simplest of cosmetics. Her face was wreathed in a tiny, kindly smile. She had the aura of an elegant young woman.

Gazing at the calligraphy scrolls of her cousin, General Qian Zhuolun, and the photographs of her own Eurasian son, I embarked on a twenty-day mission to gather bits and pieces of first-hand materials, and to bring back to light, from the shadows of age and clouded memory, the rich details of Mme Qian's life.

By that time, Mme Qian was very old, and had long since forgotten many wondrous things. I gently stimulated her, guided her, chatted with her, accompanied her on her walks and slowly awakened her long-lost memories. Some of them, though, were beyond recall and perished forever with her own death.

During my time with her, the old lady left me with many beautiful recollections.

On one occasion, she took me with her to the home of her doctor's son. On the way, the sky was suddenly filled with a flurry of snow like goose down. The big flakes drifted slowly down on us. I was afraid the old lady would be tired, and let her rest on my shoulder. As the two of us stood there, with the goose-down snow falling on us, she suddenly began to laugh loudly. It was as though my own mother were resting on my shoulder; I shall never forget the moment.

On another occasion, I was helping her put on her makeup. She complained that I was making her eyebrows look ugly, and insisted that I do them again. When I had finished, we shared a rich laugh.

And so, in this way, walking with her through her mixture of distinct and clouded remembrances, the boiling waves of a young Chinese scholar in a distant country and a series of terrifying tales became real before my eyes.

Qian Xiuling was born on 12 March 1913 to a learned gentry family in Wangpoqiao, in the county of Yixing, Jiangsu province. Her father was, by imperial appointment, the head of a rural community known as a *xiang*. His household possessed a thousand *mu* (about one quarter of a square mile) of good farmland, and he was known far and wide as an enlightened member of the local gentry. The Qian clan were kindly to one and all, and all the children of the village, even those without a penny to their names, came to the clan school to study. The Qian clan enjoyed the affection and esteem of all the local residents.

I paid a visit to Yixing. It is the home of a distinctive purple pottery, a remarkable place that has produced outstanding people. Since ancient times, the culture of Yixing has valued cultural achievement, and placed a premium on literacy and learning. This little community, over the long course of China's history, produced ten scholars who made the top score in the highest-level imperial examinations; ten 'prime ministers' in imperial governments; twenty imperial academicians; more than seven thousand professors; presidents of China's two greatest universities, Tsinghua University and Peking University; and two ministers of education (one on the mainland and the other on Taiwan). Such renowned figures as the Marxist scholar and high official Jiang Nanxiang, physicist Zhou Peiyuan, the painters Xu Beiheng and Wu Guanzhong, and Pan Hannian, a well-known communist who suffered political destruction in the 1960s and 1970s but who was politically rehabilitated in 1982, all hailed from Yixing.

Qian Xiuling's upbringing in a household rich with culture but modest of bearing exerted a powerful influence upon her.

The immediate Qian family members were talented. Two became generals in the Chinese Nationalist armies. Eight earned doctoral degrees, including Qian Xiuling, Qian Zhuoru and Qian Xianren. General Qian Zhuolun served in many high military positions, including those of senior military staff adviser to the Kuomintang's Military Commission; head of the First Department of the Nationalist Defence Ministry; director of the staff office of the National Defence

Staff; and lieutenant general in charge of fortifications in the Jiangning Military District. His eldest son, Qian Xianzhang, with the rank of major general, served as chief of staff of the national government's Shanghai Military Administrative District.

But it is said that, shortly after General Qian Zhuolun moved to Taiwan, something terrible happened to his family. While he was attending the wedding banquet of a friend, several Nationalist military police burst in, seized General Qian's son Qian Xianming and his wife, and made off with them. Shortly after, the young couple, who had been reporters at the *Central Daily News*, were executed by the military police as Chinese Communist Party plotters. After that, Qian Zhuolun withdrew completely from the political stage and spent his last years at his residence.

Qian Xiuling had three older brothers. From childhood, she was extremely bright; by the age of four, for example, she was able to read the *Book of One Hundred Names*, a classic text for literacy training that lists and explains the dominant surnames in Chinese society; at five, she could read the *Poem of Mulan*. At six, she entered the village primary school with her older brothers, and at eleven she passed the examination to enter the Middle School attached to the Jiangsu Women's Normal College. Without waiting to graduate from there, she jumped to Datong University in Shanghai to enrol in college-preparatory courses, with a special emphasis on chemistry.

In 1929, Qian Xiuling learned that her brother Qian Zhuoru, who had been studying mining and metallurgy at Datong University, was planning to move to Belgium for study. She raced home to implore her mother and father to allow her also to go to Belgium for study. When her father refused, she locked herself in her bedroom and went on a hunger strike.

At that time, the Belgian government was using the Boxer indemnity payments from China to recruit and cover the expenses of students from China.

Playing Chess with the Devil

On 3 November 1929, Qian Xiuling, thanks to the effectiveness of her hunger strike, enthusiastically joined thirty other Chinese students on a French passenger ship bound from Shanghai to Marseille, to begin a new stage of her life in Europe.

For an overseas student, she was very young – only 16 – bubbly and adorable. On the ship, she spent much of her time running to and fro on the top deck, garnering the amusement and affection of her fellow passengers. Mme Song Qingling, sailing on the same voyage, called Qian Xiuling up to her cabin on the upper deck, offered her chocolates and asked her whether she could sing.

Qian Xiuling opened her mouth and sang a popular song of the moment, *Take Action*!

> The world is flooded with gushing tides
>
> Mountains and rivers are shifting
>
> The world mocks the Sick Man of East Asia!
>
> We women in particular have suffered for thousands of years
>
> Take action! Take action!
>
> Women, pluck up your courage!
>
> Take action! Take action!
>
> The Sick Man of East Asia slumbers on!
>
> Waken him quickly! Waken him quickly!

When I visited her, Qian Xiuling was still able to sing this song to me.

Song Qingling asked Qian what she was preparing to study in Belgium. Qian Xiuling blurted out: "Chemistry!"

Song Qingling asked her why she wanted to study chemistry; at the time, very few young women were doing so.

Qian Xiuling explained: "The person I admire most in the whole world is Madame Curie. I want to be a Chinese Madame Curie."

Song Qingling smiled and patted Qian Xiuling on the arm. "Study well," she encouraged her, "in the future, you will be a chemist like Madame Curie, and you will make your contributions to all mankind."

But Qian's dreams of Madame Curie were to be smashed by war.

Among 150 Chinese students studying abroad, Qian Xiuling was the youngest and the brightest, with the highest grades. After just a year of college preparatory work, her exceptional grades gained her admission to study chemistry at the renowned University of Leuven. There, she was one of only two female students, and the only student from China. Graduating from the university in 1933, she remained there as a teaching assistant while she worked on her PhD. Three years later, at the young age of 22, with an enviable academic record, she earned her doctorate in chemistry from the University of Leuven.

While she was at the university, Qian Xiuling caught the fancy of many boys among the foreign students – a pretty Oriental girl, exceptionally charming, petite and lovely, exceedingly smart, fond of singing and dancing, and extremely good at sports.

But when she was three years old, her father had betrothed her in an arranged marriage. Her fiancé was also studying at the University of Leuven. Her father allowed them to choose an auspicious day for their wedding, but the first time they met, Qian Xiuling did not like what she saw, and briskly cancelled this loveless union. Her father was extremely irritated; Qian's family and the family of her intended became enemies, exchanging hostile comments for many years.

Qian Xiuling bravely broke the shackles of her parents' feudalism and set out to seek her own love.

Two White Russian students in the department of medicine were

Qian Xiuling in her middle years.

in love with her at that time. Every day, they gave her flowers. One of them, by the name of Mikhail, told her: "You have to choose between the two of us!"

So, Qian Xiuling made her choice: a Russian boy whose French name, in Belgium, was Grégoire de Perlinghi. They loved each other deeply, and were constantly hand in hand, walking slowly through the leaves of the plane trees. He sang to her the Russian *Song of the Volga River* and she sang for him China's *Song of Action* and *The Little Sparrow*. He often went with her to the chemistry lab, sometimes staying with her through half the night. His goal was to become a physician who saved lives and helped the injured. Her goal was to become China's Madame Curie.

But not only did her love encounter the stern opposition of her parents; it also raised suspicions among a number of Chinese students: "There are plenty of us Chinese students – why haven't you chosen one of us? Why have you so perversely given your love to a foreigner?"

Qian Xiuling replied with a laugh: "Because he is the most lovable!"

Grégoire de Perlinghi was of Russian and Greek descent. He was tall and thin, with a composed demeanour. He was well brought up, and an elegant conversationalist.

On 27 October 1935, disregarding her parents' opposition, Qian Xiuling and her beloved joined hands and entered a church. Guided by the priest, they exchanged rings engraved with each other's names. On their wedding night, he embraced her and led her to the marital bed, strewn with roses. Thus began their sixty years of romantic and sincere love.

They cared for each other in times of need, and lived a long life of mutual love and friendship. They produced five children. Like a gentlemanly elder brother, Grégoire de Perlinghi loved and cherished her to the end of his days. He preceded her in death, in 1996.

After their wedding, Qian and Grégoire intended to return to China, so Qian looked for work that could be connected to Shanghai. But just as they were thinking about leaving Brussels to go back to China, Japan began its all-out aggression against China on 7 July 1937. The Japanese military not only crushed their plans to go to China, but also destroyed Qian's dreams of becoming China's Madame Curie. Qian had no alternative but to go the village of Herbeumont, 160km from Brussels, to open a country clinic.

I went to the village of Herbeumont in 2002 and found the small three-storey building in which they had lived, much changed by the years, the original owners long gone. I wandered aimlessly by the front of the building, and around the square where the fateful execution notice had been posted.

Dr de Perlinghi had been affectionately received by the villagers, both because he was a good man and because he was a fine doctor. And Qian Xiuling, unable to pursue her dream of becoming the next Madame Curie, fell into the life of wife and mother, assisting her husband and bringing up her children.

But on 12 March 1943, the notice of an impending execution by hanging utterly changed her life.

(12)

Studying that execution announcement, Qian Xiuling suddenly thought of someone.

Three years earlier, just after the Nazis had occupied Belgium, she had read in the newspapers that the Nazis were sending Alexander von Falkenhausen to be the head of the military government in the country. She realised that this man had served as Chiang Kai-shek's military adviser. She had quickly sent a note to her cousin Qian Zhuolun: Was this the same man who had been Chiang's military adviser? If so, would he transmit all of China's military secrets to Japan through Germany, Japan's ally? If he were to do this, China's defeat would be catastrophic.

She soon received Qian Zhuolun's reply: Although von Falkenhausen is a German general, he was not in league with the vicious Nazis. He is personally honourable, a man of extreme rectitude. There was no chance that he would sell China's interests out to Japan. If Qian Xiuling had any problems she should go to von Falkenhausen, who would warmly provide assistance.

And so, when Qian Xiuling saw the posted announcement of Gérard Roger's coming execution, she thought of her cousin's letter. Remembering von Falkenhausen, she pulled it out of her drawer and raced to Gérard Roger's home.

When Roger's family heard Qian's story and saw her cousin's letter, though they were besieged by doubt, they glimpsed a possible lifeline. They had no choice but to bet against very long odds.

Everyone rallied together, and the villagers sent a note, in the name of Gérard Roger's mother and father, to General von Falkenhausen. And they asked their mayor to send a separate and personal letter vouching for Gérard Roger.

The letters were filled with supplication to General von Falkenhausen, appealing to his humanity in cancelling the execution of Gérard Roger and saving the life of one young man.

That night, Qian Xiuling hastily boarded a train with her young son for the 160km trip to Brussels, bearing in her bosom the heavy assignment of the people of Herbeumont.

On top of everything else, 12 March was Qian Xiuling's 30th birthday. To that time, Qian's life had been fairly stable and quiet. Though she had taken her doctorate from the University of Leuven and had cherished ambitious goals for herself, she had really done nothing outstanding. She was just another Chinese student abroad, deprived by war of the chance to pursue her dreams, living out her ordinary life as a wife and mother in a tiny remote village in southern Belgium.

But with her bold decision to seek out Hitler's appointed military administrator to discuss with him the fate of a single resister sentenced to death, the dimensions of her world began to expand.

No one else told her to undertake this wild mission, and no one knew of her cousin's relationship with General von Falkenhausen. But her finer nature called to her and sent her on her way, to take the most critical and unshirkable step in her life. Now, on her 30th birthday, she was off on her wearying mission to save the life of another.

Was this merely a coincidence, or was it the unseen hand of Heaven at work?

Was the meaning of a birthday in one person's life to be found in the saving of another person's life?

Was the great woman who would come to be known as 'Belgium's mother' born on this very day?

The train rumbled through the night and the darkened fields. Qian Xiuling, her sleeping child in her arms, gazed through the window into the darkness, her heart heavy.

She knew well that the life of young Gérard Roger hung in the balance with her mission to Brussels. Her cousin's letter had told her that General von Falkenhausen, whom she had never met, was "personally honourable, a man of extreme rectitude", but she had no real idea of what kind of man he might be, and whether he might help her.

Just as she was drowning in her worries, a German soldier suddenly appeared in front of her. Terrified, she thought of the letters she was carrying. The soldier asked for her papers, which she quickly provided.

Because, during the war, trains started and stopped constantly, German troops often demanded to see passengers' papers. Finally, at dawn, the train reached Brussels.

Qian Xiuling tramped through the dim light of dawn, carrying her child, until she arrived in front of the door of a Chinese friend's home and knocked. Her Chinese friend, frightened, opened the door and said to her with amazement: "What are you doing, running here at this time of night?"

"Let me in and I'll explain," Qian replied.

That night, on a bed at her friend's home, Qian Xiuling never shut her eyes.

She fretted about the day to come. Would General von Falkenhausen see her? If he did agree to see her, would he agree to try to help to cancel Gérard Roger's execution? She could know nothing for sure.

(13)

The next morning, the sleepless Qian Xiuling urgently telephoned the Chinese embassy in Brussels to find General von Falkenhausen's telephone number.

Von Falkenhausen learned by phone that General Qian Zhuolun's younger cousin had come to Brussels to meet him, and he quickly agreed to a meeting. He instructed her to come to the Chateau de Seneffe that very morning.

Hastily asking her friend to call her a cab and look after her son, Qian Xiuling set out for the Chateau de Seneffe.

I myself have made the trip to the Chateau de Seneffe, about sixty kilometres from Brussels. It was originally built by a Jewish banker. With the German invasion, the banker was driven out, and the military government occupied the chateau and established its headquarters there.

When I went there, evening had fallen, the gates were shut and no one was inside. The sun's slanting rays fell upon this chateau, which had seen so many vicissitudes. Looking at this century-old structure, the effects of years of harsh weather failed to diminish its vastness and grandeur. The facade of the chateau was a two-storey main building, flanked by two smaller round turrets. Broad gardens were encircled by a wall of iron railings, while beyond the wall lay a band of fields. The palace lay still and secure; it was easy to see why the Nazis had decided to establish their military government headquarters there.

Gazing at the chateau, the image of Qian Xiuling meeting with General von Falkenhausen flooded my imagination.

At 11.15 that morning, Qian Xiuling stood before the heavily guarded chateau, bristling with security forces.

To enter, she had to pass through two checkpoints, the first at the main gate and the second within the edifice itself.

When the soldiers set out to search her, her palms sweated and her heartbeat choked at her throat. She was terrified that the letters in her bag would be discovered – not letters, but a life!

The soldiers opened her bag, found no weapons and let her go.

Guided by an attendant, she crossed the great hall on the second floor, where many officials were seated, and under their astonished gaze she made her way to General von Falkenhausen's office.

As she entered, her heart froze again. What would she read on the face of the man she was about to meet? Icy rejection? Warm friendliness? Or merely perfunctory blandness?

What she observed in the spacious office was an aged general, tall and straight, in an impeccable uniform, with deep eyes, seated in front of his great desk.

Bowing respectfully, she addressed him politely in French. "How do you do, General von Falkenhausen. I am sorry to trouble you."

"Hello, Mme Qian. Please be seated."

A trace of a smile crossed the general's stern visage as he invited her to sit down. With no further pleasantries, he began in French: "General Qian Zhuolun is a good friend. Please tell me, Mme Qian, what I can do for you?"

"Uh, yes, General von Falkenhausen," Qian Xiuling blurted out. "From Zhuolun, I know that you are a general of great rectitude, upright and kind-hearted. The matter is this. In my little village of Herbeumont there is a young man whom the Gestapo have seized and taken away. His name is Gérard Roger. They have posted a notice that he is to be hanged in three days. But he is a wonderful young man, and his parents' only child. I entreat you gaze upon the faces of the elderly residents of our village, and the faces of Gérard Roger's mother and father, and on my own feelings and the feelings of Qian Zhuolun, to save him. I beg you to give him his life by stopping his execution. He is barely 29, and is soon to be married. All of us from our village will be profoundly indebted to you."

Then she nervously drew several letters from her bag and formally presented them to the general with both hands, as though she were offering him a human life. She sat gravely before him with clasped hands.

Von Falkenhausen took the letters and glanced through them quickly. Qian Xiuling bowed her head, her gaze fixed on the general and her heart beating in her throat.

Her cousin had told her in his letter that General von Falkenhausen was a person of the highest rectitude, but at the end of the day he was now Hitler's all-powerful agent in Belgium. He carried out Nazi Germany's commands there. And now she had raced to this Nazi general to implore him to cancel an execution. He would have plenty of reasons to turn her down. He might even arrest her for sympathising with the young resistance fighter.

Oh, God! The tension was extreme. Her mind seemed as though it might shatter. She heard her deafening heartbeat. She knew that Gérard Roger's life hung in the balance at that very moment.

What she didn't realise was that in coming to von Falkenhausen to beg for the cancellation of this execution, she was neither the first nor the last to do so. People sought him out every day. In one corner of his office was a file drawer filled with appeals from relatives and friends for the pardoning of their loved ones. In reality, the Gestapo's execution orders did not fall under von Falkenhausen's jurisdiction at all; instead, they were approved directly by Gestapo headquarters in Berlin. But still, he could use his authority and influence as military governor of Belgium to change the decisions on the execution of resistance fighters.

And so, Qian Xiuling, her mind almost snapping under the tension, heard a single sentence that shook her to her core, a sentence she would never forget: "All right. I'll do everything I can to take care of this. Please return to your home and wait for news."

She stared at him, unable to believe her ears, wondering if she had heard him correctly.

"Please relax. I'll do everything I can."

Her palpitating heart finally came to rest.

"Thank you, thank you, General von Falkenhausen. My deepest thanks. I entrust the life of this young man to you. I won't trouble you further, and will say goodbye." Qian Xiuling rose and offered a deep bow to the general.

As soon as Qian Xiuling was gone, von Falkenhausen summoned his secretary and told him to contact the Gestapo chief in Brussels, and order him to send over the death sentence on Gérard Roger. He added: "Tell him that Gestapo headquarters in Berlin has phoned. They're short of labour and have ordered that the colonel convert all death sentences to hard labour."

Von Falkenhausen knew that all those sentenced to death were deeply committed resistance fighters, and he held them in admiration. As soon as he assumed his position, he exerted his utmost efforts, and used all sorts of reasons to commute their death sentences. But each time he did this he had to act reasonably and fairly, so as not to allow the Gestapo to discover any irregularity. This Gestapo boss was a vicious character who had to be handled very carefully.

Emerging from the Chateau de Seneffe, Qian Xiuling experienced relief unlike anything she had felt before – it was pure exaltation. Her footsteps were light-hearted. She had not disappointed the hopes of the villagers. Gérard Roger's life would be spared.

When she returned to Herbeumont, Qian Xiuling received a queen's welcome.

Three days later, the news arrived: Gérard Roger's sentence had been commuted from execution to hard labour. Overjoyed, the villagers ran to her, embraced her, and proclaimed her "Holy Mother Mary".

Gérard Roger was quickly transferred to a labour camp in Berlin. He was not liberated until the end of the war.

When I visited in 1999, Gérard Roger was still alive. I asked Qian Xiuling to call him and ask whether I could visit, but because his health was very poor he tactfully declined the meeting.

On the same day that Gérard Roger's sentence was commuted, another person of the same name, imprisoned in the small Belgian town of Bouillon, was also saved.

It should be understood that the Gestapo had a savage policy towards the resistance; all were to be executed without debate. The entreaties of the King of the Belgians made no difference. These two resistance fighters were spared from execution entirely thanks to a Chinese woman's appeals.

When the news emerged, it spread like a whirlwind throughout Belgium, causing great excitement. Everyone wondered: What is this woman's name? What does she do? How did she manage this so adroitly? She must have magical powers to be able to save resistance fighters sentenced to death! What is her true relationship with the Nazi military governor?

But no one had any details about Qian Xiuling. People only knew that she was a Chinese woman, of considerable talent, and that she had been able to save a resistance member sentenced to death.

The moving tale of this miraculous Chinese woman spread quietly throughout Belgium. The more it spread, the more it seemed like a miracle. The story spread farther and farther. This legendary Chinese woman became a heroine in the hearts of the Belgians, and a saviour for those imprisoned and doomed members of the resistance. Throughout the nation, the relatives of the imprisoned all knew of Qian Xiuling and sought to discover her whereabouts.

Little by little, the remote and obscure village of Herbeumont came to the attention of the Belgians. The de Perlinghi clinic became a lifeline for members of the resistance. Qian Xiuling became their great saviour. For a while, family members of prisoners throughout Belgium came to seek her out. Her good nature compelled Qian Xiuling to accede to their every appeal. On occasion, so many people came to her that she could make no commitments to them all, and had to make choices among their appeals. She placed the greatest weight on those resistance members already sentenced to death. Often, she left her child with her husband and travelled alone to Brussels.

(14)

A year passed. A slight, pretty figure could frequently be seen taking the 160km train trip from Herbeumont to Brussels, sometimes with a child in tow and sometimes by herself, but always risking danger from the Gestapo, over and over again making her way to the Chateau de Seneffe to stand before the Nazis' military governor of Belgium.

Once, on the train, Qian Xiuling overheard a whispered conversation that a guerrilla in the resistance had been taken by the Gestapo and was about to be hanged. She quickly whispered to the speaker: "What is the guerrilla's name?" A few days later, that guerrilla, a complete stranger to her, was sentenced to hard labour and sent to Berlin.

Each time she journeyed to the military governor's palace, crossing the great hall under the astonished gaze of the crowd, to meet General von Falkenhausen without any waiting, pressing upon the great brown door to enter the chamber where the lives of so many hung in the balance.

Each time, she was greeted by the same still and sombre visage, devoid of small talk, only placing a piece of paper in front of her and nodding: "Kindly write down the names of those you want to save."

Then he would place the list in his drawer.

Occasionally, he would give her advice.

Once, she wrote down two names. "Write that they are brothers," he said.

Each time she came to him, he warned her sternly: "You must beware of spies. Belgian collaborators and the Gestapo are everywhere. In Wallonia and Flanders, in the towns and in the countryside, there are plenty of Belgian traitors. They create all manner of terrible things."

Another time he warned her: "You must be sure to deliver your name lists only to me personally. Never let anyone else have them if you want to avoid trouble."

And each time she would bow her head, saying: "Please, do not fear. I certainly…"

Like revolutionaries making contact with each other, everything was done according to unspoken agreement.

Over the course of a year, countless members of the resistance, all complete strangers, were granted new lives thanks to this silent contract, undertaken amid mortal danger.

These two people – a Nazi general and a Chinese overseas student, both possessed of righteousness and the best of human nature – exerted their common efforts to save the lives of Belgians with whom they had no connection whatsoever.

Von Falkenhausen and Qian Xiuling both understood that they could lose their own lives each time they undertook a life-saving mission.

Qian Xiuling knew this, and felt deeply apologetic. More than once, meeting with von Falkenhausen, she said: "General von Falkenhausen, I feel truly embarrassed. I keep bringing these requests to you, and I know they are exceedingly hard to arrange. I know these matters are very dangerous."

And indeed, though von Falkenhausen was military governor of Belgium, he had no power to order the Gestapo to release anyone. Himmler's Gestapo was a secret police organ, beholden to no one else's commands. Von Falkenhausen fell under the direction of the Wehrmacht, Germany's army, and thus had authority over the German army of occupation, but not the field armies or the Gestapo.

Each time he received a list of names of those to be spared, he had to devise various reasons for seeking out figures in the German high command and asking them to send down the orders sparing the lives of those on the list and commuting their sentences to hard labour. Often, he used the shortage of labour in Berlin as the avenue to convince them.

Hearing Qian Xiuling's words of embarrassment and apology, von Falkenhausen would shake his head and say from the heart: "I deeply admire the patriotic activities of these members of the resistance, and I will do everything I can to save them."

"General von Falkenhausen, I deeply admire you."

"Thank you."

Actions bespeak the souls of men.

In his diary, von Falkenhausen wrote:

> I have received a great many appeals for the commutation of death sentences. It seems that this must be a Belgian national custom. When the appeals are sent by people I am acquainted with, I naturally respect those for whom they appeal, and I treat them with great seriousness. Sometimes bundles of such letters come in from the wife of an Italian embassy official in Brussels. I read each letter of appeal and answer each one. While some of my answers are denials, I nevertheless exhaust all possibilities.

But at this time, a pair of eyes sent from Berlin were secretly spying on General von Falkenhausen's every action.

When I interviewed Qian Xiuling, I asked her: "In all, how many lives did you save?" She shook her head and said she couldn't remember.

Von Falkenhausen wrote in his memoirs that none of the friends he visited in his later years could clearly say how many members of the resistance they had saved. For his part, von Falkenhausen never talked with others about saving anyone in the resistance. But I know that the final batch of hostages whom they risked their lives to save numbered ninety-six.

(15)

These events happened on 9 June 1944, deep in the night of the third day after the Allied invasion of Normandy.

That night, the sky was black, with thick clouds and not a trace of starlight.

In the pitch blackness of the village of Herbeumont, only a single faint light could be seen in the three-storey residence of Qian Xiuling.

Qian Xiuling and her husband lay in bed, talking in whispers about news of the Allied landings. Dr de Perlinghi, with loving concern for his wife, who was five months pregnant, said: "This hateful war is almost over. I am still so worried that someone will come to seek your help. My love, each time you have gone on a mission to save lives, I have been worried sick about you. If someone seeks your help now, you absolutely must not go. It is too dangerous."

"Don't worry. I will not go again," Qian replied, knowing that General von Falkenhausen was having some difficulties that prevented her from going to him again.

Four months earlier, in February 1944, the family of a doctor who had been sentenced to hang had come to Qian Xiuling, begging her to exert herself to save him. Qian had gone to von Falkenhausen's palace, but when she got there the general had not met with her, sending only his secretary to receive her.

The secretary informed Qian that von Falkenhausen had encountered some problems and that it was not possible to meet with her. The secretary asked Qian to tell him what was on her mind, so that he could pass on her message. But he also conveyed a message to her from von Falkenhausen, asking her not to seek further meetings with him because his circumstances no longer permitted him to be of assistance.

Hearing this, Qian Xiuling was deeply anxious. She did not know what difficulties von Falkenhausen had encountered. Were they because of her? In asking him to save people's lives, had she awakened the suspicions of the Gestapo?

But in spite of the difficulties he faced, von Falkenhausen did what he could to save the life of the doomed doctor, and managed to have his sentence commuted to hard labour in Berlin. The doctor was freed at the end of the war.

During my visit to the town of Écaussines, I met with this doctor. Seated in a wheelchair, his eyes filled with tears when he saw Qian Xiuling, he embraced her fiercely. He said that Qian Xiuling had given him his life. If she had not personally sought his salvation, he would have gone to meet his maker long ago.

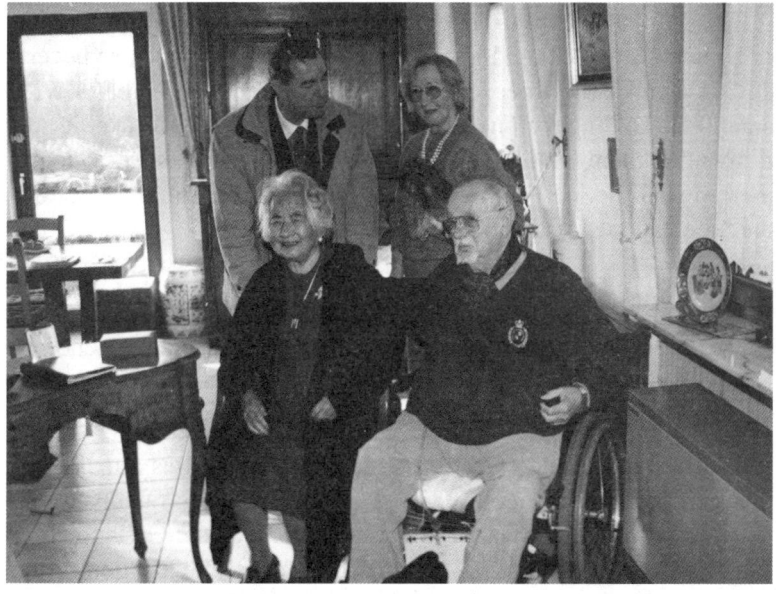

The physician rescued by Qian Xiuling (front row, right) was still alive in 1999.

At midnight on the night of 9 June 1944, Qian and her husband had just gone to bed, when suddenly there was a hurried banging on their door.

The couple threw on some clothes and raced downstairs. They leaned from a window to try to see who was outside.

All they could see was a battered Citroën parked outside. Three young men in tattered, dirty clothes stood in great agitation outside her door. They did not look like enemy agents or Germans.

Dr de Perlinghi opened the door and let them in. Together, he and Qian Xiuling heard their heartbreaking story.

At that moment, in Écaussines, 160km away, 96 lives hung in the balance. Once again, the final call for Qian's intervention arrived.

The previous day, 8 June, three Gestapo officers had been assassinated in the main plaza of the town. One of them was a colonel who headed the Gestapo in Brussels.

The chain of events had begun on 2 June, with the Gestapo's arrest of a guerrilla leader and his two daughters. The Gestapo used every device against the three captives, burning the girls' breasts with cigarettes, holding their heads under water to simulate drowning and tormenting them until they hovered between life and death, to make them reveal the location of a secret radio broadcasting station and the whereabouts of their guerrilla unit. But the three captives kept silent.

On 8 June, the Gestapo chief, sensing that defeat lay just ahead, took the captured guerrilla leader back to his residence in Écaussines, thinking that he could locate the broadcasting antenna and the guerrilla group through his prisoner.

When the guerrilla entered his home, the place was a mess, but the secret passageway connecting to his comrades was undisturbed, to his great relief. No matter how many methods the Gestapo chief used to extract information, he refused to reveal the location of the radio station or the guerrilla unit.

Unable to get any answers from his captive, the Gestapo boss had no choice but to have him driven back to Brussels and thrown in prison. As the motorcade was passing the main square in Écaussines there was an outburst of gunfire. Three Gestapo chieftains died on the spot. Only one driver, wounded in the arm, managed to drive away and make a report. What followed was a brutal act of revenge.

The following day, 9 June, at five in the morning, as the people slept before dawn, five hundred Gestapo agents surrounded the entire town of Écaussines, awakened the sleeping populace and drove them into the town square. There they seized 96 young men as hostages.

One of the Gestapo roared: "Listen to me. You have thirty-six hours to turn over the guerrillas who attacked our Gestapo officers. If you don't comply, we will execute all ninety-six of these people by firing squad. We will kill them fifteen at a time until you turn over the culprits."

But no one did turn in those who had attacked the Gestapo chief. And so, the Gestapo dragged out the 96 hostages and took them to prison in Brussels.

I went to Écaussines. It is a little town, just like so many others in Europe: sparkling clean, with single-family residences arrayed along both sides of the streets, simple and peaceful. Although it was but a little town, it was populated by heroes.

The Commemorative Hall of the Second World War displayed artefacts and photos of these martyrs, along with some of the guns, ammunition, broadcasting sets and printing equipment used by the guerrillas. The person in charge of the hall was a brother of one of the martyrs. At the gate of the hall was parked a Citroën sedan, the very car that Qian Xiuling had used, now rusted and deteriorated. But the car told people all that had happened that year.

By 9 June, everyone could hear the sound of artillery fire as the Allies advanced to liberate Brussels, and could glimpse the victory ahead. But for the families of the 96 hostages and the people of Écaussines, only 36 hours remained. In that 36 hours, if the four guerrillas who had attacked the Gestapo were not turned over, 96 people would meet their deaths, one after another. The list of names of the first 15 to be shot had already been made public. The Gestapo had drawn straws to see who would be shot in what order. In the first batch were two young boys, 17 and 18 years old. It was too pitiable.

All of the town was sunk in gloom and tearful despair.

Then, someone thought of the legendary Chinese woman. But no one knew her or even knew her name. They only knew that she lived in the village of Herbeumont. That was 160km away, and there was no car to go there and bring her back. When the Germans invaded, they had confiscated all private cars and radio sets.

Someone said that there was an old car stored in a nearby village. With that, three young men leapt up to seek help.

These three young fellows pulled an old Citroën from under a family's haystack, where it had lain for four years. After dark, with a few repairs and some petrol pilfered from the Germans' fuel tanks, with no drivers' licences or official papers authorising its movement, and under constant threat of arrest or attack, they took the ancient Citroën on the road.

At that moment, all transportation had been sealed. They dared not use the main road or turn on their headlights. They could only grope their way in the dark along rugged small roadways through the hills. The car broke down many times. It was midnight before they reached Qian Xiuling's house.

Facing the three unfamiliar callers, Qian Xiuling was seized with sadness. She explained that General von Falkenhausen had left the country.

The three replied: "Mme Qian, we beg you to see the ninety-six lives in the balance, and to see the faces of their families. Please –

make one more trip. Even if there is no hope, we implore you to make one final effort!"

"Mme Qian, we beg of you. See the faces of the ninety-six. Return with us in our car."

"Before God, please – come back with us."

Hearing the cries of the three young men, Qian Xiuling's noble heart was deeply moved. She felt there was no way she could turn them down. Ninety-six lives, ninety-six families! Even with no hope, she had to make one final effort.

"Dear one, I must go," she said to her husband. "If I don't go, my conscience will never be at peace."

Her husband sighed deeply and clutched his wife to him. For a long time, he said nothing. He was proud of his wife, a woman of such character, but he could not help worrying about the tiny life within her body. He knew that, with the Allied invasion, the two sides were locked in fierce battle. Outside, the night was cloudy and starless; only the light from artillery flashes pierced the gloom. In such a violent battle, even a good conscience would not prevent an artillery shell from landing on her head. With everyone else hiding in their homes, how could she risk her unborn child by going out into such danger?

But he knew he could not stop her. She was a woman who seemed soft on the outside, but who had a will of iron. What she decided to do, no one could prevent her from doing. From the time she saved the life of Gérard Roger, she had never ceased to tread the path of saving others' lives.

Her husband could only say to the three young men: "Listen to me. You must bring my wife safely back to my side."

"Please set your heart at ease. We three will guarantee her with our lives."

Her husband knew that these pledges were only words blowing in the wind at a time like this. They were useless. He could only pray for his wife's good luck. Only the god of destiny could smile on their beautiful and prosperous family.

At the door, de Perlinghi embraced his wife, pressing her again and again: "My beloved, you can surely return in peace. Our child and I are waiting for you, dreaming of your safe return."

"Don't worry, my love. I'll get back safely for sure," Qian Xiuling replied with a thin smile.

Dr de Perlinghi stood in the doorway, watching as his ungainly wife clambered into the beetle-like Citroën and the car disappeared swiftly into the darkness.

As the car departed, the doctor suddenly felt as though his heart had been hollowed out, as his tears welled up. He could not know whether he would ever see his wife again.

In time of war, anything can happen.

Thus, at the fiercest moment of the war, in a darkness so thick that one could not see the five fingers on the hand, a dilapidated Citroën sedan, with four people crammed inside like the filling of a steamed bun – one of them a Chinese woman five months pregnant with her child of mixed race, the other three tall and strong Belgian boys – braved the constant thunder of distant artillery and the occasional explosion of a random shell, and jolted through the Belgian night. The road was rough and potholed, and more than once the car nearly overturned as they drove the 160km back to Écaussines.

Three times the car broke down, and three times they managed to fix it in complete darkness. Finally, at 5am the next day, they reached Écaussines.

When I interviewed Qian Xiuling, I asked her: "Weren't you scared at that time?"

The old lady gave the faintest of smiles: "At that moment, I didn't think about fear."

Playing Chess with the Devil

A simple, unadorned sentence, so expressive of a person's great soul.

She didn't think about fear because 96 people and 96 families desperately waited for her to go and save them. She did not fear for her own safety. She did not fear for the five-month-old foetus in her womb. At that moment, she had no idea whether she would be able to get to see General von Falkenhausen, let alone whether he would be able to help her. Whatever the outcome, she had to brave all risks and make every possible effort.

I wonder how many people in this day and age – not only expectant mothers, but any woman or man – would brave mortal danger and race to save others. I feel that Qian Xiuling is the most beautiful woman I have ever met. Her beauty lay not in the God-given lovely appearance of her face but in the beauty of her God-given soul.

That dawn, as Qian Xiuling pulled into Écaussines in the old Citroën, everyone in the town had poured into the streets, welcoming her as though she were the Virgin Mary, embracing her and saluting her.

The townspeople hung the lives of 96 of their fellows upon her.

That morning, the mayor of the town came to meet Qian.

In the afternoon, the three young men brought Qian Xiuling, bearing the hopes of 96 families and all the people of the town, to the Chateau de Seneffe. Because the roads were sealed off, with frequent checkpoints, every step of the way was extremely difficult. It was ten at night by the time they reached the Chateau de Seneffe.

By that time, only two hours remained before the first batch of 15 hostages was to face execution.

Qian Xiuling hurriedly told the guard to inform General von Falkenhausen that she had something to see him about immediately. For a long time, there was no reply. Qian was afire with impatience. She kept glancing at her watch. She knew well that with each passing minute, fifteen people came a step closer to death.

At 11.30pm, von Falkenhausen's secretary appeared. He told Qian that von Falkenhausen was in an important military meeting and could not see her; she was to return at 11.30 the next morning to see the general.

Qian Xiuling hurriedly told the secretary why she had come, and asked that von Falkenhausen immediately order a stop to the execution of the hostages. The secretary nodded, turned on his heel and departed.

Now it was 30 minutes before the scheduled execution of the first 15 hostages. Qian Xiuling had no idea whether von Falkenhausen could issue the command to stop it.

At 11.30 the next morning, Qian Xiuling entered the Chateau de Seneffe for the last time.

Once inside, she could feel a looming and ghastly tension in the air. The great guest hall was cheerless and empty; not a single person was in sight. It was a far cry from the days when the room was full of people waiting for their meetings with government officials.

As she entered his office, all she saw was von Falkenhausen and a middle-aged general seated on a sofa and conversing. When the younger officer spotted her, he rose, nodded to her and left the room.

Qian Xiuling was astounded. Von Falkenhausen seemed to have become a different person. He was sunk in depression, his face haggard and filled with gloom. She had never seen him so dejected, and had no idea what she was facing.

Von Falkenhausen had known for a long time that what Hitler had brought to Germany was not hope but destruction. And so, for a long time, he had belonged to a secret anti-Hitler organisation. But his activities had caught the attention of the Gestapo in Brussels, acting on orders from Berlin. Now, with the Allies already on the ground at Normandy, Germany was facing mortal danger. Von Falkenhausen, a German general, was facing arrest, concentration camp or even execution. A calamity for both his country and his family was at hand; how could he not be disheartened? He had been up until four that morning pondering the question of what to do about Hitler.

Qian Xiuling knew none of this. She only felt sorry that she was bothering the general, particularly at a time like this. But she had to come because 96 lives were in her hands.

Von Falkenhausen nodded to her and signalled for her to take a seat.

Without sitting down, Qian began in a voice full of apology. "General von Falkenhausen, I feel terrible about bothering you again, but the ninety-six hostages are innocent, ordinary people, with families, parents and children. They did not kill the three Gestapo officials. Please, I implore you: save them any way you can."

Von Falkenhausen sat silently for a moment, and then said in a sombre voice: "I am in trouble. The Gestapo is secretly watching me very closely, and I am about to be removed from my position."

Hearing these words, Qian Xiuling's heart was stricken, both for the 96 hostages and for von Falkenhausen. She thought to herself: "That finishes it. General von Falkenhausen cannot help me save these hostages. He himself is in a desperate situation – how could he concern himself with the hostages?"

But then, just as she was giving up hope, she heard these startling words: "But, set your mind at ease. I can use the last powers I hold to save these innocent lives."

"My deepest thanks, General von Falkenhausen. My most profound thanks. I simply do not know how to thank you."

She knew the general was a man of his word, whose actions would be effective. He would not simply use loose words to buy her off. She knew then that the 96 would be saved.

She rose to her feet, her eyes filled with tears, and bowed deeply to the general. Sobbing, she said: "General, on behalf of the ninety-six hostages and their families, thank you. They will thank you forever."

Von Falkenhausen shook his head. "Don't thank me – they are innocent," he said.

"General von Falkenhausen," Qian said hurriedly, "if you are facing removal from office, is it because of the trouble I have brought you on behalf of those people?"

"No," von Falkenhausen cut her off. "Those people should not have been executed. They were fighting to protect their own nation's rights. I admire them a great deal. Unfortunately, I have not been able to... All right. It has come to this. I must go to join General Rommel. Farewell, Mme Qian."

"Farewell, General von Falkenhausen."

General von Falkenhausen extended his hand to Qian Xiuling, and they shook hands for the last time, before he sent her off at his doorway.

Qian Xiuling began to leave General von Falkenhausen's office and turned her head back once, thinking that this was the final time she would see the chamber where so many people had been given back their lives. As she turned, she saw von Falkenhausen in his doorway, waving to her. She quickly waved back.

Suddenly, she had a premonition; the image of General von Falkenhausen flickered before her eyes but then faded into obscurity.

The next day, when the three young men had conveyed Qian Xiuling back to Herbeumont in their ancient Citroën, she could see Dr de Perlinghi and their son standing outside their door, anxiously waiting for her return.

As soon as he saw her, her son ran to her and threw his arms around her legs, crying: "Mama! Mama! You've come back! We both worried about you!"

Qian Xiuling's first words to her husband were these: "Von Falkenhausen is in trouble."

Her husband stared at her. "Is it because you went to him often to try to save lives?"

Qian Xiuling shook her head without answering.

Several days later, none of the 96 had been killed; all were transferred to a concentration camp in Berlin for hard labour. After he received Qian Xiuling's appeal through his secretary, General von Falkenhausen had issued the order to halt the execution of the hostages, and thereby saved 96 lives.

(16)

General von Falkenhausen used the last powers at his disposal to save the lives of the 96 hostages, but sadly he could not save himself. He changed the fates of others, but could not change his own.

He had in fact participated in the anti-Hitler group for a long time. He and Wehrmacht chief of staff Ludwig Beck were good friends. Beck was the leader of the anti-Hitler conspiracy and had gathered a number of high-ranking military leaders. These fine officers knew from an early point that Hitler was a war-drunk monster. The outbreak of the war was wholly the result of Hitler's inflated ambitions to rule the world, and had nothing to do with the wishes of the German people. What Hitler brought to Germany was not hope but destruction. They plotted repeatedly to kill Hitler, but, sadly, without success.

Not only was von Falkenhausen a member of the anti-Hitler conspiracy; he was also military leader on the Western Front. After General Rommel, the famed 'Desert Fox', was defeated in north Africa, he fell into Hitler's bad graces. Von Falkenhausen and General Carl Heinrich von Stülpnagel sought Rommel out several times and finally succeeded in bringing him in to their anti-Hitler secret camp.

Because von Falkenhausen's headquarters at the Chateau de

Seneffe was far from Berlin, it became the secret meeting place for the officers and men in the conspiracy, who frequently convened there.[4]

Over time, more and more conspirators were arrested and executed. Von Falkenhausen walked a tightrope, trying to protect Germany's interests and the interests of the Belgian people.

Thus, in the fourth year of his military governorship in Belgium, he still had not carried out Hitler's orders, and was still engaged in humanitarian efforts to protect, as fully as possible, the interests of the Belgian people. He assisted in the creation of the Belgian Red Cross to provide food and medicines to the Belgians. He tried to protect the economic development of Belgium by restoring transportation facilities and buildings damaged by war. He opposed the German plan for forced labour in Belgium. He did everything he could to save the lives of Belgian resistance members condemned to death.

These measures were utterly unique in areas occupied by the Nazis.

Because of this, Goering and Goebbels had both criticised von Falkenhausen on numerous occasions for being weak and not carrying out his duties. They reported secretly to Hitler that von Falkenhausen was disloyal to him, and that he was suspected of plotting rebellion against the Third Reich. Hitler therefore sent an administrator to observe von Falkenhausen's behaviour secretly. The reason that it took such a long time to remove von Falkenhausen from his post was that he had highly placed friends in Berlin to protect him; they used every personal tie they could to save von Falkenhausen from being branded a criminal.

With the Allied landings on 6 June 1944, German forces on the Eastern Front and the Western Front fell into the direst straits. The anti-Hitler conspirators knew that time was of the essence; they would have only one opportunity. They had to eliminate this monster and minimise Germany's losses.

The conspirators met and took an oath: "We must carry out the attempt on Hitler at all costs. If we fail, we will attempt to seize power in Berlin. We will show the world and our descendants that the members of the German resistance movement are prepared to take decisive steps, and to face all dangers without hesitation. Nothing else matches the importance of this goal."[5]

But on 14 July, six days before the attempt on Hitler's life by Colonel von Stauffenberg, General von Falkenhausen suddenly received an order from Berlin removing him from all his posts, including that of military governor of Belgium and northern France. He realised that his own luck had run out. The only hope, he knew, was that von Stauffenberg's bomb might kill the monster and bring everything to an end.

At midday on 20 July, the brilliant military officer and member of the anti-Hitler conspiracy, 37-year-old Colonel Claus von Stauffenberg – one-armed, one-eyed, wearing a black eye patch and bearing the long-cherished hope of saving Germany from further destruction – managed to bring a dispatch case containing a bomb into Hitler's 'Wolf's Lair' headquarters near Rastenburg in East Prussia and placed it below the conference table only six feet from Hitler. Unfortunately, a major general named Brandt, who arrived in advance of the meeting, removed the dispatch case and set it down at the outer side of the table.

At 12.42pm, the bomb exploded. General Brandt was killed, but Hitler survived, to live nine months more.

This was the last of more than ten attempts on Hitler's life, none of which had gone according to plan.

Von Falkenhausen was not only aware of this attempt; he was a participant in the plot. But when the bad news arrived, it signalled the collapse of years of effort.

What followed was monstrous retaliation. His great friend Field Marshal Eric von Witzleben, Colonel General Erich Hoepner and several other generals were all apprehended. Von Falkenhausen knew that he would soon face the same fate.

He could have fled abroad. But he was concerned for his family members and his followers. Moreover, the Gestapo was watching him night and day, and would not have allowed him to escape. All he could do was remain in the Chateau de Seneffe, awaiting his uncertain fate.

He remained alone in his office, refusing to see anyone. Only his secretary, who had served him for so many years, could witness the general's hopelessness and bitter internal struggle.

At three in the afternoon on 29 July, the accursed moment arrived.

An officer named Canaris arrived at the Chateau de Seneffe and entered von Falkenhausen's office. To von Falkenhausen, Canaris said: "Respected General, on orders from Supreme Headquarters, I have come here to instruct you to travel to Berlin for a military conference."

"I will have my secretary make preparations," von Falkenhausen replied.

"No. No need to bring your secretary. You are to come alone."

Von Falkenhausen saw that the Devil was finally showing his face.

That evening, von Falkenhausen and his wife dined privately at a grand restaurant in the Plaza hotel for the final time. They held hands and chatted long into the night. For four years, the von Falkenhausens had lived in a pair of guest rooms at the hotel. Over a forty-year marriage they had always been one another's helpmates. But as her mother had told her: "My daughter, if you go with this man, you will certainly live a tumultuous life." Theirs was unquestionably a tumultuous life.

Not only because he was a military man, but also because he was born in a tumultuous time and into a nation led to bestiality by one bestial man. Now, as man and wife faced parting forever, they could not know whether they would ever lay eyes on each other again.

Von Falkenhausen said to his wife quietly: "After I am gone, you must live a good life. Whatever happens, you must live your life firmly and strongly."

His wife lay against his chest and said with a sob: "My beloved, nothing terrible will happen. Perhaps they really are asking you to come to a military meeting."

Von Falkenhausen shook his head. "Impossible. Hitler has wanted to bring me down for a long time. It is only…"

At the brink of separating, perhaps forever, the couple passed the saddest sleepless night of their lives.

At ten the next morning, Canaris sent men to relieve von Falkenhausen of his personal firearms and place him in a jeep. Before getting into the car, von Falkenhausen and his wife kissed farewell for the last time. Von Falkenhausen encouraged his wife once again: "My beloved, remember: face everything with strength. Take care of yourself. Goodbye."

His wife sobbed: "Take good care. Goodbye."

Her face covered in tears, von Falkenhausen's wife watched as the jeep bearing her husband moved away and finally disappeared in the distance, on the road back to Germany. She silently made the sign of the cross and prayed to God for her husband's safe return.

But everything is unknowable.

No sooner had von Falkenhausen's car departed when his secretary shot himself.

As the car entered Germany, the officer sent by Canaris to bring von Falkenhausen back declared: "On instruction from the highest authorities, I place you under arrest." He then handcuffed von Falkenhausen.

The date was 30 July 1944. Von Falkenhausen was transferred to a concentration camp in an out-of-the-way village to await his fate.

(17)

After the 20 July Incident, Hitler ordered bloody reprisals against the assassination plotters.

The Rise and Fall of the Third Reich states:

> Research materials show 4,980 people killed. Secret police records indicate that 7,000 were arrested.
>
> The first convening of 'People's Courts' took place on 7 and 8 August in Berlin. Among those convicted of participation in the 20 July plot were Field Marshal von Witzleben, Colonel General Hoepner, Major General Helmuth Stieff, Lieutenant General Paul von Hase and a number of lower-ranking officers who had cooperated closely with von Stauffenberg in the plot.[6]

Those sentenced to death were brutally tortured, summarily judged, tied to butcher's meat hooks and finally hanged while they were still alive. Field Marshal von Witzleben, recipient of the Iron Cross First Class and Iron Cross Second Class medals, was hanged on 8 September in the Plotzensee prison in Berlin.

Field Marshal Erwin Rommel – the highly regarded 'Desert Fox' and 'Eagle of the Reich', whom British Prime Minister Winston Churchill regarded as a courageous and skilful opponent – was forced to commit suicide at his home on 14 October; it has been said that Hitler had sent the cyanide capsule that Rommel used to end his life.[7]

Many other military officers took their own lives in order to avoid trial and judgment. According to *The Rise and Fall of the Third Reich*, Major General Henning von Tresckow, serving on the Eastern Front, was involved in the plot. Before he committed suicide, it is said that he spoke to his deputy commander von Schlabrendorff in this way:

Now, everyone is going to attack us and denounce us. But my heart is unwavering. What we have done is right! Hitler is not only Germany's greatest enemy; he is the world's greatest enemy. In a few hours, I will stand before my God, who will judge my actions and my omissions. I believe I bring a clear conscience and can defend myself for everything I have done to oppose Hitler.[8]

And what of the fate of General von Falkenhausen, facing the same crowd of demons and the same remorseless machinery of death? Could he somehow escape this massive destruction of lives?

After his arrest on 30 July, von Falkenhausen was placed in a concentration camp. For some unknown reason, he was not tried immediately. He was transferred from one detention centre to another near Berlin, including Tegel and Potsdam.

It was always the same: a stinking cell with no window to the outside, crawling with lice and insects. All communication forbidden. The sun's rays blocked. The prisoner unshaven and dishevelled, surviving on potatoes alone, driven wild by pain and despair, beset by morbid fears. He contemplated suicide and wrote a will. Curled up in a corner of his cell, he sat alone, awaiting fate. He sternly kept himself under control to avoid losing his mind.

His wife remained in Belgium, with no word of her husband. Not knowing whether he was alive or dead, her days were filled with torment, until 24 October.

On that afternoon, von Falkenhausen was taken for the first time into a frigid reception room in his prison. As he entered the room, he was stupefied to see, standing in front of him, his wife, looking aged and wan. He had no idea how she had found her way to this prison. He could only weep, and embrace her in silence.

Hand in hand, they poured out their hearts to one another. Though regulations allowed them only half an hour, they extended their time together to two hours.

In 1944, the wintertime dawn was frigid, and in the jail cell it was colder still.

Like the other prisoners, von Falkenhausen huddled, shivering like a leaf in an icy wind, listening to the distant rumble of artillery, suffering through the days that seemed to pass like years.

On 5 December, von Falkenhausen's jailers summoned him to stand trial. As he left his cell, he looked up at the grey sky and wondered whether this would be the last time he would be able to see it. Most of the prisoners taken from their cells in this way were put before firing squads and executed.

Von Falkenhausen was taken into an austere interrogation room, where he immediately noticed that the interrogators standing before him was not the old crew but a new set of military guards with ugly attitudes. The questions they put to him were a shock, and he even began to feel just a little bit lucky.

They asked him: "Whom did you have contact with and what did you talk about with them in the several months preceding the 20 July attack?"

He realised that they had found nothing to prove that he had any connection to the 20 July plot. It appeared that no one among the plotters had betrayed him. With a great sense of relief, he offered only perfunctory responses.

Next, they asked him: "While you were in power in Belgium, why did you save so many Belgian resistance members who took Germany as their enemy? What made you provide so much aid to the Belgians and the French?"

Von Falkenhausen put them off with uninformative replies about friendship and personal relationships and the labour shortage in Berlin.

After two days of interrogation, nothing had been settled.

After that, he was locked up in a concentration camp or another prison. He was transferred back and forth, starving and freezing, continually suffering and wondering when – what year, what month – all this might finally come to an end.

The fourth of May 1945. A very special Friday.

For Nazis, this was a dark Friday indeed. It was the end of the world. But for everyone else in the world, and especially for those locked in Nazi concentration camps, this was the Friday they would never forget, a Friday of incomparable good fortune.

At that time, according to what some prisoners at the Niederdorf prison in Italy's South Tyrol recounted, they were in a living hell, completely cut off from the outside world and unaware of what was happening there.

They could not know that the Soviet Red Army had entered Berlin on 30 April, and that Hitler, with no way out, had committed suicide with his mistress in his underground bunker. On 27 April, Mussolini and his lover Clara Petacci were discovered by two partisans near Lake Como as they tried to flee. They were shot to death on 28 April, and their bodies were hung by furious crowds at a street corner.

The war in Europe, which had raged for six years, had finally ended.

At that moment, extinction staring them in the face, the leaders of Nazi Germany were not thinking about what was happening in distant prisons. Though the Nazi secret police guards did not realise that the Third Reich was already demolished, the bones of their raving chieftain had already been burned to cinders.

But the last insanities before annihilation can be the greatest expressions of evil in human nature.

That morning, although the head of the secret police guards at the Niederdorf prison in the South Tyrol, whose name is lost, had received no orders from Berlin, he knew that the Allied armies were at the gates. The sound of Allied artillery was drawing ever closer. He had a premonition that the end was at hand. He decided to slaughter all of his many prisoners and destroy all evidence of the crime, just as had been done in the slaughter of the Jews at the Auschwitz concentration camp.

At dawn, he ordered all his prison guards: "Attention. We will kill all prisoners this morning."

Just as he issued his order, the sound of furious firing cut him short. The Americans had broken in to the camp!

The Rise and Fall of the Third Reich states:

> Many people in the South Tyrol Niederdorf prison were liberated by the Americans on the morning of 4 May 1945. At that time, the secret police guards at the prison were planning to shoot all prisoners.[9]

And so it was that all those imprisoned at Niederdorf were saved. Among the prisoners were some renowned Germans and well-known people from other countries, including Kurt von Schuschnigg, Fabian von Schlabrendorff, General Franz Halder, Leon Blum and Dr Hjalmar Schacht.

A number of important members of the 20 July plot were among the prisoners there.

When the American troops entered the cells, they found these senior generals of the Third Reich, filthy and dishevelled, their clothing tattered, their bodies mere skeletons, their eyes vacant and staring, gaping at the soldiers who had just broken in.

At this point, I must add a comment. There was another reason that von Falkenhausen and other 20 July conspirators were still alive.

The Rise and Fall of the Third Reich states:

> On the morning of 3 February 1945, at the very moment when

First Lieutenant Fabian von Schlabrendorff was led into the courtroom, an American bomb killed the chief judge of the 'People's Court'. The bomb destroyed the file containing the names of most of those accused who were still living and awaiting trial. Thus these trials were aborted, and von Schlabrendorff's last bequest was to save their lives. He was one of the few 20 July plotters on whom destiny smiled. He was finally freed from his captors at the prison in the South Tyrol by the American forces.[10]

Thanks to this fortunate turn of events, General von Falkenhausen survived.

But these high German officials of the Nazi period were not freed.

(18)

On 2 September 1945, the second world war finally, after six years, came to a formal end. All of the vast number of people incarcerated in concentration camps were freed to return to their homes.

General von Falkenhausen remained in an Allied prison camp, awaiting his fate. When he heard of Germany's unconditional surrender, he could not stifle a sigh of grief. The great enterprise for which the German people had suffered so much was forever lost, reduced to ashes. And all this was because one insane man had brought about this accursed war.

On 1 June 1945, a group of haggard but happy men left Berlin in a Soviet truck for their return to Belgium and a reunion with their families.

Gérard Roger, rescued by Qian Xiuling, was among them.

Of the 96 hostages of Écaussines, five had succumbed to illness or died in bombings, but the remaining 91 all came back. Many others, saved from execution, also returned. The people of ravaged Europe began to arise from the destruction, and started to rebuild their hearts, their souls and their towns. They cherished the memories of the brave and brought judgment to the war criminals. They punished the collaborators and brought honour to the heroes who made their contributions to the nation and the people.

The twenty-first of July 1945 was Belgium's National Day holiday.

Écaussines was bathed in unusual bright sunlight. The town government held a large and festive commemorative event in the central square in honour of the resistance heroes who had attacked the Gestapo chieftain the previous year. Qian Xiuling was invited as the most honoured guest, along with her husband and child. When she arrived, the entire square boiled over with excitement. The 91 rescued hostages and their families rushed to embrace her, tears rolling down their cheeks. Their saviour!

They said that, without Qian Xiuling, they would not now have their day. Without Qian Xiuling, 91 families would not now be enjoying their restored lives together.

Qian Xiuling, garlanded with flowers and thronged by the applauding crowd, was invited to the podium. A special government representative from Brussels expressed deepest gratitude to Qian Xiuling on behalf of the Belgian government.

He said: "So many lives fortunately preserved, thanks to the efforts of Mme Qian Xiuling. So many families, thanks to her racing back and forth, are now together again. She is a hero of the Belgian people, and forever the pride of Belgian and Chinese people." Then he placed a national heroism medal upon her chest.

The mayor spoke: "In order that the people of Écaussines may forever remember the name of this Chinese woman, and in order that they never forget the grace that Qian Xiuling has bestowed upon the town of Écaussines, I hereby declare that the street on which the 96 hostages were arrested shall henceforth be named after Qian Xiuling."

The entire square burst into prolonged applause.

Then the mayor presented a Chinese copper incense burner to Qian Xiuling as a gift; he had purchased it especially for her at an antiques shop. I saw this copper censer myself when I visited Qian Xiuling's home many years later.

During my visit, I accompanied Qian Xiuling to Écaussines, where we were warmly greeted by Mayor Jean Dutrieux. The mayor invited a local historian to explain to me in detail the story of the 96 hostages.

In his office, I spied two precious photographs. One showed the 91 surviving hostages as they departed from a concentration camp. The other showed Qian Xiuling and the mayor's father together. That man, father of the Mayor Dutrieux with whom we met, was one of the 96 hostages.

That year, as I was working on materials involving Qian Xiuling and General von Falkenhausen, I wrote a television play called *A Chinese Woman Under the Guns of the Gestapo*. At the celebration of the start of production in Beijing, the mayor of Écaussines attended the ceremonies. In his remarks, he said: "I have two mothers. One is my Belgian mother. The other is my Chinese mother. Without Mme Qian Xiuling, I would not be here today."

This television drama *Gestapo* was filmed in Écaussines, and many of the extras were inhabitants of the town.

At that time, Qian Xiuling was a household name in Belgium. Print and broadcast media alike prepared many stories about her and her photo appeared in many publications. This Chinese woman, pretty and delicately built, wearing a permanent faint smile on her face, was known to the Belgian people as 'Belgium's mother' beloved by them for her heroism.

But Qian Xiuling merely said: "It was what I ought to have done. And I repeat: without General von Falkenhausen's assistance, I could have done nothing."

She knew well that, if von Falkenhausen had not exerted all his efforts to help her, in the face of enormous danger, she would not have been able to save so many people. The more she received the adulation of the Belgian people, the more it reminded her of the general's unhappy plight.

But where, in fact, was General von Falkenhausen?

Qian Xiuling tried repeatedly to learn his whereabouts, but no one had any news of him.

(19)

At that time, von Falkenhausen was in a prisoner of war camp.

After the Allied forces arrived, the crimes for which he was charged changed, and his own identity changed as well.

No longer was he accused of crimes because of his involvement in the plot to assassinate Hitler. Now he was a general from the defeated Germany, a high-ranking war criminal from the Nazi invasion of Europe.

Once he was in the hands of the Allied forces, von Falkenhausen's situation improved somewhat. He would be dealt with according to law as a prisoner of war. But reality soon shattered his illusions. Conditions for the POWs were even worse. Human dignity vanished. Thousands of prisoners were thrown together in dilapidated wooden structures with tiny rooms, fetid air and food fit only for hogs. All written materials were confiscated, even the last words of those who had died, as well as books and any kind of paper. He was continually transferred from one prison to another, from the Number 326 Camp in Italy to another camp in Wiesbaden, and then to a prison in England, another in Paris and finally to the prison in Nuremberg. As he was going through all of this, he learned that his home had been bombed, his possessions destroyed or scattered, and his family members dispersed.

He later wrote in his memoirs:

> The hardest thing for a prisoner of war was not to be treated like a human being, but instead to be regarded as an animal, an object of no value. Your guards fed you as they would feed animals, with the same dishes used for feeding dogs. You are cursed as a dog or cat might be cursed. Tossed from jail to jail, from cell to cell, you become a ping pong ball. You don't know to where you will be flung next, where your body will end up. You lose all ability to defend yourself. All you can do is await your fate, forgotten and trampled.[11]

When von Falkenhausen was transferred to a prison in Britain, the Pacific War had not yet ended. An American major general engaged von Falkenhausen in conversation and let him express his own views on the war in the far east. How would the situation develop? When would the war end?

Von Falkenhausen replied: "By now, Japan has exhausted its human and material resources. It will only take a minor attack to bring her down. The Allies should amass five hundred bombers to attack the major Japanese cities. If that is not enough, more troops might be needed to bring the war to the Japanese home islands and secure a rapid victory."

The exact date of those remarks by von Falkenhausen was 7 July 1945, barely a month before the Americans dropped the first atomic bomb on Japan, on 6 August. On 15 August, Japan announced its unconditional surrender.

The American major general listened to von Falkenhausen's views with admiration, and gave him the thumbs-up sign, saying: "Okay!"

General von Falkenhausen was an extremely capable military man. The long period of incarceration had not impaired his analysis or his judgment. But even as a brilliant general he could do nothing to determine his fate.

Von Falkenhausen's name, with the names of many other captured Nazi officers, was placed on the list of Nazi war criminals. He could not know what verdict awaited him.

On 23 August, he was told to get ready; in ten days, all war criminals were going to be shipped to the US.

On 24 September, a large group of prisoners was taken to the docks and prepared to board a ship bound for the US. But as it happened, von Falkenhausen's name was not on the list, and he alone stayed behind as all the other POWs sailed away. He remained in his filthy cell, awaiting his uncertain destiny.

Once he tried to escape, but he did not succeed.

He was placed under even more stringent observation and suffered humiliating treatment. He was stripped naked and placed in a freezing, damp and dark cell.

Von Falkenhausen developed heart trouble and serious intestinal problems. Despite severe pain, there were no doctors and no drugs for him. He could only grit his teeth and, with death by his side, trust in prayer to God to sustain his fragile life.

On the 5 May 1947, von Falkenhausen's health deteriorated, and he was transferred to the military hospital at Marburg, where he was found to have pneumonia and weakened heart function. He remained in the hospital for five months.

When his wife learned of this, she came to be at his side. Already, on 10 May, one of her legs had had to be amputated after she was shot by an American soldier while walking near the home of one of her friends.

Misfortunes cascaded upon them, one after another. At about this time, all of von Falkenhausen's assets in Dresden, including those in a bank safe deposit box, were looted.

When husband and wife met again, one with an amputated leg

and the other bedridden with heart problems, they sat in silence, hand in hand, as tears fell from their eyes.

(20)

On 21 March 1948, after three years and eight months of repeated transfers to German, English, French and Dutch prisons, von Falkenhausen was sent to the capital of Belgium as the number one war criminal, to be incarcerated in the tightly fortified St Leonard prison while he awaited the judgment of the Belgian military court.

Finding himself back in his old location, von Falkenhausen was filled with complex emotions. In those years, he had been the all-powerful military governor, and now he was a prisoner, denounced by all. How life casts one to the highest of heights and the deepest of depths.

His transfer back to Brussels led to a Belgian uproar.

People hung all the crimes of the Nazis, and all the hatred of the victims' loved ones, on this former military governor. Wave after wave of demands for his hanging welled up.

Though he had done all in his power to protect the Belgian people, he was after all the highest Nazi official in Belgium. The people understandably insisted on settling accounts with him.

Von Falkenhausen was placed in a damp and unlit cell in the St Leonard Prison, totally sealed off under tight surveillance. He was allowed no contact with the outside world.

Starting on 21 May, he was subjected to unending interrogation by the military court, before the final, life-or-death verdict arrived in April 1950, after 130 days.

During that 130 days, more misfortune arrived.

In December 1949, Von Falkenhausen's elder brother died. In January 1950, his wife, with whom he had shared everything, became seriously ill after so much anxiety over her husband's wellbeing, and required surgery.

On 12 February, the military court finally agreed to von Falkenhausen's repeated requests for permission to visit his wife in the hospital. Several days later, under tight guard, he was able to reunite with his wife at her bedside. She did not have long to live.

On 23 February, von Falkenhausen again appeared beside her, took her hand and comforted her. She shook her head. Her main concern was not herself, she said, but whether he would be judged fairly by the military court, and whether he would be hanged like so many other Nazi officials. She told him she prayed for him each day. God was just; He had seen this fair-minded man of conscience. She believed that the military court would treat him fairly.

Von Falkenhausen wept as he told her: "Beloved, we have been together through thick and thin. Now you are old, but still you agonise over me. I beg your forgiveness."

His wife replied: "Dearest one, I love you. Being your wife has been the greatest gift of my life. It is so sad that I was not able to bear a child for you."

"No! Finding you and making you my wife has been my life's greatest good fortune."

"Thank you, my beloved one."

They could not know that this bedside meeting would be their last. That afternoon, von Falkenhausen was led away. A week later, his wife passed away on the operating table.

When von Falkenhausen was taken back to the hospital by his guards on 4 March, his wife's lovely eyes had already been closed. He was sorely grieved. His wife was buried at Hünfeld in the German state of Hesse.

During this long period of waiting for the judgment of the court, it was Qian Xiuling who brought the greatest comfort to von Falkenhausen.

When Qian learned that von Falkenhausen had been transferred back to Belgium, she quickly sought out the relevant authorities and asked permission to visit him in prison. She and her family had moved to Brussels at the end of the war, but because von Falkenhausen was a top Nazi war criminal he was prevented from seeing anyone. Qian Xiuling sought the help of the Chinese embassy in Brussels, asking that a Chinese friend be permitted to visit him. The Chinese embassy stepped forward, pressing the appropriate Belgian authorities repeatedly, until, at last, Qian Xiuling was allowed, as a Chinese friend, to visit von Falkenhausen in prison.

She was his first visitor.

She did not retain clear memories of that day. She only remembered the shock she had felt on entering the tightly guarded prison, carrying some fruits and other snacks, and went into his damp and frigid solitary confinement cell instead of seeing him in a meeting room.

She could hardly believe that the man in front of her had once been the all-powerful Military Governor General von Falkenhausen. Now he lay curled in a corner, dishevelled, in a tattered uniform, with a scrap of blanket, the very image of despair.

Von Falkenhausen was equally stunned. He had not imagined seeing her. He was a major war criminal, forbidden to see anyone.

Qian Xiuling, her eyes swimming with tears, was swept by powerful currents of emotion. Life was so fleeting, so changeable!

She said, sobbing: "General von Falkenhausen…"

Hearing that unfamiliar voice from so long ago, von Falkenhausen said with darkened eyes: "Thank you, Qian Xiuling, for still being willing to visit me at this terrible time."

Qian Xiuling was heartbroken to see the reduced circumstances of her old friend, a man who had given her so much aid. To her, though von Falkenhausen had been the Nazis' top official in Belgium, he was a man of humanity and great righteousness who understood true friendship. She squatted next to him and took his emaciated hand in hers. Seeking to comfort him as best she could, she said: "General von Falkenhausen, I am so grateful for the help you gave me. I believe that many people in Belgium will thank you as well. Please trust that the people of Belgium will treat you with fairness, and that the military court will deliver a fair verdict."

Von Falkenhausen shook his head. Did he feel that nothing mattered, or that the court would not bring down a fair verdict? Either way, he remained sunk in deep depression.

Qian Xiuling told Falkenhausen that her cousin, Qian Zhuolun, had written to her to say that Chiang Kai-shek had already sent a representative to meet with Allied commanders and plead for a reduction of von Falkenhausen's sentence. Chiang had also said that if von Falkenhausen wished, he was welcome to come to live in China. But von Falkenhausen shook his head and politely declined.

"Thank you. Now I have nothing. I have no family. I have no possessions. All I have now is old age. It doesn't matter what happens. Please ask General Qian Zhuolun to pass my thanks to Chiang Kai-shek, and thank your cousin for his goodwill."

Qian Xiuling asked: "General von Falkenhausen, do you harbour any regrets now for all the assistance you provided to me in those years?"

"No!" This time, von Falkenhausen answered firmly. "Absolutely no regrets. I believe what I did was right. If I could have, I would have done even more." After that he remained still for a moment. Then he uttered a sentence pregnant with meaning: "Alas. A man cannot choose his era."

Playing Chess with the Devil

Qian Xiuling could sense the depths of von Falkenhausen's soul, filled with profound and painful regret.

Soon their meeting would run out of time.

Taking his thin and bony hands in hers, she said to him: "General von Falkenhausen, I will come again to see you many times. I want you to know that I will never forget everything you have done. I will write an essay telling the whole world all that you did to help me."

Hearing this, the general again shook his head and merely said: "Thank you."

Emerging from the prison in tears, Qian Xiuling could not set her mind at ease.

She knew that she had received the highest tributes for her role in saving many Belgians, and that she had been showered with love by the people of Belgium. But the man who had helped so greatly, General von Falkenhausen, was languishing in prison awaiting the judgment of the military court. To her, his treatment was so unfair!

"No! I must save him. I must think of a way to rescue General von Falkenhausen!"

And so, as with the 96 rescued hostages, a deep sense of responsibility called to her and propelled her to spring into action to save a Nazi general.

She realised that her own voice was weak and inadequate and would be unable to sway the court. But still she had to issue her call. She resolved to do everything she could for von Falkenhausen, just as he had done everything he could in those years to save the hostages, no matter how great the danger. Even if she failed, she would have no regrets.

Fundamentally, she was a woman of conscience. Just as in the past, when she had made her way to von Falkenhausen's chateau at great peril, she now had no fear of public criticism or pressure. To call attention to the Nazi general's situation, she held press conferences, answered reporters' questions, published articles, gathered signatures from resistance fighters who had been saved during the war and boldly placed her own views before the public.

I found one of her articles in a Belgian newspaper from 1948. It read:

> If it be said that I managed to do something for the people of Belgium during the war, and thus gained a national award from the Belgian government and the affection of the Belgian people, I must say to everyone: this was the result of my hard work, to be sure, but these results were the gift of General von Falkenhausen! It was he who exerted his maximum efforts, in the face of great peril, to achieve the results we achieved. Without his help, I could have done nothing. Moreover, it was thanks to General von Falkenhausen's maximum efforts to protect the zone over which he held power that Belgium did not suffer the tragic fate of Holland, Norway or Poland. As for what will befall General von Falkenhausen, I have no way of knowing. But I hope he will be able to read this article and to know that I will always hold in my heart the greatest feelings of reverence for him. Though he was a Nazi general, he was a man of deep human ethics, a man who understood true friendship and a man of integrity. I will be forever moved by him. I will continue to speak out, no matter what verdict the military court pronounces on him.

She continued to press her activities, which were simply unheard of in Belgium. Her articles made waves throughout society. Some people praised her, and others denounced her bitterly. Some went so far as to accuse her of Nazi sympathies, and to denounce her as a fake heroine.

It was gratifying that her articles gained wide attention, even among the judges. They saw that, although von Falkenhausen was the most powerful military administrator placed by the Nazis in Belgium, and undeniably committed many crimes, they had to recognise that his actions were based on ethical motives. He acted in full realisation that Hitler could fire him, or even kill him, as he expended every effort to protect many members of the resistance, and to defend the interests of the Belgian people.

Unexpectedly, Qian Xiuling's article moved the heart of a heroine of the resistance.

During a later prison visit, von Falkenhausen said to Qian Xiuling: "Lately, someone has been sending me gifts of baked goods and fruit. I am deeply grateful to her, but I have no idea who she is."

That same day, a tall woman of about forty came to Qian Xiuling's house, walked in and introduced herself. Her name was Cecile Vent. Born in 1906, she had married in May 1926, but later divorced. Because of her anti-Nazi activities during the war, she had received an award from the Belgian government. Her entire family despised the Nazis. But when she read Qian Xiuling's article, she was struck by von Falkenhausen's sense of right and wrong, which transcended national borders. She herself had been seized by the Gestapo, and a friend had appealed to von Falkenhausen to save her. She knew that no resistance heroine should harbour affection for a Nazi general. Her family opposed her sympathies for this man, but she could not conquer her heartfelt feelings, and felt an almost insane love for him. She had run more than once to the prison to try to meet him. The guards refused to let her see von Falkenhausen, so she left gifts of food for him with the guards.

Qian Xiuling was deeply moved by this, and felt admiration for this person who loved and hated at the same time, this woman who bravely broke the shackles of hatred. Qian Xiuling said to her: "How can I help you?"

Cecile Vent quickly pulled a letter out of her bag and asked Qian Xiuling to deliver it to von Falkenhausen. In the letter, she told him that she loved him and that she would wait for him no matter how long his sentence. She wanted to spend the rest of her life with him.

Qian Xiuling was profoundly affected by this resistance heroine's true feelings. She told her: "Set your mind at ease. I will most certainly deliver your letter to General von Falkenhausen."

"Thank you, oh thank you!" cried Cecile Vent. She pressed Qian over and over again.

On her next visit to the prison, Qian Xiuling delivered the letter to von Falkenhausen. When he finished reading it, he shook his head. "I am a war criminal hovering between life and death," he said. "How could I possibly accept a woman's appeal for my love? But I am deeply grateful to this woman. Please tell her how much I thank her for all she has done for me."

At that time, von Falkenhausen was deep in grief at the loss of his wife. In addition, he did not know whether he would live or die. He could not possibly accept this unrealistic expression of love.

But Vent was passionately in love with von Falkenhausen. She often sent him gifts of food, and tried desperately to see the German general, shut away in prison awaiting the verdict of life or death.

(21)

The military tribunal convened on the case of General von Falkenhausen a total of 56 times, from 25 September 1950 to 27 January 1951.

In the courtroom, all of the testimony presented was detrimental to von Falkenhausen. All the media – broadcast and print alike – excoriated him; the Nazis' military governor in Belgium had committed heinous crimes.

At this, von Falkenhausen was deeply wounded. He felt the Belgians did not understand him. While he was in charge in Belgium, he had done many things that benefited them, and had defended their interests as much as he could. Facing the accusations of the witnesses against him, he felt he could only submit to God's will.

Perhaps this was the ultimate court of judgment.

If it was the last session, it would have been 27 January 1951. Qian Xiuling only recalled that it was a winter morning. Not a seat in the courtroom was empty. All jurors and observers were present. She knew that all Belgians high and low were focused on this still-undetermined case and the fate of the number one war criminal in Belgium. All were watching to see whether he would meet the fate of Arthur Seyss-Inquart, Hitler's top military ruler in the Netherlands, who had gone to the gallows.

Needless to say, among those most intensely focused on the case were two women: Qian Xiuling and Cecile Vent.

Over fifty sessions of the military court to that point, all of the witnesses had denounced von Falkenhausen from the depths of their souls for his monstrous crimes during the Nazi occupation of Belgium. But on this day, a very different sort of witness approached the court.

Qian Xiuling, dressed in a short woollen coat, approached with steady footsteps and took the witness chair. The court fell utterly still, and all eyes turned to the face of this attractive Asian woman.

Qian Xiuling read her lengthy testimony in a strong voice.

She said: "Honourable members of the Court, this German general could not but follow higher orders. But from the first time that I went to meet him in 1943, drawing on his higher ethics, he faced enormous risks time after time as he sought ways to save the lives of members of the resistance who had been sentenced to hang. Only a month before he was dismissed, he used the last powers in his hands to save the lives of ninety-six hostages."

As she testified, Qian Xiuling offered both human and material evidence. She submitted as evidence the letter signed by many of those von Falkenhausen had saved from death. She asked the 91 surviving hostages from Écaussines to offer their testimony to the court.

Finally, she called on the court: "Confirm that von Falkenhausen made great efforts for the people of Belgium. Treat him with fairness, and bring down a fair verdict."

Her testimony shook the entire courtroom, including all the judges on the tribunal. Most of all, her words shook the heart of von Falkenhausen himself, sunk deep in discouragement.

For von Falkenhausen, Qian's testimony was not only a call for the court's fair verdict; it was a message of consolation for his despair. It helped him to realise that, in human affairs, true feelings and friendship still existed, and that voices of righteousness could still be heard!

At that moment, tears fell from his eyes, which had been dry for so long.

For Qian Xiuling, von Falkenhausen forever cherished the deepest emotions and respect. Years later, when he was near death, he still recalled the life-saving grace that she had bestowed upon him. In the home of the aged Qian Xiuling, I saw the letter that Cecile Vent had written to her: "General von Falkenhausen has died. To the end, he cherished the deepest feelings of friendship and emotion for you."

In the military court, before the eyes of all in attendance, a foreign woman courageously stood up to offer testimony in defence of the number one Nazi war criminal in Belgium. In all the war crimes courts following the second world war, it is unlikely that anyone else came forth so bravely to speak on behalf of such a man.

When I went to see the aged Qian Xiuling, I asked her: "Mother Qian, those people had neither family ties nor bonds of longstanding friendship with you. Why did you risk your life time after time to save them? Weren't you afraid that the Gestapo would seize you?"

"No! No!" the old lady said with a smile, shaking her head vigorously. "I didn't think much about that. I only thought about saving their lives. They were good people, and they deserved to live."

I asked her: "When you testified in von Falkenhausen's defence at the military tribunal, weren't you afraid that the Belgians would denounce you as a Nazi collaborator?"

"No!" she answered clearly. "Von Falkenhausen was a person who embodied humanitarianism and friendship, and who possessed deep feelings of righteousness. He deserved to be treated justly by the tribunal."

As I spent time with her, I was eager to discover that courageous heroine, that righteous individual who presented such rousing testimony to the tribunal. But it was not to be; the old lady's face retained a quiet and placid trace of a smile.

She said again: "I was not a heroine. I only did what needed to be done."

As I write this, I am reminded of what the author Herbert Steinhouse said after his visit to Oskar Schindler: "Schindler's great deeds arose from his sense of right and wrong and from his essential nature. But once we grew to adulthood, we could hardly believe these things."

Many of life's greatest events are rooted in the fundamental nature of individuals and in their sense of right and wrong.

In those years, von Falkenhausen helped Qian Xiuling to save the lives of many resistance members. Now, in a clear voice, Qian called on the military tribunal to render a just verdict upon him. Two righteous individuals, each calling out for justice and fairness for the other!

In early 1947, an Englishman who had fought in the war had written a letter to the authorities, arguing that keeping von Falkenhausen in military detention was unjust because he had acted out of humanitarianism. He had helped the Chinese to resist Japan. Ultimately, he expended supreme efforts to defend the interests of the Belgian people. He had participated in the plot against Hitler.

That letter had had some influence at the time, but it had not changed von Falkenhausen's fate. He had still languished in a POW camp.

On 27 January 1951, the military tribunal conducted a final review of each criminal count on which von Falkenhausen had been charged and each item of testimony it had heard. It then issued its final conclusion:

"Over a long period, in word and deed, von Falkenhausen displayed great humanitarianism. All strata of Belgian society and the Belgian media have testified to this…"

On 9 March 1951, after seven years in prison, von Falkenhausen sat awaiting the final verdict. Although Qian Xiuling's testimony had praised his righteousness, he had nevertheless been the supreme Nazi military commander in Belgium, with wartime responsibilities no one else could bear.

The final sentence of the tribunal was for 12 years of hard labour.

The trial, which had lasted three years, was over.

That night, von Falkenhausen again lay in his frigid, damp and filthy cell, his dimmed eyes searching for the dawn, his heart chilled, as he contemplated the blackness.

He was 73. How could he fill the 4,300 days ahead of him?

He could not know that God would take pity on this old general, whose fate seemed so grim.

Two weeks later, he was told: "General von Falkenhausen, you are free to leave this prison."

Von Falkenhausen's eyes were full of doubt. Why had this happened?

The answer was straightforward: Belgium and Germany had reconciled. Because relations had warmed, von Falkenhausen's sentence had been reduced.

Dawn, 26 March 1951.

The 73-year-old von Falkenhausen ended six years and eight months in prison. Facing the chill winds of the northern European winter, bearing all the injuries that history had imposed upon him, he walked with steady steps from the St Leonard Prison and journeyed by car to the town of Hünfeld in the state of Hesse. He stood before his wife's grave and offered a floral wreath, saying: "My beloved, I am free. Your soul, in heaven, can rest in peace."

Soon after, against the strong wishes of his family, he brought Cecile Vent with him to Bonn.

Before they left, Qian Xiuling saw him for the last time. She congratulated him on his freedom, and wished him and Cecile Vent happiness and prosperity in their late years.

Von Falkenhausen once more expressed his gratitude to her for her grace in helping to save his life. He asked her to send his best wishes to her husband and their children. He said: "I love children. Where there are children, there is hope."

Qian Xiuling knew that von Falkenhausen had not become a father himself.

The two old friends embraced and said farewell. They did not see each other again, but continued to correspond, and sustained their treasured friendship.

From that time on, Qian Xiuling and her family lived in Brussels. Her husband continued to practise medicine. In 1951, harking back to her early education, Qian Xiuling became a researcher in chemistry at the United Nations Nuclear Energy Research Institute in Brussels. Later, she opened a Chinese restaurant in the city named The Confucius Restaurant, which proved very successful. She and her fellow Chinese pooled their resources and founded the first Chinese language school in Brussels, the Zhongshan Primary School. Qian became the first chair of the board of the school, which brought Chinese language and culture to the children of Chinese parents in the city.

In 1990, she was recognised by the Queen of the Belgians and praised by the media covering the Chinese community in Belgium for her work in generating financial support for the queen's charitable foundation. To express their appreciation, the king and queen sent her a photograph of themselves.

On 1 August 2008, Qian Xiuling passed away peacefully at the age of 95.

Kindness was at the core of her long life, and mercy was her most cherished value. For this, she gained the esteem and affection of the Belgian people and Overseas Chinese in Belgium.

(22)

In order to trace the footprints of General von Falkenhausen's last years, I completed my final visit. In the summer of 2004, I sought the help of Ms Li Wen, a cultural attaché in the Chinese embassy in Germany, in locating von Falkenhausen's final place of residence. He had lived in the town of Nassau in the state of Rhineland-Pfalz.

I flew from Beijing and travelled to Nassau in search of my 'friend of many years'.

On the evening of 4 August, I took the train from Frankfurt to the old border town of Nassau.

When I reached Nassau, dusk had fallen and the station was deserted. In the fading light, the feeling of late summer was already in the air amid the stillness. The dying rays of the sun lit the twin ribbons of the railroad, and touched the heart of a stranger from far away.

In the twilight, I cast my glance into the distance and gazed at the little town, nestled between two hills. I could barely make out some small buildings, alternating between red and white, and a few cottages, lying quietly in the sunset, with pots of red flowers decorating each home's terrace or windowsill. The little town seemed so distant from the cacophony of modern day life. Except for the occasional sound of someone using a mobile phone, it was as though all the devices of modernity were absent. On the railway, hand-operated switches still shunted trains from track to track, without the use of computers. There were no high-speed trains. There were no high-rise buildings. There were not even any taxicabs.

Standing alone at this tiny railway station in a foreign land, a person could feel very strange indeed, solitary and isolated. I could not help asking myself: "Did you come all this distance to look for the former residence of a German general and listen to stories of his final years? What kind of valuable materials will the people who receive you tomorrow be able to provide? Will they be overbearing and arrogant, and keep you at a distance?"

I passed a restless night in a tiny hotel.

The next morning, in the reception room of the mayor, three elderly gentlemen with white hair and genteel appearance welcomed me warmly. All three were notables of Nassau. Two of them were former mayors, now bearing the title of 'honorary mayor'. One of them, Herr Schōnrock, 83, had formerly been in charge of a school for the disabled; he was a historian. Another, Herr Bruchhäuser, 84, had been von Falkenhausen's neighbour, and had advised the general on his family taxes. The youngest of the three, Herr Wenzel, was the current mayor and a former teacher. After his retirement from teaching, he had twice been elected mayor.

This was quite different from China. In Nassau, mayors were usually elected after their retirement to serve the townspeople. The mayor received a modest compensation of €1,700.

Alongside these three gentlemen in the reception room, I also met a retired journalist who was living in the house formerly occupied by von Falkenhausen.

My visit to the mayor's reception room began in a warm and friendly atmosphere, the room graced with fresh flowers, and refreshments served to us all. Deng Weixing, a Chinese diplomat stationed in Frankfurt, travelled specially to be with me on his day off to serve as my interpreter.

The mayor, sporting a full beard and wearing eyeglasses, began very warmly, in a very cultivated way: "Ms Zhang, you are the first foreign journalist or author to come to Nassau to gather information about General von Falkenhausen. You are most welcome! We want to provide every assistance, and we hope that your search for information will be a complete success!"

And in that manner, the little-known story of the last years, in obscurity, of a German general who had been tossed about by the vicissitudes of world war began to unfold on that cool and lovely day.

Some of the older gentlemen took me to see von Falkenhausen's former home, a two-storey wooden building of dark brown colour. By the front door was an ancient and tall tree. In front of the building was a broad expanse of lush green grass. This was the home of descendants of an old aristocratic German family, who had lent it to von Falkenhausen as his residence. After the death of the general and his wife, the retired journalist had rented it; he had lived there for 37 years when I visited. Here, in this small two-floor building, General von Falkenhausen and his wife had passed their final years in obscurity.

Herr Bruchhäuser, von Falkenhausen's one-time adviser on household tax matters, took me to see his garden home and showed me the gifts the von Falkenhausens had given to him before the general died: an 'Eight Immortals' table that could accommodate seating for eight people; several photo albums, including two containing photos of his years training the Chinese armies, and three paintings given to von Falkenhausen by Chiang Kai-shek. I only spied these paintings hanging in a dim stairwell. One was a

Xu Beiheng painting of a cat. Another was a painting of a drooping branch by the late Qing painter Chen Ziqing. The third painting was signed with a seal which I could not understand, so I was unable to figure out who the artist was.

General von Falkenhausen had enjoyed Chinese calligraphy, curios and other works of Chinese art. In his memoirs, he wrote: "Chinese paintings stirred my soul. Each brushstroke, each painting, each poetic inscription brought satisfaction to my soul. Each was a profound work of art."

Some of the elderly gentlemen told me that von Falkenhausen had few interactions with others in his last years, and spoke little. It was as though he never emerged from the painfulness of history.

But Herr Bruchhäuser did say to me: "Von Falkenhausen opposed Hitler from 1933 right up to the time of his arrest in 1944. This was a significant red line." He spoke those two words – *red line* – with special emphasis.

The meaning of this term, so little known by the world, was fully recorded both in von Falkenhausen's memoirs and in *The Rise and Fall of The Third Reich*.

In his later years, though General von Falkenhausen was accompanied by his wife, no one could really know the magnitude of his interior grief. This was not the tragedy of one man; it was the tragedy of an era.

Like a leaf that drifted soundlessly down upon the little town in autumn, von Falkenhausen spent his last days in silence, seemingly forgotten by the world.

The twenty-ninth of October 1958 was von Falkenhausen's 80th birthday. Only Cecile Vent knew that. That morning, no one came to congratulate him. Vent's own family members had broken relations with her over her marriage to von Falkenhausen, and they remained estranged for the rest of her life.

Nevertheless, on the afternoon of that day, several respected Chinese figures arrived at his home, amid gentle laughter, bringing flower baskets, cakes and various medals of honour to commemorate the general's 80th birthday.

When the general realised that these visitors were diplomats from Taiwan, sent personally by Chiang Kai-shek to wish him well on his birthday, and to present him with medals of recognition, along with a sum of money in US dollars as a means of thanking him for his assistance during the War of Resistance, his withered spirits were stirred as they had not been for many years.

"Thank you! Thank you so much! I had no idea that the Chinese would remember me!" The old general's voice was choked with sobs.

It was true. Though the general never dreamed of it, 20 years after he had left China, people in China remembered the birthday of this German general, leader of the military advisory group, and sent representatives to greet him, decorate him with medals of appreciation and provide him with financial support.

In his 80 years, this was the general's most memorable birthday.

The coming of these Chinese guests, in the flickering darkness of von Falkenhausen's final years, brought a shaft of light, briefly shining like a shooting star and offering a bit of comfort to him in his desolation.

Von Falkenhausen's last years passed amid sad memories and reflections. In his memoirs, he re-examined himself, his nation, the wars and humanity itself, finally completing his *Memoir from Beyond the War* in 200,000 words.

He pondered many heavy questions, as a German army general living in a very distinctive historical era: nation and world, nationality and righteousness, solemn oaths and betrayal. His heart torn and conflicted, his soul perplexed, until finally he made his difficult choices.

In his re-examination, the questions that he raised most often were these: Why was a madman able to drive a strong German nation to destruction? Why did so many high officials carry out his orders when they could so clearly see Hitler's barbarity was leading Germany not to glory but obliteration? Why did they swear loyalty to him?

He wrote that, because of the oaths they had sworn, many generals dared not resist Hitler's commands, thinking that that was what so-called loyalty was all about. Organising these oaths in the name of 'the people', Hitler was in fact only pursuing his own interests. If an oath no longer represented a commitment to the service of the people, but became a commitment to crimes that harmed the people, then violation of such oaths and resistance itself became moral obligations!

In the face of impossible choices, the American president Thomas Jefferson, in the Declaration of Independence, included this short but inspiring passage:

> But when a long train of abuses and usurpations, pursuing invariably the same Object evinces a design to reduce them under absolute Despotism, it is their right, it is their duty, to throw off such Government, and to provide new Guards for their future security.

In governing occupied Belgium, von Falkenhausen adopted the view of Montesquieu:

> The conqueror is obligated to repair and make good the destruction and losses imposed on the occupied area. This is the clear power of the conqueror. He must make vast compensation for the human and natural destruction he has wrought. This power is not to be resisted; it is consistent with the law. But it is still a matter of regret.

As an author, I have pondered the tortured questions thrust upon the soul in time of war.

I pondered the distinction between the nature of man and beast in wartime, and the relationship between an individual and fate. How could I find the boundary between good and evil in mankind, or between the nature of man and the essential nature of the beast?

In my interviews, I asked the elderly German gentlemen a number of pointed questions arising from reality itself: How did they view the war in those years? What was their opinion of the German chancellor prostrating himself before the memorial to the murdered Jews of Warsaw? What attitudes did the German people hold now with respect to the Nazis? What attitude did they hold towards the maniac who fomented the war? What did young Germans know about the war? How did the German government educate the young about the war? Did the government carry forward the re-evaluation of the war? What was the meaning of present-day neo-Nazi right-wing extremism? And so on. These were the important questions I tried to understand on my trip to Europe.

My own deepest feelings were divided, like two surging currents in the sea. One was like the turbulent waves on the surface of the ocean, beneath the glare of the sun. As I looked for powerfully moving stories, I found example after example of man's loftiest nature. But the other current was darker, hidden in the depths of the sea. These were my own heart's deepest thoughts.

I wanted to understand the Germans. How did they themselves understand the crimes of aggression in those years? How did they perceive neo-Nazism and the extreme right? Were they like the militarists in Japan who, to their dying days, would never acknowledge their aggressive crimes or else would only superficially acknowledge them while, in the depths of their souls, their viciousness lay undisturbed as they kept their eyes open for the chance to return?

This was my attitude as I followed the footsteps of a Nazi general and sought to understand the thinking about those times of war in the minds of those whom I questioned.

My questions were sometimes sharp, and I could only express myself directly, even though I was concerned that I might offend these elderly gentlemen's sense of national respect. If worst came to worst, they might give me the cold shoulder, or simply refuse to answer my questions.

But I was wrong.

I underestimated the high standards of these men.

The answers from these three old men completely confounded my expectations:

> Those wartime years not only brought disaster to Europe and irredeemable catastrophe to the Jews; they brought disaster to the German people! When the German chancellor prostrated himself before the memorial to the Jews in Warsaw, his was not a decorative act or some sort of performance. It was an expression, from the deepest sense of their own crimes, of the German people's profound repentance. Only from genuine repentance might Germany find the understanding and forgiveness of the peoples of the nations that Germany had so wounded. As for today's neo-Nazis, right-wing extremists and hypernationalists, they will never run rampant again in Germany. They will not take an important role in our national legislature and will never cause serious turmoil. This crowd of Nazis will never go unhindered in Germany. The people have already made up their minds, after much pain, about the war and Germany's aggressions. They thirst for a life of peace and stability. The people need peace, not war! Because Europe has known peace for seventy years, it has succeeded in building the European Union.

Mayor Wenzel told me that, in teaching his students, he never avoided the subject of the second world war, but tried to instil in his pupils an opposition to war and a love of peace by showing them the catastrophe that this conflict had unleased upon mankind.

These old men never steered clear of matters of history or their own nation's crimes, and never pled failing memories. They viewed the present through their broad and far-reaching views of history. Through these elderly men, I came to see the wisdom in the hearts of the German people, who had a clear understanding of plain truth.

That plain truth was that history can neither be changed nor falsified. Whether you be good or bad, it can neither be modified nor erased. Only by staring history in the face can we hope to make the right choices. A people that is brave enough to stare history in the face is worthy of the respect of mankind. A people with such broad and far-reaching vision is a great people with great hopes for the future.

As my visit ended, Herr Bruchhäuser presented me with a set

The graves of General von Falkenhausen and Cecile Vent in Nassau.

of freshly printed photographs of the general in his later years, including one taken on his 80th birthday, when the Taiwan authorities presented him with their medals and ribbons of commendation.

The three elders also gave me a copy of von Falkenhausen's *Memoir from Beyond the War* privately published in French, signing their names on the flyleaf of the book.

This memoir was extremely important for me. When I got back to China, I asked Fan Xiu, the vice chairman of the student association at the Translation Institute within the Tianjin Foreign Languages University, to translate it. As I read the translation, it was almost like hearing the voice of a Nazi general telling of his own complicated life and his soul's bitter struggles against a turbulent fate.

As we concluded, the mayor hosted me at a sumptuous banquet of western food.

As we parted, I bowed deeply to the elderly gentlemen, and to Mr Deng, and thanked them all for their assistance in making my visit completely successful.

Early the following morning, I got out of bed and made my way quietly to the cemetery that the gentlemen had led me to the previous day. There I bade silent farewell to the soul of General von Falkenhausen.

The cemetery was very near the home of Herr Bruchhäuser. There were very few graves and tombstones. A small copse shielded a simple tombstone. A pot of emerald green flowers stood in front of the stone. On the stone itself were inscribed the names of von Falkenhausen and his widow with their dates of birth and death. Von Falkenhausen was born in 1878 and died in 1966 at the age of 88. Cecile Vent was born in 1906 and died in 1977, aged 71.

At that moment, the sky was cloudless and there was no wind. There were no rumbles of artillery. Between heaven and earth, all was tranquil. The chirping of some small birds was the only sound to be heard.

I stood before the grave, bowed deeply and offered to the general and his wife the respects of a Chinese author. I reflected on a Nazi general, expelled from his high office, his life at risk, who had made such efforts to save his 'enemies'. This great spirit transcended nation and race. It surpassed the understanding of ordinary mortals. It was unprecedented in the entire history of human warfare. And it deserved to be cherished in the memory of later generations.

History tells us that Hitler changed the fate of Europe. The career of Tōjō Hideki altered the destiny of Asia. That a magnificent Chinese woman like Qian Xiuling and a magnificent German general like Alexander von Falkenhausen could emerge amid this gigantic war that practically extinguished human nature itself, tells us something important. Qian Xiuling could not choose her own era, or nation, or race. Neither could Alexander von Falkenhausen. But they chose their own pathways through life. Each of us can do the same.

Even when the sky is dark, the glimmer of a few stars is visible. Even when mankind is overwhelmed by bestiality, a few great souls can still remind the world of the sublimeness of human nature.

I write of them not only for the sake of remembrance, but for the future.

"Hitler is dead. Tōjō was executed. But there is no guarantee that others will not arise to substitute for them in such positions in the future."

These words, from an editorial in a Philippine newspaper on 13 December 1948, merit our very deep contemplation.

PART 1 NOTES

(1) Translator note: This English translation is from *The Chinese Classics*, tr. James Legge, vol. II: The Works of Mencius, Bk. VI, Pt. II, Ch. XV, p. 447. Copyright reissue by Hong Kong University Press, 1960

(2) (胡平著《一百个理由》157页，长江文艺出版社2005版) Hu Ping, *One Hundred Reasons*, Changjiang Wenyi Chubanshe, 2005, p. 157

(3) (中国第二历史档案馆，民国档案史料) China Second Historical Archives, Republican Archive Historical Materials

(4) (《第三帝国的兴亡》下卷第1000页) *Rise and Fall of the Third Reich* (Chinese edition) vol. 2, p. 1000

(5) (世界知识出版社2012年版《第三帝国的兴亡》下卷第1011页) *Rise and Fall of the Third Reich* vol. 2, Shijie Zhishi Chubanshe, 2012, p. 1011

(6) Ibid., pp. 1036-38

(7) Ibid., pp. 1043-44

(8) Ibid., p. 1039

(9) Ibid

(10) Ibid., p. 1037

(11) Von Falkenhausen, arr. 乔·杰拉德 *Memoir from Beyond the War* (Chinese version: Yishu yu Lvxing Chubanshe, for internal circulation), p. 244

PART 2

Angel and Devil

The Perpetual Game

The heavily armed Japanese military, with its ideology of militarism, knows no love of mankind and has no humanitarian ethos. The goal of war is victory. Victory is righteousness. Our troops become 'living weapons'. Our creed is Loyalty to the Emperor, and Glorious Death in War!

– Words of the invading Japanese army, taken from *The Diary of Azuma Shirō*

Outside the gate of the Memorial Hall for the Compatriots Murdered in the Nanjing Massacre by the Japanese Invaders.

(1)

A morning in early August 2014. The air crystalline and clear. Tired and dusty but full of anticipation, I arrived in a hilly residential district in Heidelberg. At the door of a small building, decorated with flowers, a smiling old man gracefully appeared in front of me.

Suddenly, the past came flooding back. In front of me stood a figure from history: a red necktie, a white shirt, thin white hair, small and hooded eyes, a ruddy face, brimming with good nature. Only such a person could smile as he did.

For a moment, I thought I was mistaken, and my heart chilled: could this be Herr Rabe?

I stood as though in a trance, my thoughts disordered, all my preparations forgotten. I forgot that I was in Heidelberg, Germany, and not in Nanjing, at the Memorial Hall for the Compatriots Murdered in the Nanjing Massacre by the Japanese Invaders.

In an instant, hallucinations and reveries flooded my mind, tearing at my sensitive feelings and smashing at my jumbled feelings. Scenes of blood-drenched history cascaded through my mind. Suddenly, sobbing cries filled my ears: "Herr Rabe, Herr Rabe! Save me! Herr Rabe, quick! Save me!"

Before my eyes appeared a vision of mountainous heaps of bones – the bones of my 300,000 compatriots.

I had been to Nanjing, and had stood for a long time before the image of John Rabe in the Memorial Hall for the Compatriots Murdered in the Nanjing Massacre by the Japanese Invaders. I had braved torrential rains and gone to the home of Herr Rabe at 1 Xiaofenqiao on Guangzhou Road in Nanjing. (Now it is called the John Rabe and International Safety Zone Memorial Hall.) For a long time, I could not leave that place.

A foreigner of about fifty-five, afflicted with diabetes, repeatedly refused invitations to leave Nanjing. Instead, leading about twenty righteous foreigners, like a giant standing amid the rivers of blood and heaps of human bones that filled China's land, Rabe had spent every ounce of his strength to save Chinese lives. His actions saved the lives of a quarter of a million of Nanjing's people.

Two hundred and fifty thousand. Hardly a small number.

For saving the lives of 1,200 Jews, Oskar Schindler became famous throughout the world. Rabe and his team saved 250,000!

How do we measure something like this? My weeping heart is time and again moved, shaken to the core, and cries out when I contemplate Rabe's deeds.

And so I came. I came to search for the traces of this great man. I came to explore the life of this extraordinary figure.

The man who greeted me was Young Rabe. He and John Rabe were born of the same family line. He was the grandson of John Rabe, the son of John Rabe's son Otto Rabe. This grandson went by the name Thomas Rabe. For the sake of economy, I'll simply call him Young Rabe.

I could see the resemblance between grandfather and grandson. Even the voice, the face and the smile of the younger man seemed to link him to his forebear.

When I entered Young Rabe's two-floor home, once again I seemed to be viewing an illusion. Chinese objects were everywhere. A photo showed Young Rabe and his wife decked out in imperial jade belts, their heads bearing imperial-style crowns. On their bookshelves were displayed a number of Chinese books: *The True Face of the Nanking Massacre, A History of the Republic of China, Eyewitness Accounts of the Nanking Massacre, The Biography of John Rabe*. Chinese artworks adorned the walls. A huge ornamental cabinet housed all sorts of Chinese handicraft items: enamelled housewares, a cloisonné pen, a jade Guanyin... If it had not been for the genuine foreigner who greeted me, I would have thought that I had entered the wrong house, a Chinese home filled with beloved curios.

I crept delicately inside, touching these objects so loved by John Rabe. It was as though I were entering John Rabe's very soul, stepping into a moment in history now so far away but nestling close to Rabe's heart, silently communing with him, quietly feeling the presence of the great man's soul – and touching the souls of the German, the Japanese and the Chinese races. What every individual does, what every race does, is the extension of the inner soul.

Touching the inner soul is a big part of what my searching and my writing is all about.

Young Rabe took me to see the John Rabe Communication Centre next door to his house. He told me that people often came here to talk about war and peace with him, or to remember and cherish John Rabe's great soul, and to remark upon John Rabe's manifest greatness.

In Young Rabe's garden, we sat before a bust of his grandfather.

On this visit to a parlour so filled with the aura of China, I asked a Chinese overseas student named Li Xiaoxuan, a fine young girl, to serve as my interpreter.

Our conversation began with the photographs displayed on Young Rabe's bookshelves.

Young Rabe told me quietly that he had three children and a dog. His two daughters were twins, studying medicine at a university. His son was also in college, studying architecture. His wife was studying child psychology. He himself was a professor at the University of Heidelberg and a gynaecologist. He had published more than thirty medical articles and a book about his grandfather. His late father, Otto, had been born and raised in China, and had also studied medicine.

As the conversation turned to his grandfather, Young Rabe told me that he felt pride in having such an ancestor.

On the subject of Chancellor Willy Brandt dropping to his knees before a memorial to the Jewish victims of the Warsaw ghetto uprising, Young Rabe said to me: "He is a man of peace. He opposes militarism and he opposes war."

In an article he later gave to me, he developed his views. To be a German, one had to face history squarely. Although the Third Reich was over, what happened during that era had not been totally relegated to the past. After the war, the German people had searched hard for the causes of their tragedy, and had gone through a profound process of contemplation. Germany, he said, had to offer its profound apologies to Poland, Israel and all invaded nations, and seek their forgiveness. Only this could become the foundation for resolution of conflicts and the building of genuine links between Germany and such countries.

Of John Rabe, Young Rabe said: "At the price of his own health and his very life, John Rabe rescued those Chinese people. Every person must ponder the question: 'Under similar conditions, would I be able to act in a similar way?'"

Young Rabe had never known his grandfather, who died a year before he was born. What Young Rabe knew about his grandfather came from the many stories his father had told him.

(2)

Before August 1937, John Rabe was an ordinary businessman, assigned to China by Siemens, the German company. Few Chinese had heard his name, and even fewer knew him personally. Black-framed eyeglasses, dark-hued western-style clothes, a bow tie, bald, with a good-humoured mouth – a middle-aged foreigner, and little more.

But when Japanese airplanes began bombing Nanjing and set out to lay waste to the city and exterminate a million lives, the humble Chinese people suddenly discovered a polestar guiding them to escape from death and evade the devils' lethal pursuit.

John Rabe was born in Hamburg, Germany, an old and lovely city.

The city had a famous seaport, and the 13th and 14th century churches of St James and St Catherine. It was the birthplace of great figures such as the renowned composer Felix Mendelssohn (1809-1847), the distinguished poet and writer Gotthold Ephraim Lessing (1729-1781) and physicist Heinrich Rudolf Hertz (1857-1894), who contributed greatly to the field of electromagnetics.

On the blustery and snowy early winter evening of 23 November 1882, with a newborn's lusty cry, an adorable new life came to the household of Markus Rabe in their home at Number 4 Stubbenhuk.

On the roof of their house was an unusual symbol: a sculpture of a crane, balancing on one foot, the other claw grasping a ball, standing over the house night and day. According to local lore, this sculpture was created to commemorate a long-lost ship's crew. The crane's message to the populace was to remain always vigilant and never to slumber, lest the ball in the crane's talon fall to earth.[1]

Markus Rabe named his new son John, in memory of his younger brother, who had been a mariner.

John Rabe's arrival brought joy to the Rabe family, which until then had only had a single child, a daughter. The parents carried their young son to the Church of St Michael to be baptised. Young John became a Christian.

John's father was a calm, kind and strong sea captain on the South America route. He was young John's cradle of good fortune, his safe harbour when John was evading a slap from his mother. He was also a key source of John's inbred kindness, calmness and joy in helping others.

John's mother was smart and capable. She had a penchant for slapping people, and when young John, whose studies were mediocre, would try to avoid school altogether, he could expect a blow from his mother. His father was his greatest protector. Whenever John received a slap from his mother, he would run to hide behind his father's broad back. John cherished many happy memories of his father, whose face was adorned by a full beard. Sadly, however, the elder Rabe died of cancer at the age of 48, ending the years of the young boy's childhood happiness and paternal love.

With the death of his father, the 16-year-old John Rabe had to drop out of school and take his first steps into adult society. He became an apprentice in an export agent and sales representative firm. At 19, he went alone to the Portuguese African colony of Mozambique, where he worked for a well-known English firm. While there, he learned to speak beautiful English. After three years there, malaria forced him to return to Germany.

In 1908, at the age of 26, Rabe went to Beijing as a sales representative for a German company. Then he joined Siemens as an accountant and copy clerk. Thanks to his intelligence and talent, he soon rose to become general manager of Siemens' Beijing office.

The move to Beijing put John Rabe in contact with eastern culture for the first time. The ancient walled city of Beijing, the seat of the kingdom of Yan in the Warring States period and the capital of the Liao, Jin, Yuan, Ming and Qing dynasties of later times, kindled the most positive feelings in him. For Rabe, Beijing stood as the embodiment, and a rare treasure, of Oriental culture. Everywhere around him were ancient and undisturbed relics. Rabe raced here and there, to all the ancient sites, taking photographs, writing in his diary, even writing a book.

He wrote many letters to Dora Schubert, the young Hamburg

neighbour of whom he was fond, urging her to come to Beijing by herself. On 25 October 1909, Rabe led his beloved Dora to a church, and they became husband and wife. Thus began their life of mutual love and support as expatriates in a foreign land.

Dora was a gentle and pretty woman who enjoyed writing poetry. Rabe, for his part, was humorous and upbeat. He enjoyed writing in his diary, writing articles and taking photos. Thus, *The Diary of John Rabe* and other writings on China sat upon Young Rabe's bookshelves. I looked at a dozen of his works, written between 1913 and 1945, including *The Autobiography of John Rabe, The Maitreya Buddha, Ancient Residences of Tianjin, The Beijing I Have Seen* (in four volumes), *Collected Writings at My 25th Wedding Anniversary, Enemy Aircraft Approaching Nanjing* (in six Chinese *zhuan* settings and eight western-style volumes), *The Bombing of Nanjing* (in two parts), *A Draft Diary Written in Berlin* and *A Myriad Memories Never to be Forgotten*.

In China, the Rabes enjoyed a happy and tranquil life, and Dora gave birth to their daughter.

In March 1919, after the defeat of Germany in the first world war, nearly all Germans abroad returned to their homeland. Rabe did not want to go back, but he had no choice but to leave Beijing with his wife and child, and return to the country that he had left eleven years before.

The Germany he had left had been under the feudal rule of Kaiser Wilhelm II. He discovered as soon as he returned that it had become a bourgeois republic. But in the Germany he saw before him, the environment was terrible. Political life was in chaos. Violent factional struggles occurred constantly. On many a night, Rabe had to rise from his bed and take cover from the danger of random bullets. Inflation was rampant. Hunger was widespread as well. Electricity was frequently interrupted, and even water and coal were in short supply. Beggars and ruffians were everywhere. He himself watched as a gang of thugs beat up the editor of a prominent Hamburg magazine. Rabe knew the editor to be a good man, and he rushed to his defence, only to be beaten himself by the gang. The two of them had a hard time escaping from their attackers. On another occasion, Rabe saw a woman collapse from hunger on the tram. He rushed to give her some of the bread he had himself obtained only after much difficulty. He saw a small girl selling matches, so overjoyed at the bit of bread and sausage that a gentleman had given her that she dropped her matches in the street and ran home. For a long time, as the girl disappeared into the distance, he stood unmoving at the spot.[2]

Rabe was eager to get out of Germany and return to China where food and clothing were plentiful. Finally, in June 1920, he found an opportunity to go there. And so, in transit with his wife for several months, he returned to Beijing and resumed his work for Siemens.

Rabe lived in China for 30 years, from 1908 to 1938. He and his wife celebrated their wedding anniversaries there. Rabe's daughter Gretel and a Siemens employee named William Schlegel were married in Tianjin on 3 August 1930.[3]

Over his three decades in China, the political stage saw tumultuous changes: the imprisonment of the Guangxu Emperor; the Empress Dowager Cixi's hurried flight from Beijing to the west; the successful revolution of 1911; the end of the Qing dynasty; the creation of the Chinese national government; the rampant military conflicts of the Warlord Era. But no matter what political changes swept over China, they had no effect on the Rabe family's life. Wherever they lived – in Beijing, in Tianjin or later in Nanjing – they occupied a simple western-style house of two or three stories, attended by several servants. They maintained an automobile and generally lived a comfortable, upper-class life in which food and clothing were never in doubt.

In 1933, in Nanjing, Rabe founded a German School. In order to secure funding for the school, in March 1934, he applied for membership of the Nazi Party.

But Rabe's quiet and pleasant life continued uninterrupted until the summer of 1937. That summer, the people of China fell into disaster.

(3)

As Japanese bombers began striking Nanjing in mid-August 1937, Rabe was not there. He was in Beidaihe, hundreds of miles from Nanjing, on vacation with his wife and daughter. In those days, Beidaihe was a summer resort for foreigners and wealthy people. When news arrived of the bombing of Nanjing, Rabe made no move. But on 28 August, in spite of his wife's objections, he bade her farewell and boarded a train alone for the south. The trip normally took hours, but because of the war it took more than ten days.

As he made the slow journey back to Nanjing, the sights he saw shook him deeply and filled him with sorrow.

Rabe had lived in China for 30 years. He was a China Hand. He knew that Nanjing was one of the Six Ancient Capitals of China, with a long history and filled with historical sites. So many renowned historical figures had revealed their brilliance there: the kings of the states of Wu and Yue in the Warring States era; the great General Han Xin of the Western Han; Sun Quan from the Three Kingdoms era; Zhu Yuanzhang, the founder of the Ming dynasty; Hong Xiuquan, creator of the Taiping Heavenly Kingdom; and so many great literary figures including Li Bo, Wang Anshi and Li Yu – all had left their historical footprints in Nanjing.

Now this world-renowned and ancient city had fallen into terror in the face of impending catastrophe.

The enemy airplanes arrived like swarms of locusts, obscuring the skies and blanketing the ground, on their bombing assaults on the ancient city. The unexpected sound of the air raid warning signals threw the spirits of the inhabitants into panic. The air filled with the choking odour of gunpowder. Every home, every garden, every street, every park was filled with people frantically seeking protection in air raid shelters. And after the deafening explosions of the bombs, through the smoke-filled air came the wailing and the groaning, the torn and bleeding bodies – some missing arms or legs or simply turned into shattered corpses – strewn about on the wide avenues and in the narrow alleys, scattered in every corner of the ancient city. The bombed corpses of many Chinese lay close to Rabe's own company office.

This was the tragic scene that greeted Rabe when he managed to return to Nanjing. In his own courtyard, someone had managed to display a small Nazi Party banner, six metres wide and three metres high. In the office's air raid shelter, built to hold about a dozen people, he found thirty or forty souls. All his German office colleagues were preparing to return to Germany or to flee Nanjing in search of safety elsewhere. They all rushed to Rabe: "Herr Rabe, Herr Rabe, hurry! Gather up your belongings! If we don't get out now, who knows when Japanese bombs will land on our heads?"

Meanwhile, the Siemens office in Shanghai was sending repeated messages to Rabe, ordering him to leave Nanjing for his own safety. The German embassy in Nanjing also sent people to him: "Herr Rabe, if you do not leave now, it will be very difficult for our government to guarantee your safety."

The embassy posted a notice:

> The Jardine Matheson steamer Kut Wo, chartered by the German government, reached Nanjing yesterday and is docked at Xiaguan, two miles north of the city. The steamer shall provide emergency shelter for all German citizens.
>
> – Embassy of Germany, Nanjing, 1 October 1937[4]

The battle for Shanghai commenced on 13 August, and after three months of bitter fighting the city was lost on 12 November. On 22

Playing Chess with the Devil

November, the national government issued the announcement of its evacuation to Chongqing. Chiang Kai-shek left Tang Shengzhi and about a hundred thousand troops to guard Nanjing.

Still, no matter who tried to get him to leave, Rabe was unwilling to depart. He transferred his household possessions, including several boxes of his diaries, to the waiting steamer as though preparing to go, and kept behind only a couple of western suits and insulin for the treatment of diabetes.

By that point, everyone knew that to remain in Nanjing was to stand at death's door. Anyone with the money or the power or the cleverness to do so rushed to escape. Only the poor civilians, lacking official positions or power or money to escape, were left behind. They could only wait in terror in Nanjing, through hours that seemed like years, awaiting the fate that they could not know.

John Rabe, this businessman with his money, his connections and his German backing, had countless reasons for fleeing Nanjing before it became a charnel house.

Why did he not leave? At the end of the day, what was he thinking?

In his diary, Rabe wrote:

> Times are bitterly hard here in the country of my hosts, who have treated me well for three decades now. The rich are fleeing, the poor must remain behind. They don't know where to go. They don't have means to flee. Aren't they in danger of being slaughtered in great numbers? Shouldn't one make an attempt to help them? Save a few at least? And even if it's only our own people, our employees?[5]
>
> I absolutely would not risk my life casually for materials things, whether belonging to the company or to me personally. But this is a question of morality. As an 'ordinary German businessman' I cannot leave. My Chinese employees and teachers and their families number about thirty. They are all watching 'the boss'.

> If I remain, they will all stand together to the last. To this point, I cannot make such a decision and face the people who trust me. How these people can place their trust in me, a useless person who in ordinary times would not merit their gaze – how can I not be moved by this?
>
> Anyone who has held in his arms a trembling Chinese child, curled up in an air raid shelter for hours under the rain of bombs, would have the same feelings that I have.[6]

It is easy to see in Rabe's writings that what filled his soul was neither religious faith nor concern for his company's interests. What filled his soul was the simplest and worthiest of all feelings, the feeling of common humanity. The feeling that every life was worthy of preservation lay at the heart of Rabe's conscience, and made it unthinkable for him to leave others behind.

Of himself, he wrote: "I cannot leave. Were I to leave, what would become of so many Chinese who are depending on me?"

His way of thinking was simple, not animated by anything particularly elevated or grand. Did he understand what it would mean to stay behind? It meant that life and death were intertwined, that at any moment he might be destroyed by an incoming shell. It meant sharing the lives of the Chinese – their hunger, their pain, their wounds, even death itself.

Nevertheless, he stayed, firm in his decision. He directed his staff and servants to strengthen the air raid shelters, assemble supplies of food and medicine, and provide necessities for the long term.

Over the next several weeks, Rabe and everyone with him lived a life suspended between sudden terror and abiding extreme tension. At every alarm, dozens of staff gathered the women and children and rushed them into the air raid tunnels dug in Rabe's garden. In the shelters, masses of people were packed like canned sardines. Crouched in the tunnels for hours, people gasped for the deteriorating air. The children, terrified, trembled and shook like tufts of grass blown in a frigid gale, their tiny hands grasping for Rabe's big hands, trying to absorb some of the warmth of his large body into their tiny bodies. Each time that exploding bombs shook the air raid tunnels with earth-heaving violence and the terrified people sensed that death was at hand, Rabe would rally their spirits with jokes: "Hey! Who has gotten the gods so angry again?"[7]

He gave the safest places inside the tunnels to the women and children. When he saw that some of the Chinese men were taking those places of safety for themselves, he posted a conspicuous notice, in German, Chinese and English at the entrance to the tunnels:

Notice to our guests and our Company staff:

Anyone using my bomb shelter must obey the rule giving the safest seats, meaning those in the middle of the dugout, to women and children – whoever they may be. Men are to make do with other seats or stand. Anyone disobeying this instruction may not use the dugout in the future.

– John Rabe, Nanjing, 19 October 1937[8]

Meanwhile, the big Nazi flag deployed in Rabe's garden served many purposes. Throughout the entire bombing campaign against Nanjing, not a single bomb landed in the garden. Japan and Germany were allies, and when the Japanese bomber pilots saw the flag, they left it alone.

Later, a Japanese adjutant asked Rabe: "What made you want to remain behind? Why did you stick your nose into our military affairs? What did all this have to do with you? You could have left and suffered no damage!"

Rabe responded: "I have lived in China for thirty years. My children were born here. I have lived a happy life here, and my work has been successful. The Chinese people have been good to me, in this time of war as always. If I had lived in Japan for thirty years and the Japanese people had been as kind to me, I can guarantee you that, in a time of crisis like the one now looming in China, I would not abandon the Japanese people."

Hearing that, the Japanese officer stiffened his legs together and bowed to Rabe.[9]

This man of good heart, John Rabe, would not abandon the Chinese servants and staff members whom he had long lived beside, day and night, as part of a larger family. He knew they had no place to go. War and violence were everywhere; where could they possibly find the safety of home?

Rabe had lived in China for thirty years, starting in the prime of life and continuing into his sixties. From an ordinary employee of Siemens, he had risen to become the Siemens agent in Nanjing. To him, protecting these Chinese people was his duty.

I tried to search for the bases of Rabe's deeds in his thoughts, something pulsating deep in his soul. I could see that he harboured a deep sense of gratitude towards the land where he had lived for three decades and the people who had received him so graciously. But naturally, something even deeper drew me into yet more exploration.

The twenty-fifth of October 1937 marked the Rabes' 28th wedding anniversary. They had originally planned to celebrate together, but on this day they were separated, one in Shanghai and the other in Nanjing. Other than the endless sound of exploding bombs to greet their happy day, only a poem, mailed from Dora to John, reflected on the day:

> To Commemorate the Day, 25 October 1937
>
> Our hazy predictions have become crystal clear,
> Fate is never the product of good luck.
> Man's life is like the tracks of the wandering stars,

Guided in the universe by a Higher Wisdom who determines
What will join together and what will move apart.

– Dora, Tianjin, 9 October 1937[10]

The poem itself is somewhat obscure, but one can clearly see Rabe's wife's fears for the future in it.

When Rabe received the letter, he kissed it again and again, as though it were itself his wife's fragrant lips.

(4)

On 22 November, the day that the national government announced its decision to move to Chongqing, a group of foreigners from many countries took advantage of a break in the bombing to gather at 5 Ninghai Road in Nanjing's Drum Tower district.[11]

The people of Nanjing must never forget the compound at 5 Ninghai Road.

Begun in 1935, the compound included a two-storey structure in classical style. Its grounds, covering 4.17 *mu* (about two thirds of an acre), contained a garden in the Southern style, with swooping roofs of the ancient Xieshan style, glazed roof tiles, upturned eaves and carved rails. On the second floor of the main structure were eleven rooms. Below ground, there were additional rooms. All the appointments were of the greatest elegance. There was a handsome plot of green, as well as a flower garden decorated with pebbles of red, white and black that formed ornamental images of tigers, lions, eagles and other birds.

This had been the estate of Zhang Qun, foreign minister of the national government. Before the fall of Nanjing, Zhang Qun had offered the property to the German government for its use. Before the German embassy evacuated from Nanjing, it had turned the property over to serve as headquarters for an international committee.

Rabe called it 'our palace'. In May 1946, when the US president sent General George Marshall to Nanjing to mediate negotiations between the Chinese Nationalists and the Chinese communists, Marshall lived in this guest house. After the founding of new China, great figures whose identity was not revealed to the public stayed there.

But the historical value of 5 Ninghai Road did not lie with the great figures who stayed there. Rather, it was significant because, during the Nanjing Massacre, it was the headquarters of the International Committee. A quarter of a million Chinese compatriots found protection and survival in that Noah's Ark of a compound.

Day after day, through the many weeks of Japanese bombing, crowds of hungry people whose homes had been destroyed gathered at the front entrance to 5 Ninghai Road. On winter days, they gathered to await a bit of edible food, while trying to avoid the raids and killings that the Japanese forces could unleash upon them at any moment.

The man in charge of this Noah's Ark was a 55-year-old German with a severe form of diabetes, completely dependent on insulin: John Rabe.

During Rabe's time in the city, a group of about twenty foreigners who had been working in Nanjing ignored the appeals of their embassies and remained in the city. The Chinese called them 'The Good-hearted and Righteous Foreigners Who Do Not Fear Death'. Remaining behind, they concluded: "We must unite together and demand of the Japanese that we and our rights be respected."

They discussed what the French Catholic priest Robert Jacquinot de Besange[12] had done during the Battle of Shanghai: establish a 'neutral zone' (known in Chinese as the Nanshi Refugee Zone and in English as the Jacquinot Zone), which took in as many as 200,000 refugees. They decided to set up a similar safety zone in Nanjing and a 'Nanjing Safety Zone International Committee' as well as a Nanjing International Red Cross to try to give the maximum protection to the humble inhabitants of Nanjing. All voted to elect John Rabe as head of the International Committee.

Rabe was astonished. "Why elect me? You are all better people than I am," he said.

In fact, none of the foreigners who established the Nanjing Safety Zone International Committee was an ordinary person. The majority were professors, missionaries, doctors, businessmen – all successful in their fields. The key reason that they voted for Rabe, in addition to his organisational skills, good heart, enthusiasm and excellent relations with them, was his nationality. He was German – the Nanjing representative of Siemens, the German company. And he was a Nazi Party member. No one else possessed those credentials.

As early as 25 November 1936, Japan and Germany had signed the Anti-Comintern Pact and created the Tokyo-Berlin Fascist Alliance. In November 1937, Italy joined Germany and Japan to form the Axis.

Everyone understood that having the German Rabe as chair of the International Committee would be valuable in dealing with the Japanese and would help with the work of creating the safety zone. Thus, chairmanship of the International Committee went to Rabe. Once he was convinced that the group's choice was sincere, he accepted the responsibility. He said: "Since you all consider that my German nationality and my membership of the Nazi Party might be useful to us in dealing with the Japanese, I accept your recommendation."

The first session of the Nanjing Safety Zone International Committee took place at 5 Ninghai Road at five in the afternoon on 22 November. From that moment, the lives of hundreds of thousands of residents of Nanjing were inextricably bound to this group of foreigners.

The meeting resolved to create the safety zone and elected Rabe as their chairman. Rabe addressed the group in a strong voice:

> My thanks to everyone for their confidence in me. I will do my utmost to carry out this work. Since you have chosen me to be chairman, I must have no hesitation whatsoever. Germany and Japan are allies, and because I am a German this should help in negotiations with the Japanese. I came to this eastern nation at the age of 26, and have happily spent the best years of my young life here. My children were born here. My professional work here has achieved some success. I have always been received warmly by the Chinese people. I will extend every possible effort to carry the responsibility of your hopes and expectations.

Rabe's speech received the warmest applause.

The International Committee's mandate was to make recommendations to the Chinese and Japanese governments for the establishment of a Safety Zone for the Ordinary Residents of Nanjing, for the purpose of protecting those residents' lives.

Their tasks were to negotiate for Japanese recognition of the safety zone; to protect the people from murder or rape; and to handle problems of food supply and transportation.

The committee laid out the dimensions of the zone, occupying 3.86 square kilometres in the northwestern part of the city and bounded on all four sides by major roads. The location plans were laid out in detail. They designated this particular area because a number of embassies, including those of the US, Japan, Italy and the Netherlands, were located there, as well as the missionary institutions Ginling University, Ginling Women's College, Ginling Seminary, Ginling Middle School and the Drum Tower Hospital. The Japanese bombers would have to exercise restraint there.

The committee set up 25 Refugee Reception Centres in the zone, in buildings originally housing Ginling Women's College, Ginling

University, the Chinese Supreme Court, the Ministry of Justice, the Ministry of Communications, the Military Academy, the Ginling Seminary, the Ginling University Library and the Hankow Road Primary School, among others.[13]

On the day of its creation, the committee issued its first proclamation, in Chinese and English, conveying it to the Chinese government and Japanese authorities through the American embassy. The proclamation read:

> In light of the outbreak of hostilities in Nanjing and the surrounding area, the Danish, German, British and American members of the Safety Zone International Committee make this urgent appeal to the Chinese and Japanese authorities in the hope that, for the duration of this unfortunate war, the Committee will be able to create a Safety Zone in Nanjing and its near suburbs to serve as a place of refuge for the fleeing residents of the city. The Committee guarantees that, if the following conditions are met, security can be implemented within the Zone. No military installations, including telecommunications offices, are to be established within the Zone. No existing buildings within the Zone are to be used for such purposes. Except for sidearms carried by police, no firearms are permitted within the Zone. No soldiers or military officers are permitted to enter the Zone...
>
> The International Committee earnestly hopes that, so long as these provisions are met, the Japanese military authorities will act in a humane way and respect the civilian nature of the Zone. The Committee believes that the Chinese and Japanese, by acting out of their concern for the residents of the city, will earn the honour and respect of both sides.
>
> To achieve the necessary steps with the Chinese authorities in the shortest possible time, and in order to make appropriate preparations for the protection of refugees, the Committee

entreats the Japanese authorities to respond to this message at the earliest moment.

The Committee is confident that this appeal will be received with understanding by all sides.

Finally, each member of the committee signed his name:

Miner Searle Bates	American professor	University of Nanking
JM Hansen	Danish businessman	Texas Oil Co.
J Lean	American businessman	Asiatic Petroleum Co.
Iver Mackay	British businessman	Butterfield and Swire
John Magee	American missionary	American Church Mission
Rev W Plumer Mills	American missionary	American Church Mission
PH Munro-Faure	British businessman	Asiatic Petroleum Co.
JV Pickering	American businessman	Standard-Vacuum Co.
John Rabe	German businessman	Siemens Co.
Charles Riggs	American professor	University of Nanking
G Schultze-Pantin	German businessman	Shingming Trading Co.
PR Shields	British businessman	International Export Co.
Lewis SC Smythe	American professor	University of Nanking
Eduard Sperling	German businessman	Shanghai Insurance Co.
Dr CS Trimmer	American doctor	Nanking University Hospital
Dr George Ashmore Fitch	American	YMCA[14]

It is probably true that not many people knew the names of these strangers, or that few of the 250,000 compatriots saved knew their names either. Some research materials only show the names of a few of them; the names of others seemed lost to time and circumstance, or simply forgotten. These figures from history have all passed away. Even their children and grandchildren are now old. Actually, the story of each one of them is moving and worthy of being written down. I had hoped to write them all. But I am now 70 myself and my energies are limited. My inkwell is running low. I can only write a few words and mention their names so that others will remember them forever.

They came from different countries, and pursued different vocations. They were professors, doctors, missionaries, businessmen. Most were well educated; quite a few held doctorates. All had lived for years in China, and some had been born there. Some had worked in China for ten or even twenty years. Towards this land, at once so backward and impoverished but also so honest and warm-hearted, they all felt deep and burning emotions. They had felt the tolerance and generosity of the Chinese people, and had led fine, respectful lives. They deeply loved this land. Watching the viciousness of the Japanese, something not seen before in history, as they launched themselves murderously against the unarmed and defenceless Chinese and laid waste this thousand-year-old city, they felt overpowering indignation. They decided to remain in the city and do whatever they could to help the Chinese compatriots who had no other assistance.

In the words of the American Professor Searle Bates of Ginling University, in letters to his friends, we can gain a deeper understanding of these people's universe:

> The events of the past year and a half make it difficult for a thinking person to believe in the benevolence of Heaven or the goodness of faith. In the tides of cruelty and greed engulfing the world, I see no sign of God. But the values of humanity, the demands of man's existence, and the visions made clear by Jesus, are never bleak. To battle for the utterly defenseless, knowing that you yourself could at any moment be incinerated by some force that escaped your attention, and still to uphold truth and human morality – that is a kind shock and stimulation to the spirit.
>
> Grant peace to the world, and charity to all mankind. But

can the peace we see before us become a charitable peace? Everyone's spiritual outlook seems crushed under these merciless conditions, unable to resist and subject to profound testing. But I know that cannot be misplaced and bent out of shape. Do not allow yourself to be overpowered by evil. That is the truest call from the heart of man.[15]

By coincidence, 22 November was the day before John Rabe's birthday. The next day, he received the biggest birthday gift of all. His Chinese assistant, Han Xianglin, told him that a Chinese friend of his had learned that Rabe had established a safety zone for residents of Nanjing and had decided to send him two trucks, 100 barrels of gasoline and 200 bags of flour.

Hearing this, Rabe was overjoyed and leaped up to embrace Han Xianglin. "My God," he cried, "this is the best birthday gift I have ever received!"

He knew that the International Committee, so recently set up, desperately needed this food and these vehicles. He could use them to rescue so many people. Sadly, in the end, only a part of these birthday gifts became a reality.

(5)

On 23 November, the day after the International Committee's establishment, a German war reporter named Wolf Schenke arrived in Nanjing from Shanghai, and prepared to move on to Wuhu to board the river steamer Kut Wo on his way out of China. He visited Rabe.

Later, in 1943, this journalist published a book entitled *Travels on the Yellow Front Line: A German War Reporter's Observations*. In it, he wrote:

Rabe's decision to remain in Nanjing did not stem from

commercial considerations. He had in mind the creation of a safety zone in Nanjing for several hundred thousand people, similar to what Father Jacquinot had done in Shanghai. I had grave doubts about his plans. Rabe said to me, 'I have lived here for thirty years, and I will go through fire and water for this.' In our brief conversation, Rabe displayed his humour, but now I felt it was little more than gallows humour.

The reporter made fun of himself with black humour: "While others threw themselves willingly into the jaws of death, I myself headed for the safety zone." Schenke brought forth the true dimensions of the man John Rabe.[16]

Rabe's words – *I have lived here for thirty years, and I will go through fire and water for this* – expressed the hearts of many of the foreigners who remained behind.

The proclamation from the International Committee drew a rapid response from the Chinese government, committing to sending 80,000 *yuan*, 20,000 bags of rice and 10,000 bags of wheat flour as an expression of support for the creation of the safety zone.

Ultimately, because of transportation difficulties, the committee did not receive that much. The national government also sent 200 policemen "to guard the borders of the Zone, and take responsibility for internal security within the Zone".

But from the Japanese government, the International Committee received no reply at all.

At that moment, thanks to a careless mistake by the Reuters news agency, it was widely reported that the US embassy, rather than civilians, had created the safety zone. The Japanese government immediately raised a sharp protest, and the International Committee had to spend a great deal of valuable time explaining what had happened.

With the lengthening delay in the Japanese response, Rabe became increasingly alarmed. Newly named to head the International Committee, he felt himself losing face. Thus, he bethought himself of a really powerful figure: Chancellor Hitler. "You'll buy this if it comes from Hitler!"

On 25 November, Rabe sent Hitler a telegram via the German consulate in Shanghai and the head of the Nazi Party cell there, urging Hitler to persuade the Japanese to agree to the establishment of the safety zone.

In his first letter, he wrote:

> Chancellor Hitler,
>
> As head of the Nanjing City Nazi Party organisation and chair of the city's International Committee, I request that you urge the Japanese government to agree to establishment of a safety zone for ordinary residents of the city. Otherwise, the battle that is about to break out in Nanjing will threaten the lives of more than two hundred thousand people.
>
> My deepest respects to Germany,
>
> Rabe
>
> Siemens Agent in Nanjing

His second message was a telegram to the German consulate in Shanghai:

> To Consul General Kriebel:
>
> May I ask for your support of my message of today, requesting that Chancellor Hitler encourage the Japanese government to support the creation of a Zone of Neutrality. Without it, the outbreak of battle in Nanjing will result in the needless loss of vast amounts of life and blood.
>
> Long Live Hitler!

Rabe

Siemens Representative

Chairman, Nanjing International Committee

(If necessary, I will cover the cost of the necessary telegram. Please bill my account at the Siemens Office in Shanghai.)[17]

After he had sent the telegrams, Rabe waited anxiously day and night for Hitler's response. No matter how much he hoped his chancellor would put in a good word for him and his colleagues with the Japanese to obtain their agreement on creation of the safety zone, cruel reality demolished his fond expectations. He received no telegram from Hitler. Instead, he received this message from the German embassy, sent to his Siemens office in Shanghai:

To the sender of the original Siemens message:

Attention Siemens: Please advise whether you yourself will leave Nanjing to escape from physical danger. We recommend that you remove to Hankou and await your return message informing us of your plans.

Rabe wrote back:

For transmission via Siemens Shanghai:

Your message of 25 November received with thanks. I have decided to remain in Nanjing to handle the work of the International Committee, create the Neutral Zone and protect 200,000 ordinary citizens. Rabe.[18]

Regardless of what Japan's view might be, the International Committee under Rabe did not delay its work to establish the safety zone, actively working on the many urgent tasks involved.

By 1 December, the great flight from Nanjing was underway. All the great and petty officials of the national government and the Nanjing city government were making their preparations to get out. Rabe's International Committee was meeting and making its own preparations, planning supplies and assigning tasks. Rabe as chairman, Dr Smythe as secretary, George Fitch as director general, Hang Liwu as deputy director general and Tang Zhongmo as Chinese director of the secretariat.

A chart of the International Committee's tasks read like this:

1. Funds
2. Police
   a. Inspectors for entry to the Zone
   b. Boundary guards
3. Matters involving soldiers or armies
   a. Withdrawal orders and their inspection
   b. Measures when troops begin to flee, and care of wounded
4. Food
   a. Food quantities
   b. Food storage and distribution
5. Transportation and transportation equipment
6. Refugee housing
   a. Supervision
   b. Use and management of housing facilities
      i. Public structures (government buildings)
      ii. Schools and other missionary buildings
      iii. Vacant residential facilities

iv. Reed huts
7. Public Facilities
   a. Water, electricity and telephone
8. Public Health and Medicine
   a. Specially designated toilets
   b. Garbage and nightsoil management
   c. Hospital and medical facilities

Five working committees were established:

Inspector General – Eduard Sperling.

Food Committee – Han Xianglin, director; Hubert Sone and Sun Yao, deputy directors.

Housing Committee – Wang Ting, director; Charles Riggs and Su Chang, deputy directors.

Health Committee – Shen Yushu, director; Dr CS Trimmer, deputy director.

Transport Control – EL Hirschberg, chairman; RR Hatz, associate.

As the great enemy assault neared, this city, this national capital of a million souls, was under the oversight of twenty foreigners. What had happened to all our Chinese 'father and mother officials'? Where had they all gone?

On 2 December, Rabe received a postal letter from the French priest Robert Jacquinot de Besange containing a telegram from the American Embassy:

> In response to your message of 30 November, see the following response with respect to the Nanjing Safety Zone:

> The Japanese government has received your request to establish a safety zone. With regret, it declines your request. The Japanese government accepts no responsibility in the event that the Chinese armies treat civilians or their property inappropriately. But so long as Japanese military orders are obeyed, the Japanese government will work to respect the relevant Zone.
>
> Father Jacquinot (Shanghai) Gauss (US Embassy official)[19]

When he finished reading this telegram, whose message was clear through all of its evasive wording, Rabe was speechless for half a day.

He feverishly drafted another telegram to be sent through the US Embassy to Father Jacquinot, imploring the priest to do everything in his power to advocate for Japanese agreement to the creation of the safety zone.

On 5 December, the Japanese sent another message through the US Embassy, with their formal response to the International Committee on the matter of the safety zone: "We have already refused the request relating to the safety zone!" But there was also one confusing sentence: "We will do everything possible to protect the entire area."

The work being carried out by Rabe and his colleagues did not cease, in spite of the Japanese attitude.

On 8 December, the International Committee posted a formal announcement to the people of Nanjing:

> Recently, during the Battle of Shanghai, the International Committee there contacted the Chinese and Japanese authorities to recommend that a portion of Nanjing be set aside for creation of a Civilian Safety Zone. The Zone would be secure, and could save the lives of ten or more million people.
>
> Now the Nanjing International Committee has made similar recommendations. The boundaries of the Zone are as follows...

They will be marked by flags. On the top of the flags will be a red cross, surrounded by a red circle. The words 'Refugee Zone' will be written on the flags. We believe that, if the two sides carry out their commitments, those within the Zone will be far safer than those outside the Zone. We therefore invite people to enter within the Zone!

Nanjing International Committee, 8 December 1937[20]

Rabe had the committee secretary, Dr Smythe, pass a document entitled 'Temporary Measures for Housing and Food Distribution Within the Safety Zone' to the media:

1 Housing

    a. Everyone is encouraged to make private housing arrangements within the Zone. Rents, if any, must be kept low and must never exceed peacetime levels.

    (b, c, d...)

2. Meals

    a. Rice and flour stocked by the Committee will be allotted for sale to private merchants only with special permission of the distribution committees.

    b. Meals for the poor, including rice gruel, will be provided at low cost by the Red Cross and by facilities under the Red Cross responsible for cooking the gruel...

The next day, 9 December, the International Committee sent another document to the media: 'Security Measures Within the Safety Zone'. This was divided into ten sections and contained telephone numbers for ambulance and fire brigade services.

This series of announcements was aimed at making the location of Noah's Ark clear to the world. Thousands of impoverished refugees, including women, children and the aged, struggled into the zone, seeking the one place where their lives might be saved.

According to the Nanjing Safety Zone archives, in a single week the number of refugees reached 51,000. By 17 January 1938, this had risen to 250,000.

(6)

The eighth of December 1937, the day of the committee's message to the people of Nanjing, marked the opening of a tragedy unprecedented in the history of the Chinese people.

The Japanese had begun to breach Nanjing's walls on the seventh. Chiang Kai-shek and his wife left Nanjing by plane that morning, and the senior members of the government still left in Nanjing followed suit.

Furious debate had raged within the Chinese Nationalist Party on the question of whether or not to evacuate. In the end, Chiang Kai-shek appointed Tang Shengzhi military commander, with Luo Zhuoying and Liu Xingwei as his deputies, to protect Nanjing, using about 110,000 officers and men drawn from the remnants of the crack 36th, 87th and 88th divisions from the Battle of Shanghai and including 35,000 cadets from the army military academy,

Though Tang Shengzhi issued a ringing pledge to his officers and troops – "We swear to live or die with Nanjing! Our forces must swear to fight to the death to protect every inch of the front lines!" – Tang's forces, which included the exhausted and depleted units from the defeat at Shanghai, faced 50,000 of Japan's highly trained, well led and better-armed troops as the battle for Nanjing opened. The results can be easily imagined.

Thus, on 11 December, Tang Shengzhi received orders from above to act as he saw fit and immediately to abandon Nanjing.

Two urgent messages from Chiang Kai-shek quickly followed:

"Tang Shengzhi must relinquish Nanjing this day!" and "The Yangtze must be crossed by nightfall."

With that, General Tang Shengzhi, a veteran of twenty years on the battlefield as well as the Northern Expedition that had led to the establishment of the national government, his heart filled with grief and shame, issued the evacuation order at 5pm on 12 December. Reluctantly abandoning the hundred thousand men under his command, he watched the soldiers mingling with a vast crowd swarming the bank of the river, pushing and squeezing, shouting and cursing, screamingly helplessly, as boats overloaded with the fleeing capsized and sank. In deep pain and remorse, Tang Shengzhi boarded a steam launch, leaving behind an unprecedented scene of collapse.

All this took place on 12 December, within only one day – within hours, actually – of the start of the Great Nanjing Massacre.

Even then, on the front lines, the Chinese forces fought the Japanese, ignorant of what was happening elsewhere. Countless men died under Japanese swords and tanks in one of the worst catastrophes in Chinese military history.

I have no way of knowing exactly how many officers and men perished. Some have said ninety thousand; others have estimated seventy or eighty thousand. In his memoir, *Invasion – The Words of a Reporter with the Army on the China Front*, Ōbata Yukio, the reporter for Japanese newspaper Yomiuri Shimbun, wrote that "more than a hundred thousand were taken prisoner".

Tang Shengzhi later wrote bitterly: "I had been in many battles, but never one as disorganised as this. I have shamed myself before the nation, and I shamed myself in my own eyes."

On 8 December, Rabe produced a long catalogue of problems urgently requiring solutions: funding; the police force; handling of soldiers and other military matters; food supplies; transportation resources; housing for refugees; overall compliance supervision;

other housing questions; water and electrical supplies; latrines; medical care, and so forth.

Prior to this, Rabe had sent telegrams repeatedly to the Red Cross in Hong Kong, Shanghai and Hankou, begging for doctors and medicine to be sent to Nanjing – they were in desperately short supply and people were dying in the streets for lack of urgent medical care. Many people's homes had been destroyed, leaving their inhabitants with nothing and no place to go. In the cold of the night, whole families, young and old, lay at the base of the city walls or under the eaves of buildings, sometimes in the open air by the roadsides, ignored in their misery.

These tragedies tore at Rabe's kindly heart. He felt that as the chairman of the International Committee he must himself somehow solve all the problems that these people faced.

On the evening of 12 December, when Tang Shengzhi received the order to board ship and leave Nanjing, at the door of the Rabe family home at 1 Xiaofenqiao on Guangzhou Road, a crowd of destitute and homeless civilians gathered. Refugees knelt in the roadway, or hammered on the door begging for help. "Rabe, Rabe, save us. Offer your grace! Mr Rabe, find a way out for us! You are a living Buddha of infinite mercy and compassion! We beg you! Let us in!"

In his diary entry for 12 December 1937, Rabe wrote:

> The sky above Nanjing glowed red from the great fires. In the yard, masses of refugees had crowded by the sides of the air raid tunnels. Some had tried to force the Double Fan gates. Women and children begged me to let them enter. Some bold young men came over the courtyard wall from the German school on the other side, hoping to find protection in our yard. These heart-rending pleas for my help never stopped. Finally, I opened the Double Fan gates, letting inside all the people who were trying to enter.[21]

By then, the sky over the southern part of Nanjing was a sea of fire. Everywhere the air was filled with deafening artillery and machine gun fire and screams. The great Nanjing Massacre was only hours ahead.

Rabe's own home was jammed with people, squeezed together like canned fish. But Rabe could not bear the anguished cries for help outside his door. He allowed all the refugees in, packing them into every nook and cranny, inside and outside every room. The toilet closet held nine people. Many more filled the bath chamber. People jammed the stairways and all the hallways. More passed the icy nights on the grass in the garden.

After several weeks, Rabe's house and yard, of no more than a thousand square metres, held five to six hundred people – more than six hundred and fifty if his own company staff and their families were added in.

When the Japanese assault on the city began on 13 December, Rabe had been without sleep for 48 hours.

The exact moment of the Japanese army's advance into Nanjing through the Zhongshan Gate was 3.10am.

On 3 July 2015, a New China News Agency story reported that an old man named Zhang Guangsheng was in possession of two bandanas left behind by the invading Japanese soldiers. One of the bandanas read: "Eyewitness to the China Incident. The Nakajima Forces, Ōno forces, Tsunehiro forces, Ishibashi forces, Nakano forces and Sakamoto units, each occupied the Zhongshan Gate at 3.10am, 13 December." On the banner were also printed the words: "Die for the Nation!"

On that day, as the Japanese forces began their entry into the city, Rabe hurriedly had his staff post an 'Important Announcement for All Refugees at Refugee Receiving Stations':

1. Do not linger in the streets.

2. In times of maximum danger, it is recommended that you huddle in your homes or in other places where you cannot be seen.

3. You must note: The Refugee Safety Zone is only for refugees. With deep regret, we must point out that the Safety Zone has no power to provide protection to Chinese soldiers.

4. If Japanese soldiers come to the Safety Zone for investigation or on patrol, you must let them proceed. You must offer them absolutely no resistance.[22]

The horrific Nanjing Massacre, unprecedented in human history, began on 13 December.

As the Japanese army torched, slaughtered and raped everywhere, even the safety zone was not spared.

From 16 December onwards, Rabe had his secretary Lewis Smythe keep a record of the crimes committed by the Japanese. The first part, entitled 'The Violent Actions of Japanese Soldiers in the Nanjing Safety Zone', in fifteen sections altogether, provides detailed data on their crimes.[23]

Then, Rabe, disregarding the mortal peril, took Smythe, his secretary, and went out into the bloody streets filled with corpses, holding over their heads the flag bearing the sign of the safety zone. Their intent was to present to Japanese military authorities their documentation of the Japanese troops' atrocities, and to demand an immediate halt to the indiscriminate slaughter and a guarantee of the safety of civilians.

But not one of the five top Japanese commanders on the scene was willing to accept this documentation.

Next, Rabe took this evidence to the Japanese secret police unit. The top Japanese officer in the secret police, General Harada, took the materials and offered his sworn guarantee: "The Japanese Army is virtuous, and under no circumstances will commit indiscriminate massacres."

But no one could believe such lies, and the crimes continued.

On 17 December, Rabe went once more to the Japanese embassy and personally delivered his 'Urgent Announcement' and his letter of protest.

On 18 December, Rabe sent an even more strongly worded letter of protest titled 'Letter of Protest to the Japanese Embassy', replete with revelations of atrocities. It read, in part: "Because of your troops' unending plundering, violence and rape, the entire city is in a state of terror."

That same day, Rabe received a message that filled him with grief. It was from 540 refugees at 83 and 85 Guangzhou Road, and was addressed to "The International Committee of the Nanjing Refugee Zone":

> Our homes have been ransacked and pillaged by small bands of Japanese soldiers. All our jewellery, money, wristwatches and clothing have been stolen. Young women are being raped every day. The screams of women and children fill our ears. The situation is beyond words. Please, please rescue us!
>
> – Refugees, 18 December 1937[24]

"Herr Rabe, please save us!"

"International Committee, come to our aid!"

Such appeals for one final chance to board Noah's Ark filled the city.

On 19 December, Rabe wrote in his diary:

> Six Japanese soldiers climbed the wall of our courtyard, aiming to open our main gate from the inside. I came out and shined my

flashlight on the face of one of the raiders. He drew his pistol. I shouted at him sternly and showed him my Nazi Party armband. He quickly put his weapon away. Those six soldiers went down from the wall the way they came up, and disappeared. The main gate to our yard could not be allowed to let the bandits in.[25]

As I wrote this, my hands stood still. For half a day, I could not touch the keyboard. My heart seemed to stop, holding back an enormous wave of emotion, unable to quiet down for what seemed an eternity. An immense grief overcame me. A Chinese person, I was drowned in a sadness beyond relief, for my people and for my nation. I could only think of the words of our national anthem *The March of the Volunteers*: "Arise, Ye who refuse to be slaves! With our very flesh and blood, Let us build our new Great Wall! The Peoples of China are in the most critical time…"

In the past, I had never really pondered the content of our national anthem. Singing the national anthem was just something everyone did. I had not really thought about the meaning of the words. But that day, as I wrote about the people of Nanjing being massacred by Japanese soldiers, I pondered for the first time this question: Why had the Chinese nation come to this last extremity? Why did rapacious foreign powers invade and slice away at China time after time? How did it come about that the Japanese militarists seized and occupied the three northeastern provinces in 1931, and then in 1937 opened a full-scale invasion of China? Over and above the aggressiveness at the root of imperialism itself, what problems and what ills lay deep within our own people?

Once these questions stood before me, I had to ponder them further.

I thought about the hundred years of humiliation of the Chinese race, the endless succession of treaties great and small, and the degrading terms that foreigners used when they talked about the Chinese: 'swine', 'a heap of loose sand', 'warlord chaos', 'slumbering lion', 'internal strife'. I recalled all the countless revolutionaries who had shed their blood and given their lives in the struggle to awaken the Chinese nation.

What happened in Nanjing in December 1937 only made me ponder further.

When the ferocious Japanese forces advanced into Nanjing, throwing humaneness to the winds, the President of the Republic of China and every high official of the national government fled. The national army withdrew in defeat. The lower-ranking officers and officials all melted away. The several hundred thousand people who remained became helpless children, innocent sheep at the mercy of others, mere objects of bestial brutality, consuming their rations from their food bags. Their cries unanswered, they could only take their women and children and wander aimlessly in the streets or curl up in any nook or cranny, at the mercy of a fate they could not foretell.

Just at that time, a group of foreigners, complete strangers to one another, stayed behind, risking their lives to form the International Committee and create the safety zone in order to try to help those humble Chinese who had no place to go. They took up the responsibility for protecting these Chinese compatriots. They were like mothers guarding their children, or like protective gods. Out of their humanity, they opened their beautiful arms and spent all their strength and efforts to save the lives and souls of hundreds of thousands who might otherwise, at any moment, have lost their lives to the monsters.

As for Herr Rabe, the chairman of the International Committee, he could not but take up the duties of Nanjing's police chief and mayor, since in all of the city there were no longer any high 'officials'. He was but a single German, and the members of the International Committee, were only a bunch of highly educated foreigners.

I had to ponder this question, too: Why did our Chinese officials – our 'father and mother officials' – leave their children in the care of the foreigners while they themselves made their escape? Why did not a single Chinese official remain behind, to live or die with his own people? Although I loathed to admit it; although I looked for all sorts of high-sounding reasons to justify ourselves; although Chiang Kai-shek's forces did certainly later begin to fight in earnest; nevertheless, the history of this earlier phase could not be altered.

It was simply out of the question to deal with this as the Japanese militarists had done: by denial, by slowly erasing it, by covering it up.

History is history. The historical truths carved into the historical memory of mankind are tombstone inscriptions that can never be washed away.

Rabe and the other foreigners had lived for a long time in Nanjing, and they had strong feelings for the city. But they had no blood ties to the people of the city; they shared no common race. Why did they stay behind, in the face of mind-warping danger, labouring uncomplainingly to save the Chinese compatriots? What was their ultimate purpose? What power, what spirit, raised them up to make these selfless decisions? Simply resorting to nice-sounding traditional phrases – 'The Path of Humanity', 'Universal Love', 'Loftiness', 'Higher Goodness' – is not remotely sufficient. I exhausted my limited resources of intelligence and knowledge, attempting to fathom the deepest souls of these people, and now can only write my own shallow views.

I first considered religion. All of these men were Protestant or Catholic believers. A number of them were missionaries. Truthfully speaking, in the past I had no positive feelings about missionaries; to me they all followed the political orders of the imperialists, using religion to wash the brains of the Chinese people. Some of them were international spies as well. Now, facing the fact that so many missionaries stayed in Nanjing at mortal risk to try to rescue the Chinese, I had to view them with fresh eyes.

Was it the influence of their childhood New Testament teachings, which instructed them to "love thy neighbour as thyself", and imbued the belief that all living creatures deserved to be delivered from torment? Was that what led them to try with all their heart strength to redeem these innocent souls?

Universal love was their core value. Most devout Christians would say that suffering calamity was God's way of putting them to the test. But then I wondered: Do Japanese people not believe in religion in the same manner? Why did the teachings of religion have no restraining effect on the Japanese armies? Japan was a country of many religions, principal among them Shintō, Buddhism and Christianity. In worshiping the Goddess of the Sun, they believed that they were worshiping the original ancestor of their emperor. Moreover, the teachings of both Buddhism and Christianity taught doctrines of compassionate conduct, prohibiting killing or evil acts, without too many strictures. But then, as they were carrying out this massacre that extinguished all humanity, the Japanese approached the Chinese as though they were 'slicing tofu', bloodily lopping off the heads of humble Chinese people as though they were trash, finding amusement in killing them, even having contests to see who could kill the most. If religion really did seek to restrain man's conduct, wouldn't these Japanese soldiers fear Heaven's wrath? Wouldn't they tremble lest the Lord of Heaven rain catastrophes down upon them and their descendants as punishment?

The most absurd meaning of all was that, when he was sent to be executed after the Tokyo international war crimes trials, the highest-placed architect of the Nanjing Massacre, General Matsui Iwane, turned out to be a Buddhist. Buddhist scripture states: "Killing is a sin." Having soaked the soil of Nanjing with the blood of 300,000 Chinese, he returned to Japan and put up a three-metre statue of the goddess Guanyin and named it 'The Goddess of the Rise of Asia'. He had an inscription carved on the statue:

> In the China Incident, friends and neighbours fought one another. Taking masses of lives – truly a tragedy of the ages. I worship life. Transferred to the battlefields of Jiangnan, lives

and souls without number were lost. I cannot bear the pain and regret. To propitiate these souls, especially those whose blood soaks the soil of Jiangnan, I erect this statue of the Guanyin Calmly Views All Living Things in order to earn virtue and deliver all things from torment.

General Matsui Iwane prayed daily to Guanyin. Committed to prison, he hung images of Guanyin on the walls of his cell. Each day he read from the Sutra of Guanyin to atone for his crimes. And yet, the Bodhisattva Guanyin never forgave this butcher. In the end, the international war crimes tribunal sent Matsui Iwane to his death.

As to the nature of man, not only did I ponder long and hard; so did the author Herbert Steinhouse. After calling upon Oskar Schindler, he said: "Schindler's brilliant deeds arose simply from his fundamental righteousness and humane nature."

Using religion to explain people's behaviour can never be completely convincing.

It is clear from Rabe's diary that what claimed his heart was not religious conviction and not a determination to advance the interests of his company, Siemens, or the power of the Nazi Party. Instead, his inborn sense of humanity and chivalry, rooted in his purest and most compassionate emotions, was just as expressed in the inscription on a silken banner presented to him by the refugees: "Chivalrous Knight with a Buddha's Heart."

For myself, I think that religion was just a kind of pretty self-ornamentation for these Japanese militarists, to whom aggression was second nature. Savagery had long since wiped their hearts clean of any shreds of compassion. What remained was only animal savagery and slaughter.

As I write this, a deep torment shakes my being. Do we dare to reveal the depths of our own ugly courage? Do we ourselves have the courage to take up the burdens of morality and feelings of responsibility for others? In a word, do we dare to face the very depths of our own souls and speak what must be said – a kind of self-recognition, or a perspective drawn from our own self-examination?

I am just an ordinary writer. My inner heart is not particularly strong, and I don't have any particularly lofty ideals. As I write these modest paragraphs on my keyboard, my heart continually endures an interrogation about conscience and bravery, a bitter battle in which the 'Big I' pitches the 'Little I' over and down into a corner, until finally, at the end of the struggle, my fingers return to the keyboard.

These heavy topics torment not only me but my race. They compel an interrogation of our ancient land with its history of thousands of years.

With the fall of Nanjing, what was it that led these foreigners to risk everything to remain in the city, at immeasurable risk, and try to shield the Chinese? And we Chinese, and our 'father and mother officials', all born and raised in this land where we sought to make our names and our fortunes – why was not a single one willing to remain behind? Why, when many of Nanjing's surgeons had fled, did a single foreign doctor remain behind, at his post day and night, performing operations and caring for thousands of injured civilians and wounded soldiers?

Why, when our Chinese 'fathers and mothers' had fled, did a group of foreign professors and missionaries remain in the city, preserving photographs of the massacre and keeping records in their diaries, so that the world could learn the truth of the Japanese fascists' crimes?

Robert Wilson, an American surgeon from the University Hospital, was born in Nanjing in 1904. His missionary father taught in a middle school in the city. His Greek mother started a school for missionary children in Nanjing. To Wilson, Nanjing was his beautiful home, where he passed a happy youth and learned to speak perfect Chinese. He received a fine education at Princeton and Harvard in the US, but did not remain there to develop his career. Instead, he brought his new wife to his old home, Nanjing, and became a surgeon at the Ginling University Hospital. When the frantic Japanese bombing of the city began, he felt that Nanjing was a part of his life. He sent his wife and their daughter, still in swaddling clothes, back to the US, and remained in Nanjing himself. He was one of a very few surgeons still in the city. The people in Nanjing requiring surgery, and the wounded soldiers, numbered in the thousands. Wilson could only labour on, performing surgeries night and day, fatigued to the point of collapse. At times, shells exploded within fifty metres of his operating room; he and his staff were close to death. In his diary for 30 December, Wilson wrote: "This is simply enormous news. In this inferno of a city, I am the only surgeon!"[26]

He was a doctor, and he witnessed more tragedies than anyone should have to see.

A gang of Japanese soldiers grabbed a group of teenaged Chinese girls, overcame their struggles and desperate cries, threw them down into the muddy water and raped them in the middle of the street. Some of the girls died from loss of blood. Some of them, though clinging to life, had lost all will to struggle. Soon, news arrived that they had killed themselves, putting an end to their budding lives.

Scenes like this infuriated Wilson, but he was powerless to stop them.

All he could do was continue secretly performing surgery in his operating room. The scenes he saw there were even more pitiful and heart-rending than those he witnessed in the streets. Some of the people brought to him were covered with blood; some were missing arms or legs. The intestines of others were protruding from their bodies. Others had lost a buttock. Some were missing half of their faces. Others, shot, had miraculously survived and climbed out from heaps of corpses, their bodies torn by many bullets. Some came with scorched faces, their features entirely missing. Some young girls arrived, their genitals drenched with blood, pieces of wood rammed into their vaginas.

For Wilson, the most unforgettable case of all was a young woman whose neck had been nearly severed; her head wobbled from side to side on the remains of her neck. She had been forced to launder clothes for the Japanese soldiers by day; at night, she was the troops' sex slave. Every night, twenty to thirty Japanese soldiers bestially assaulted her. On that particular day, the soldiers had amused themselves with her, and then dragged her to an out-of-the-way place to destroy her with an axe. They slashed at her neck but did not kill her. She pretended to be dead, somehow avoided the soldier's detection and struggled to Wilson's hospital.

Wilson wrote this in his diary for 18 December 1937:

> Today was Day 6 of modern mankind's hell, a day written in blood and obscene words. My diary is filled with accounts of blood and plunder. Batch after batch of people have been slaughtered. Thousands of women have been raped. There is no power here that can stop the cruel, obscene and barbaric acts of these beasts.[27]

On 30 December, Dr Wilson wrote this single sentence: "Within the city, so many have been slaughtered that they are running out of people to kill."

He said that he had removed enough bullets and shell fragments from the bodies of his patients to fill a military museum.

John Magee was an American missionary, born to a lawyer's family in the US in 1884. He graduated from Yale and from Episcopal Theological School in Cambridge, Massachusetts. In 1912, he was dispatched to China for missionary work in Nanjing at the Episcopal Daosheng Church. At the time of the Nanjing Massacre, Magee was serving as the head of the Nanjing Committee of the International Red Cross. An avid photographer, he risked his life to shoot film with his 16mm movie camera and recorded eight reels of film showing the immeasurably horrible conduct of the Japanese troops.

George Fitch, another American in Nanjing at the time, smuggled Magee's films to Shanghai on 19 January, at great risk to himself, thus preserving invaluable eyewitness materials on the Japanese massacre. These materials provided ironclad testimony in the trials of Japanese war criminals by the International Military Tribunal for the Far East in 1946.[28]

In November 2007, in the counter-testimony of Xia Shuqin, a survivor of the massacre, against a Japanese right-wing author's claim of infringement upon his reputation, the films taken by John Magee were a crucial element in the author's legal defeat. In the film, Xia Shuqin, who was then eight years old, fainted after being struck by the Japanese troops' swords. When she regained consciousness, she discovered that of her family of nine, seven had been murdered; only she and her four-year-old sister had survived. John Magee had filmed the slaughter of Xia Shuqin's family as it happened. Seventy years later, Magee's films returned to serve the path of justice.[29]

George Fitch, born in Suzhou, was working for the YMCA in Nanjing. His American missionary parents had come to China much earlier. Risking his life, Fitch concealed Magee's films of the Japanese atrocities in his overcoat and managed board a boat for Shanghai after somehow getting through Japanese military inspection. In Shanghai, he made four copies of his films at a Kodak photo development shop and brought them back to the US as quickly as he could. His films gave the American media a graphic look at what the Japanese had done. His influential materials showing the truth of the Japanese atrocities provided ironclad testimony at the post-war trials of Japanese war criminals.

(7)

On 1 December 1937, the American embassy summoned the few US citizens left in Nanjing to a meeting, and warned them: "If you refuse to leave, we will not be able henceforth to guarantee your safety."

A bespectacled woman in her fifties, of sober demeanour, said firmly: "We cannot abandon China now." Then she took a huge brush and signed her name – Minnie Vautrin – in a witness book, provided to her by an embassy worker, entitled 'We Will Not Leave Nanjing No Matter What'. That was the fourth time that she had refused the American embassy's appeal to her to leave Nanjing.

"We cannot abandon China at a time like this!"

What kind of courage, what kind of admirable qualities, defined a person who would say this?

These words, which could shake the world, came not from the lips of a Chinese person but from the bottom of the heart of a 51-year-old American woman: head of the teaching department at Ginling College. (Later, Minnie Vautrin became head of the college.)

The American embassy, once Vautrin had made herself clear, had no choice but to see her remain behind, and gave her one final lifesaving symbol: an American flag, nine feet in length, to try to protect her school from Japanese air attacks. They also provided her with a length of rope that she could use to scale the city walls if the gates of the city were shut.

The American missionary Minnie Vautrin was born in the small Illinois village of Secor on 27 September 1886. After graduating from Illinois State Normal University, she arrived in 1912 in Anhui, where she started the San Qing Girls' Middle School. Some years later, she took up the post of president of Ginling College, where she handled tasks such as academic administration and construction of the university's new campus. Realising that the majority of Chinese women were illiterate, she decided to devote herself to women's education, working diligently to advance their education, encourage them to step beyond the confines of their homes and commit themselves to the larger society. By 1937, she had lived half her life – 25 of her 50 years – in China.[30]

I could not help asking myself: Why were these foreigners so courageous? Why was she so determined? Why did she love China so ardently?

Vautrin said: "I cannot leave China at a time like this."

Rabe said: "Having worked here for thirty years, I will go through fire and water for this."

The wife of Robert Wilson said: "Robert Wilson considers this his calling, and he considers the Chinese people his brothers and sisters."

In these foreigners, I discovered a sense of gratitude, a bravery of spirit and a righteous valour – indeed, the very measures of a person.

In comparison to these people, the inadequacies of our Chinese race over the past hundred years have lain in these very qualities: the failure of courage to take on heavy tasks, the lack of a bravery embedded in our blood and the lack of a moral integrity expressed as "uncorrupted by wealth or honours, undistorted by poverty, unbent by coercion". Our Chinese people were mired the day long in opium and lust, wreathed in ignorance, terrified of death and obsessed with self-preservation, disorganised like a sheet of loose sand, with perpetual conflicts and power struggles among warlords, finding pleasure in internal strife. Only when the enemy invaded, and the Chinese stood at the edge of annihilation, did some far-seeing figures shout: "The Chinese race has reached its critical moment! We are forced to roar furiously, to awaken our entranced and slumbering people!"

"Brothers may quarrel within the walls / But they will oppose insult from without." These words, from the classic *Book of Poetry*, tell us that even when brothers have disputes among themselves, they must resist as one all humiliations from the outside.

But both before and after Japan seized the three northeastern provinces, Chiang Kai-shek was not determined to resist Japan, instead concentrating on eliminating the Chinese Red Army of

Workers and Peasants led by the Chinese Communist Party. From October 1930, February 1931 and July 1931, Chiang gathered a huge army of anywhere from 100,000 to 300,000 troops to 'exterminate the bandits' of the Red Army, only to call an end to that after repeated failures. When Japan invaded China's northeast in September 1931 and 30 million of our countrymen were lost to the nation, Chiang responded by ordering Zhang Xueliang and his northeastern army of 300,000 to leave the northeast and relocate inside the Great Wall, turning them to 'communist suppression' and away from resistance to Japan.

With national disaster staring him in the face, the supreme commander Chiang Kai-shek did not act to support those 300,000 northeastern brothers who had fallen into terrible travail. Instead, in October 1932, he launched his fourth extermination campaign against the communists with an army of several hundred thousand, only to fail yet again. After that failure, in September 1933, Chiang assembled a force of a million men and a hundred warplanes, to launch the fifth extermination campaign against the communist base areas, forcing the communists to evacuate and set out on the Long March.

Chiang's military methods not only infuriated the people but led General von Falkenhausen, leader of the German military advisory group, to send Chiang a message of forthright criticism on 20 August 1935, entitled 'Recommendations on Strategies for Dealing with the Present Situation'.

But Chiang Kai-shek did not accept these recommendations. Instead, he clung to the ideas of 'pacification first, then resistance' and carrying out the bloody war against the communists to its final conclusion. Then, on 23 November 1936, the government arrested seven leaders of the National Salvation League – Shen Junru, Zhang Naiqi, Zou Taofen, Li Gongpu, Sha Qianli, Shi Liang and Wang Zaoshi – on charges of 'endangering the nation', in what became known as the Incident of the Seven Gentlemen, imprisoning them for the next eight months. It was only after Japan launched its full-scale war in China in July 1937 that the government, under pressure from all sides, released these prisoners.

In an attempt to shake Chiang out of his 'pacification first, then resistance' stance, General Yang Hucheng and General Zhang Xueliang launched the earth-shaking Xi'an Incident on 12 December 1936, attempting to use military force to compel China to turn away from civil war and towards the task of uniting in resistance to Japan.

For this, the 35-year-old Zhang Xueliang was held in captivity for half a lifetime. Yang Hucheng spent the next 13 years in prison. On the eve of China's national liberation, he still had not seen the end of Chiang Kai-shek's retaliation. Yang and seven members of his immediate entourage, including his secretary and his secretary's wife, and eight of his former subordinates were murdered by Chiang's secret police.

What a tragedy!

In ancient times, King Hui eliminated the reformist Lord Shang. In Qing dynasty times, the Daoguang Emperor banished Lin Zexu, Deng Tingzhen and Yang Fang. At the end of the dynasty, the Empress Dowager killed the Guangxu Emperor and his favourite concubine. Now, two renowned patriotic generals of China's modern history were thus eliminated by the country's commander-in-chief. How very similar.

Zhang Xueliang's and Yang Hucheng's only 'crime' was to try to force the nation's powerholders to cease their domestic battles and unite against the Japanese militarist threat, at the critical moment when the enemy was at the gates and the very survival of the people was at stake.

But the mind of the supreme commander was so parochial, and his inability to understand present realities too entrenched. He utterly lacked the spirit to take up the heavy tasks the people and the nation required. He found satisfaction in the squabbles and struggles of party factions. With leadership like this, how could the Chinese people not be bullied by an invading army?

What made this tragedy even worse was that as the Japanese invaded, all sorts of traitors great and small emerged to creep to the feet of the Japanese 'puppet regime'. On 1 March 1932, the deposed Qing emperor Pu Yi established the so-called Manchukuo (literally, the 'Country of the Manchus'), at Changchun in Jilin province (the city was renamed Xinjing, or 'New Capital'). In 1940, Wang Jingwei created a traitorous regime in Nanjing known as the Nanjing government. During the Japanese invasion, various 'provisional governments' made their appearance. For example, the Autonomous Government of the Mongol Alliance was established at the point of Japanese guns in October 1937 and later known as the Mongolia-Xinjiang United Autonomous Government. The day after the fall of Nanjing, 14 December 1937, Japan established a Provisional Government of the Republic of China in Beiping, relying on Chinese traitors. On 28 March 1938, after they had massacred 300,000 people in Nanjing, the Japanese established a Reform Government of the Republic of China under one Liang Hongzhi. On 10 June 1939, at a banquet convened by the Japanese consulate general in Nanjing, a courageous Chinese servant named Zhan Zhanglin slipped poison into the liquor, poisoning the entire leadership of the reform government and killing two Japanese officials. In March 1940, this reform national government was merged into the phony national government in Nanjing. After the Japanese surrender, Liang Hongzhi was executed on charges of treason and rebellion.

It is well known that during the Japanese invasion many Chinese living under the control of the puppet government served in puppet armed forces that served as frontline cannon fodder. Thus, a further tragedy was created: Chinese went to war against Chinese. And most of those who sold Chinese lives to the Japanese were themselves Chinese. In a county capital in the northeast, only two or three Japanese might be needed; for the rest, those who substituted for the Japanese in exercising Japan's control were all traitorous Chinese.

A race lacking in backbone, lacking in blood, lacking in cohesive strength, up against a hardened and savage-spirited race, was bound to be trodden upon and slaughtered.

On 29 August 1842, the Qing government and the British government signed the first Unequal Treaty in China's modern history of national humiliation: the Treaty of Nanjing. Nearly six decades later, in 1899, shortly before becoming US president, Theodore Roosevelt, in a speech about the central importance of living 'The Strenuous Life', issued a warning to Americans, using China as a negative example:

> We of this generation do not have to face a task such as that our fathers faced, but we have our tasks, and woe to us if we fail to perform them! We cannot, if we would, play the part of China, and be content to rot by inches in ignoble ease within our borders, taking no interest in what goes on beyond them, sunk in a scrambling commercialism; heedless of the higher life, the life of aspiration, of toil and risk, busying ourselves only with the wants of our bodies for the day, until suddenly we should find, beyond a shadow of question, what China has already found, that in this world the nation that has trained itself to a career of unwarlike and isolated ease is bound, in the end, to go down before other nations which have not lost the manly and adventurous qualities.[31]

We have to admit that this portrayal of the failings of our race makes for a very profound analysis.

(8)

The crimes committed by the Japanese military in Nanjing are too numerous to record and without precedent.

They dwarfed human imagination. Their barbarism exceeded anything comparable in the written annals of humanity. These actions went far beyond the bounds of war fought for territorial aggrandisement, or expansion of the people's Lebensraum (living space), or for the seizure of others' wealth and property. They revealed the bestial nature of man. Worse, even than that; they were more bestial even than wild animals, despicable, violent and shameless.

In the Japanese occupation of Nanjing, a third of all buildings in the city were destroyed. How much property and wealth were plundered is beyond calculation.

In the Memorial Hall for the Compatriots Murdered in the Nanjing Massacre by the Japanese Invaders, there is one room bathed in darkness and mottled sunlight. Standing there without breathing, every twelve seconds a visitor can hear a deep faint sound of water dripping.

Each water drop symbolises the loss of a Chinese compatriot's life.

In the six weeks following the Japanese invasion of Nanjing, 300,000 Chinese died under the slaughtering swords of the invaders. That comes to a loss of life every twelve seconds.

What kinds of physical torment and torture did these victims face before they died?

As I was writing this draft, the television showed a number of events in which terrorist groups killed people. The atrociousness of their actions aroused widespread anger, and the United Nations declared that terrorist groups required concerted attacks by the entire world.

If we compare the Japanese crimes in Nanjing with these contemporary terrorist acts, are the former lesser, or do they far exceed the latter?

The terrorist organisations committing horrific acts proclaim their responsibility for them. But 77 years after the Nanjing Massacre, the

Japanese government doggedly refuses to accept responsibility, tries by every means to obliterate this stage of history and vainly tries to blot from human history the crimes committed during Japan's war of aggression against China.

Now, let us go back to that period of bloodstained history and examine the sufferings of the Chinese compatriots in Nanjing.

At 3am on 12 December 1937, after 100,000 Japanese troops in eight divisions (some counted 50,000) marched into Nanjing, they broke into small groups, entering every home, burning, killing, looting and raping. There was no evil that they did not commit: entering, they looted; seeing someone, they killed; seeing a woman, they raped. They dragged off any possessions they could. Then they set fire to the homes; day and night, Nanjing's sky was lit red by the spreading firestorms.

John Rabe said this in his diary:

> It is estimated that 300,000 Chinese have been beaten to death, killed, decapitated, burned alive, or buried alive. At first, the mountains of corpses lay unburied. Then, perhaps fearful of epidemics, the Japanese took to pouring gasoline on the corpses and setting them alight. But only partly reduced the putrid stench of rotting corpses.
>
> In the space of two months, 20,000 women were raped. The Japanese made off with the women in the crowds of refugees they had assembled...[32]

The variety and cruelty of the methods of execution used by the Japanese arouse our fury.

They did not merely kill Chinese civilians and soldiers with a single shot. With their abnormal psychology, like cats toying with mice, they subjected their prey to all kinds of torture and humiliation. They nailed male Chinese to boards and had tanks run over them, turning them into 'meat buns'. They pierced the shoulder blades of others with wire and hung them from trees. They stripped others of their clothing and bound them, naked, in the trees or from electric poles, cutting out their eyes, their noses, their ears, their genitals. They carved pieces of flesh from their victims to feed to dogs. They used pointed tools to pierce the faces and bodies of their victims in many places, drenching themselves in blood. The troops even ate the hearts, livers, lungs or genitals of some of their victims.

They rounded up groups of Chinese compatriots, poured gasoline on them and lit the fires. Then they watched as the victims screamed and struggled, until they became a single giant fireball, burned alive. The soldiers sated their bestial dispositions, standing on the sidelines and joking as they watched the Chinese, at the moment of death, screaming and wailing.

They strung large numbers of Chinese captives like tethered grasshoppers with ropes or wires, and divided them into groups. The first group would be forced to dig a pit and then jump into it. When the second group of Chinese had been half buried, still alive in the pit, they would stop and unleash dogs. The dogs would leap into the pit and devour the heads of the Chinese victims. The soldiers would stand around, rubbing their arms and grinning, as the Chinese screamed in their death agonies, until finally all the captives had been killed by the dogs. Then they would order another group of captives to be buried. Round and round they went, until finally all the Chinese compatriots had been buried alive. Later, the Chinese discovered tens of thousands of these burial pits. That is how all this came about. Countless families were completely exterminated by the Japanese troops. In some families of eight or ten people, only one woman survived, driven completely out of her mind.

What is so tragic about this is that so few of the Chinese, whether soldiers or civilians, rose to resist. The Japanese army slaughtered them like sheep.

The soldiers stripped the Chinese naked and forced them into the icy river or ponds, watching as they gradually froze, then finally strafing them with gunfire until the water turned red and the surface was filled with corpses.

They conducted killing contests, dividing into teams to compete in killing large groups of Chinese soldiers and civilians whom they had rounded up. They cut off heads with their swords, one sword per person, as though they were chopping the green tops of radishes, to see which team killed the most and which team killed the fastest. The severed heads were piled like mountains. When the contest was over, the soldiers would dance for joy, raising their bloody hands in salute to the team that had killed the most.

Contests like this did not go on for a few minutes; they went on for one or two hours. They didn't happen at only one spot; they went on at many places. The aged Mr Tang Shunshan was one of the few who came out alive.

These actual killing competitions were written up in true records retained worldwide, written not in Chinese memoirs but in news reports in the Japanese newspaper *Nichinichi Shimbun*.

On the 13 December 1937, the Tokyo *Nichinichi Shimbun* printed an article entitled 'A Great Beheading Contest. Brave warriors! The Two Lieutenants Mukai and Noda', accompanied by photos of the two killers standing side by side with their swords. The article reported in detail on the illustrious exploits of these two fiends.

The two killers belonged to the Katagiri army. Both were graduates of the Tokyo Military Academy and both were lieutenants. One was named Mukai Toshiaki and the other was named Noda Takeshi. They made a bet in a Shanghai night club, before the attack on Nanjing, to see who could kill a hundred Chinese first.

On 10 December, the two men each drew their long swords, proudly displaying the nicks in the blades. Lieutenant Noda said: "I have already killed a hundred and five; how many have you killed?" Lieutenant Mukai replied: "I've already killed a hundred and six!" The two shared a hearty laugh: Lieutenant Mukai had beaten Lieutenant Noda by one victim. But they could not prove who had reached the target of 100 killings first. So they decided to hold a second contest, this time to see who could kill 150 people first. The contest began on 11 December with the goal of killing 150 people.

If it had not been for this report from two boastful Japanese soldiers, Chinese people would not have been able to learn that the Japanese army was holding such killing contests. And the world would not have been able to learn that the Japanese army, with its bowing and its apparent gentility, was in reality carrying out such murderous activities.

On 18 December 1947, the war crimes tribunal of the Chinese national government Defence Ministry in Nanjing sentenced Mukai Toshiaki, Noda Takeshi and a third Japanese named Tanaka Gunkichi, who had killed three hundred people, to death. Before being executed, each asked for a final cigarette.

How many of these murderous amusement contests took place during the Japanese invasion of China? There is no way to count them, because no one was willing to confess to his own crimes. Today, 77 years later, how many Japanese officers and soldiers could stand up and admit their crimes before the world, as Azuma Shirō did in publicly recognising his?

An old writer from the China's northeast doesn't have to look at quantitative data. My father's generation personally experienced Japanese aggression in the northeast, and suffered the results. For them, the so-called 'Three Alls Policy', which the Japanese employed against the Chinese, was not hearsay; they personally experienced it. What they knew of the 'kill all, burn all, loot all' policy does not bear repeating by authors and scholars now. These people experienced the pain of it themselves. When my father was alive, the words he said to me more than any others were these: "The little devils are so vicious. Their hearts are not made of human flesh. They are more vicious than wolves. Never, ever believe them!"

These were the words of warning passed from the older generation to successor generations.

To come to the subject of rape, as a woman I do not know what to write.

When the Japanese soldiers spied a female, whether an old woman of seventy or eighty or a child of six or seven, they never released her. The troops were like rutting animals. When they spotted a female, no matter her age, no matter the place, they pulled off her pants, hauled out their tools and raped her on the ground where she fell. Several men would rape a single woman, and when they had satisfied their lusts, they would wound or maim her in every sort of degrading way, splitting her in two, slicing off her breasts or ramming bottles, bamboo shards, pieces of wood or kindling into her vagina, ruining her genitals forever; one such victim had to live out her life forever after in nappies. Some children were too small, so the soldiers cut them with their swords, the better to rape them. Sometimes, when their games were over, they would put firecrackers inside their victims' vaginas and light them, exploding their victims to death. They never let a pregnant woman go. After raping her, they used their swords to open her belly, rip out her living foetus and impale it on the ends of their swords. They would tip the head of the foetus in gasoline and light it, watching the foetus burn to death like a fireball on the ends of their weapons. Sometimes, after finishing their rapes, they would force their victims to lick their penises clean. Some tied women to chairs and raped them in succession. Some women could not survive the abuse, dying amid torrents of blood. Some young women were unable to walk for days after being assaulted.[33]

Not only did the Japanese soldiers themselves commit these sexual offences; they also forced Chinese to commit sexual atrocities against other Chinese, forcing fathers to rape their daughters or sons to rape their mothers, or Buddhist monks to commit rape. Anyone who refused was killed.

The female victims of these assaults were housewives, students, schoolteachers, university professors, Buddhist nuns, office workers, little children.

The rapes took place in the streets, in haystacks, in residences, in nunneries, in churches, in schools, in hospitals – anywhere and everywhere. They went on 24 hours a day. At every moment, our sisters were being violated and gang raped.

Even more pitiful was the fact that a tenth of the rape victims were pregnant. Their shame was unendurable. Many chose to kill themselves or to kill their unborn children.

The members of the International Committee recorded all of this in their diaries. They shot still photos and movie film. It all went into their records of these events, to become evidence when the world set out to punish the crimes of the Japanese military.

A number of the members of the International Committee, including the American professor Lewis Smythe from Ginling University and Miner Searle Bates, vice president of Ginling University, appeared as witnesses at the International Tribunal for the Far East and the Nanjing Military Tribunal.

At the Nanjing tribunal, Bates testified with powerful indignation, as reported in many media:[34]

> From the Japanese invasion of Nanjing on 13 December 1937, arson, looting, killings, woundings, and rapes of civilians happened on a huge scale. The loss of life resulting from these crimes cannot be tallied. I personally saw the Japanese soldiers shooting civilians. Throughout the city, the streets were filled with corpses.

Rabe wrote a report to Hitler about the situation:

> They have not stopped raping women and girls. They are killing anyone who puts up any resistance or tries to flee, at any time.

No one who appears anywhere at the wrong time is spared. From the smallest girl of eight to the oldest woman of seventy, the victims are routinely beaten or tortured after they are raped. Some women are penetrated with bamboo stakes. I have seen these injured victims with my own eyes. I have talked with some of these dying women, and have had their bodies sent to the mortuary inside the Drum Tower Hospital...

How many Chinese women were raped after the Japanese invaded Nanjing? How many of our sisters died at the hands of the Japanese? How many were turned into 'comfort women' sex slaves on the scene? How many took their own lives, unable to endure such unendurable shame?

"Not a single soldier failed to rape a woman. After raping their victims, they killed them." This was the testimony of a Japanese soldier named Tadokoro Kōzō at the International Military Tribunal for the Far East.

According to some scholars' statistics, 80,000 women were raped after the Japanese army entered Nanjing. I think this number must be approximate; China has no way of developing precise statistics on this. Data on such shame-filled and bloody matters is hard to compile. This is not a matter of numerical data. It is about the unspeakably humiliating, a history too blood-soaked even to mention in accusations, a humiliation that all women in the world are unable to face. To me, that even includes women from the violators' own home – Japanese women.

I put it to the women of Japan: how would you feel if you were facing men who had abandoned humanity for bestiality – men whom Rabe had dubbed the 'Japanese animal soldiers' – when they are stealing not the chastity of your sisters and mothers and even grandmothers, but their very lives, and robbing you of the most elemental dignity and respect? Would you be like me, struck speechless with furious indignation, rising to my feet to denounce the violators?

As women, you too must feel the humiliation, arising from your need to protect yourselves, or from your love of country. For you surely must love your own race, and even love those men, though they are of bestial nature.

(9)

It is said that roughly 600,000 to 700,000 people did not escape from Nanjing when the Japanese invaded the city. Approximately 250,000 crowded into the international safety zone. Another 300,000 were killed by the Japanese army.

The International Committee headed by John Rabe was face to face with this hell on earth, a mob of soldiers of unparalleled bestiality. Murder, fire, rape and plunder consumed the entire city for six weeks without let-up. The international safety zone, of less than four square kilometres, took in a quarter of a million refugees through the 25 points of entry. Everything involving this quarter of a million people – food, water, sanitation, housing, sleep, health, medical care, safety – confronted the International Committee.

Rabe served as 'mayor' and 'police chief' and even needed to serve as 'fire chief'. To the refugees, he was the Star of Salvation, because Nanjing lacked any kind of higher 'official'. He had to resolve the life or death problems of a quarter of a million lives. Even though he was a Nazi, in the same circle as the Japanese, he sought to protect that quarter of a million people from destruction at the hands of the Japanese military. His travails are not hard to imagine.

Without vehicles, it was impossible to bring grain, stored outside of the city, into town; a quarter of a million souls could go hungry at any time. Without enough sanitary facilities, human waste piled up. Without enough housing, many refugees slept in the open air, in the cold nights of December in Nanjing. Without enough medicines, many of the injured and sick could not be treated, simply crying out in pain and dying at any time. Worse still, the safety zone was not safe. From time to time, Japanese soldiers forced their way in, dragging off large groups of young males and shooting them.

Rabe used every channel he could and activated every possible power within the International Committee to find vehicles and arrange special passes to bring grain into the city. He even paid high prices to some Japanese who were holding the grain they had stolen in the first place from the Chinese inhabitants. He made every room available for refugee use, and oversaw refugee construction of temporary latrines. He sent people everywhere in search of medicines to deal with the problems of those suffering from diseases. He pressed the Japanese to adhere to international custom by not killing their captives.

Rabe took at face value the words of Japanese officers who promised him that they would stop killing captured Chinese soldiers. But in the blink of an eye he personally saw bodies of a thousand Chinese soldiers, led away and shot by their Japanese captors. He was overcome with grief and remorse, seeing himself as the cause of the soldiers' deaths.

In his diary for 15 December he wrote:

> A detachment of Japanese troops sought to take away a group of Chinese soldiers who had already laid down their weapons and fled into our Safety Zone. I gave the Japanese officer my guarantee that these men would never again wage war if he would free them. I had just returned to the Safety Committee office when one of my servants gave me the bad news: the Japanese had returned and bound 1,300 refugees. I joined with Professor Smythe and Reverend Mills in trying to arrange the captives release again, but the Japanese refused us. A group of about a hundred armed Japanese soldiers surrounded them, bound them and led them off, as they reached for their firearms.
>
> Smythe and I drove again to see Fukuda at the Japanese embassy to plead for the captives. Fukuda told us that he would do his

best, but he cautioned us not to be too hopeful. I pointed out that if these men were killed, it would be hard for me to recruit labourers to serve the Japanese. He told me perfunctorily that he would act on this the following day. I was grief-stricken at the sight of these men, led away like animals. It was awful.[35]

The members of the International Committee saw batch after batch of Chinese soldiers, who had taken refuge in the safety zone, led away to their deaths. Among the others were coolies who had pulled rickshaws, policemen and physical labourers, led away because their hands and feet were callused or because the marks on their heads revealed that they had worn hats for long periods. Within the zone, eight thousand cases of rape occurred. A hundred of the zone's guard forces were killed. Thirty thousand people were harmed within the zone.

Rabe was incensed. He wrote message after message to the Japanese embassy, ranging from calm to agitated and accusatory:

> The 22 westerners in the city, and all the Chinese masses here are infuriated by the looting, raping and murdering beyond any comparison that your forces are committing...
>
> Yesterday, in broad daylight, several women from the Seminary were raped in a room crowded with men, women and children! We 22 westerners have no means of nourishing and protecting 200,000 Chinese day and night!

In the six weeks of Japanese slaughter in Nanjing, the International Committee sent 60 reports to the Japanese embassy, detailing thousands of atrocity cases and placing the blame on the Japanese military.

But the Japanese side paid no attention.

The killing, raping and looting all continued without let-up.

The members of the International Committee led by Rabe were not only witnesses; they were harmed themselves. Their own homes were not exempted; almost every one was looted by the Japanese.

On 23 December, a day before Christmas Eve, Rabe and Kroeger were tallying up the foreigners' losses to Japanese looting. Thirty-eight buildings belonging to Germans had been plundered, including one hotel burned to the ground. One hundred and fifty-eight buildings belonging to Americans had been looted. Just at that moment, one of the servants from Rabe's household rushed in, shouting: "Terrible! A Japanese soldier has forced his way into Herr Rabe's home and is forcing open the strong box!"

Rabe and Kroeger dropped their work and rushed back to Rabe's house in their car. Understand: the cash in Rabe's strong box was money for saving the lives of the refugees. When Rabe got home, he found that the soldier had tried for half a day to open the strong box but had failed and finally run off. Rabe treated it as nothing serious, and had just sat down to lunch when his servant rushed in again, crying "Terrible! Three Japanese soldiers have scaled the wall and are inside. They are coming for the strong box!"

Rabe rushed to confront the three Japanese soldiers, showing them the Nazi symbols on his sleeves and furiously shouting at them: "I am a German! Hitler! You had better get out of here at once!" The three robbers beat a hasty retreat back over the wall.[36]

Japanese troops came over the wall into Rabe's home more than twenty times. Each time, Rabe dispensed with his usual humour. He rushed at the looters and troops thinking of violence, brandishing the Nazi symbols on his sleeves and shouted angrily at them: "Out, you hooligans! You scoundrels!" Like an angry guard dog, he furiously drove them away.

Once, as he was returning to his compound, Rabe heard the sound of a girl crying loudly. He rushed to open the door to the courtyard, and discovered several Japanese soldiers who had come over the wall into the yard. One of the invaders had already taken off his belt and his uniform and was about to rape the girl. Rabe rushed at him and grabbed him shouting: "How did you crawl in here? You had better get out fast the way you came in!" The soldier saw Rabe's Nazi insignia and fled, scared out of his wits. Still carrying his pants, he raced over the wall in panic.

It was better when Rabe was at home, but worse when he was not.

Rabe did everything in his power to save each and every Chinese compatriot. He only owned two suits, but lent one to a refugee. The wife of one of his servants, named Zhang, was ill and several times stayed in Rabe's compound. Rabe drove her to the hospital in the dark of night. He gave his straw mats and door planks to the refugees to help them build a rudimentary shelter to shield them from the cold as they camped in his courtyard.

In the humble shelter in Rabe's courtyard were two tiny lives, brought into the world at this most unsuitable time, one baby boy and one baby girl. There were no doctors, no midwives, no swaddling clothes, just a few dirty rags. Rabe gave the infants' parents 10 yuan and suggested the name Dora, after his beloved wife, for the girl. The boy's parents named him Johnny, after Rabe himself.

The two couples shed tears of gratitude and reached for Rabe's hands. They sat silently weeping. They knew that the most precious gift Rabe had given them was not the 10 yuan but the gift of life itself. If Rabe had not opened his gate to them, the pregnant women would soon have fallen victim to the swords of the Japanese soldiers.

On Christmas night, Rabe played the role of Santa Claus, giving each of the 126 children in his compound two jiao, or a fifth of a Chinese yuan. But as soon as he started handing out the money, the crowd grabbed for it so urgently that the money was nearly all torn up, and he had to stop.

The refugees sought to give Rabe a Christmas gift. Rabe answered: "I have already received the best Christmas gift of all – the lives of more than 600 people."[37]

(10)

While the Japanese were manufacturing evil on the one hand, on the other hand they were working hard to cover up their crimes, using airplanes to dispense false propaganda everywhere. The content of their propaganda messages was absurd enough to make men laugh.

The leaflets read: "All good Chinese folk who return to their homes will receive food and clothing. To those people who were not hoodwinked by the devils of Chiang Kai-shek's armed forces, Japan will be a good neighbour!"

On the bombed-out walls and shattered utility poles, brightly coloured posters appeared with messages from the Japanese forces: "Please trust the Japanese military! They will protect you and provide you with food!"

Their posters showed pictures of Japanese soldiers taking care of Chinese children, and mother and child kneeling in gratitude at the feet of Japanese soldiers, thanking the soldiers for bringing them rice.

On 1 January 1938, the Shanghai newspaper *New Life Journal* printed an article titled: 'The climate in Nanjing is Harmonious, and Developments There Are Bringing Happiness to the People.' The article said:

> Once the Japanese forces were in Nanjing, they sheathed their swords and extended their hands benevolently to see to the sick, bring food to the starving and bring medical services to those falling ill. Men and women, young and old, all kneel before the Imperial Army to express their veneration. Vast crowds surround the Japanese forces flying the Rising Sun and Red Cross flags, crying "Banzai!" and expressing their gratitude. Nanjing will become one of the best places in the world, everywhere fully at peace touched by the scent of a secure and happy existence.[38]

The Tokyo *Nichinichi Shimbun* reported on 28 December:

> Nanjing's stores have hurried to reopen and have now restored their usual business. The Japanese, working with the foreigners remaining in the city, are together bringing assistance to refugees. Looting by Chinese in the city has been eliminated, and Nanjing has returned to peaceful social order.

Japanese government radio, the following March, sent a report to the world:

> The large numbers of violent offenders who caused such widespread bodily harm and financial loss have been liquidated. They were enraged troops from Chiang Kai-shek's armies. All has now returned to normal, and the Japanese army is assisting 300,000 refugees!

Never in the world had there been such absurd, ridiculous, despicable and shameless lies.

Carrying their butchering knives in their hands, taking their ninety-degree bows, smiling affectionately: "See how kind our Japanese armies are! These crimes were not committed by us! They were committed by the Chinese themselves! We are bringing salvation to the Chinese people and are building the Greater East Asia Co-Prosperity Sphere hand in hand with them!"

I think not only of Japan's actions in the 70 years since the end of the war – of their falsifications of history, their revisions of history textbooks, their many refusals to admit what happened in the Nanjing Massacre. I think of their many publicly issued materials claiming that the Nanjing Massacre never happened, that it was fiction, that it was exaggerated, hearsay, concocted.

A lying and bloodthirsty race bent on extending its territory, still uses all sorts of lies to deceive the entire world.

But the International Committee refused to remain silent about the Nanjing Massacre. A number of foreign missionaries have spent their lives exploring the true meaning of hell, and they discovered it in Nanjing. The members of the International Committee sent their diaries, their letters and their photographs out to the world and told of everything that had happened in Nanjing:

> Complete anarchy has reigned for ten days – it has been hell on earth... to have to stand by while even the very poor are having their last possession taken from them – their last coin, their last bit of bedding (and it is freezing weather), the poor ricksha man his ricksha; while thousands of disarmed soldiers who had sought sanctuary with you together with many hundreds of innocent civilians are taken out before your eyes to be shot or used for bayonet practice and you have to listen to the sounds of the guns that are killing them; while a thousand women kneel before you crying hysterically, begging you to save them from the beasts who are preying on them; to stand by and do nothing while your flag is taken down and insulted, not once but a dozen times, and your home is being looted and then to watch the city you have come to love and the institution to which you have planned to devote your best deliberately and systematically burned by fire – this is a hell I had never before envisaged.
>
> – Diary of George Fitch, 24 December 1937

> There were tens upon tens of thousands of such terrifying events. Too many. In the end, they turn a person numb, incapable of shock. It is impossible to imagine that people this cruel could exist in today's world.
>
> – Diary of John Magee, 28 January 1938

> I had never before heard of such atrocities. Rape! Rape! Rape! I estimate that there are a thousand rapes each night, and they continue into the daylight hours. People are hysterical. Each

Playing Chess with the Devil

time a foreigner appears, they kneel and touch their heads to the ground, begging for help. In the encampments of the refugees, even the most destitute are robbed of their last pennies, their last articles of clothing, their last pieces of bedding – all seized. The Japanese soldiers drag off women at all hours of the day and night.

– Diary of James McCallum, 19 December 1937

Once the foreigners' words, photos and films exposing Japanese atrocities reached the world's media, the Japanese doubted that the reports came from foreigners at all. They hated the foreigners to the depths of their souls, but for various reasons they were not able to lay hands on them.

(11)

What distinguishes human beings from animals is that humans have organised thought, culture, wisdom and a sense of shame that animals lack. But the methods of the Japanese military were enough to infuriate mankind.

The Japanese military were Asians, yellow-skinned people. Why were they so obsessed with hatred of the Chinese that they would not cease until they had exterminated them all and eradicated the Chinese race? My formal knowledge is shallow; I cannot penetrate the inner souls of the people of this island nation.

Now let us listen to the words of a number of foreign thinkers, evaluating what the Japanese did and what crimes the Japanese committed in China. Let us hear their thoughts today about Japan's unwillingness to bow their heads in acknowledgment of their crimes, and their additional, more profound and sober, views.

The great French philosopher Montesquieu said this about the Japanese:

The nature of the Japanese is highly abnormal. To European eyes, Japan is a bloody anomaly, a race that gains erotic satisfaction from slaughtering. They are headstrong and obstinate, ignorant, servile toward those above and vicious and cruel toward those below. The Japanese are easily apt to kill others or commit suicide. They do not hold neither their own lives in high esteem, much less the lives of others. Therefore, Japan is full of disorder and vendettas.

US President Theodore Roosevelt said:

In all of history, I have never seen a people more despicable and shameless than the Japanese.

French President Charles de Gaulle said:

The Japanese are a cruel race, treacherous and deceitful. In their lust for blood, they are like the Dracula of the European Middle Ages. Once they see your weak spot, your throat will be bitten, and you will not survive.

The first president of the Federal Republic of Germany, Theodor Heuss, said:

The Japanese slaughtered unarmed Chinese women and children without remorse, and would not rest until they had killed the last Chinese.

In my view, the nature of a people consists of the good and the bad. The Yamato people have their good points; if they did not, they would not have been able to become the strongest nation in Asia and form a fascist alliance with Nazi Germany. But if a nation falls under the control of a militarist group for a long while, its popular masses are indoctrinated with militarist ideals, and its education system is infected with militaristic notions of slavery, then, over the long run, expansionism and aggression come to dominate both the nation and the race. This becomes an entirely different matter. The nature of the race then changes completely and it becomes impossible to avoid the distortion and the cruelty of human nature itself.

In the book *100 Reasons*, Hu Ping offered another profound analytical view of the Japanese people:

> Without question, cruelty was an utterly obvious characteristic of the Japanese armies. Their viciousness was more than the ordinary frenzied violence; it seemed decisive, icy and final. This rose to a number of levels of 'art', as in the case of General Anami Korechika's suicide under the moonlight.
>
> This 'Way' was the Way of the Samurai – Bushidō.
>
> Japan in the 15th and 16th century was wracked by domestic conflict. Samurai warriors served different lords and struggled for dominance of territory, rivers and mountains. For two centuries, Japan was engulfed by a reign of terror. The samurai children were educated in *hara-kiri*, or self-disembowelment. A boy received his first sword at the age of seven. Small girls received the short dagger, and were taught how to defend their samurai. At fifteen, boys underwent the ceremony of becoming samurai, receiving the long sword used for killing and a short dagger to be used for *hara-kiri*.[39]

When a country is completely under the control of militarist elements, not only is it not able to see the life of other peoples; it cannot even see the lives of its own people, including the lives of its own women and girls.

Looking at their massive flight after Japan's defeat, we can gain a deeper understanding of how a populace long controlled by militarists becomes cold-hearted and devoid of tenderness.

When Emperor Hirohito on 15 August read to his nation the announcement of unconditional surrender, large numbers of Japanese people in the northeastern provinces of China were thrown into an abyss of despair. Then they began their great flight.

Japanese had been migrating to China ever since the Russo-Japanese War of 1905. With Japan's occupation of the three northeastern provinces on 18 September 1931, the Japanese government began step by step to execute a large-scale plan for invasive Japanese emigration, with a goal of moving a million households – five million people – into northeast China within twenty years.[40] With their bullets and swords, the armed force supporting Japanese development, known as the Kwantung Army, forcibly seized land at a price of one *yuan* per *mu* (a sixth of an acre). If someone refused that offer, his entire family was killed. Thus, using burning and killing as their tools, the Japanese forced great numbers of Chinese from their homes and lands, seized large tracts for themselves, brought harm to the many Chinese who had lived upon those lands for generations, and dragged away women and children into homelessness.

In just one village – Zhu River Zhangyongan East village in Fangzheng county, Heilongjiang province – the Japanese development corps seized more than 18,000 *mu* (12 square kilometres) of land, forcing more than 3,000 Chinese to flee their homes and lands to try to reclaim lands in an area with inadequate water supplies. In the end, poverty and illness claimed 200 lives. Dozens of family lines were extinguished forever.

Up to August 1945, Japanese emigrés into northeast China numbered 1,660,000. They had formed more than a thousand so-called 'development corps'. The emigrés' grand dream of migration collapsed in ruins with Emperor Hirohito's surrender announcement to the world. Among the more than one thousand development corps spread across the land, shocking scenes of cold-blooded killing erupted – not scenes of Chinese killing Japanese, but of Japanese killing Japanese.

When more than a million Japanese heard the death knell of destruction, they fell into a final desperation and began killing one another. Officials killed civilians. Leaders of the development corps forced their members to commit collective suicide. Men killed women. Soldiers killed civilians. Men in their prime killed pregnant women. Husbands killed their wives. Children murdered elderly mothers. Most horrific of all, mothers killed their young children with their own hands.

According to the *History of Manchukuo* prepared by the Japanese, there were 1.55 million Japanese in northeast China (not counting military forces and their families) in 1945. Between 1945 and 1949 176,000 Japanese perished, including 80,000 belonging to the development corps.

Historical records show that more than a hundred incidents of collective suicide or mutual shootings took place among Japanese development corps in Yilan, Anqing, and Tonghe within Heilongjiang province; the Balinyou Banner and Ulanhot in Inner Mongolia; Changchun, Dehui and Baichengzi in Jilin province; and Shenyang, Jinzhou and Anshan in Liaoning province.

Here are a few examples:

In Dongfeng village, Fengdong district, Jixian county, Heilongjiang province (which bore a Japanese name at that time), Ōe Shūji called the members of the surrounding development corps together and ordered that 280 women and children be killed, personally leading the men in murdering these victims. The few who survived were taken in by the Chinese.

On 12 August 1945, in what is now the city of Jixi, Heilongjiang province (it bore a different name then), the head of the Hada River development corps, Kainuma Yōji, led a withdrawal of five hundred women and children. Blocked by troops of the Soviet Red Army, with no hope of rescue, the corps leader committed suicide, and the soldiers mowed the women and children down with machine guns.

Out of the bloodbath, only seven children survived; they were taken in by Chinese from the area.

On 17 September 1945, 495 people poisoned themselves on orders of the acting head of the development corps. The corps headquarters was burned down. Several Japanese males who oversaw the administration of the poison fled into the hills to hide, later returning to Japan. Fifty-two of the women and children of that development corps survived and were taken in by local Chinese.

On 24 August of that year, the head of the Fenghuang development corps in Dedu county, Heilongjiang province, Fūtoku Momei, ordered two hundred elderly women and physically weakened children to take poison. Five children survived, and were taken in by local Chinese.

In August, at the development corps at Zhaopaotu in Fangzheng county, Heilongjiang province, 82 people burned themselves to death.

In the same month, the head of the development corps in Fuyu county, Jilin province, named Miyamoto, locked up 268 members of the corps and killed them with explosives, after he had killed a number of Chinese.

Again, in August 1945, in the Lijia small county development corps within Yanshou county, Heilongjiang province, the head of the development corps herded 100 corps members into a primary school classroom, locked the windows and doors, hurled in hand grenades and began shooting, killing everyone.

On 16 August 1945, at the Gaoqiao development corps in Lanxi county, Heilongjiang province, having reached the end of their rope, the corps leader Naka Yasuhiro, leading a group of 20 men, forced 299 adults and children of his corps at gunpoint to leap into the Hulan river. Only four women and children survived, and were taken in by local Chinese.

On 14 August, at the development corps at Gegenmiao in the city of Ulanhot, Inner Mongolia, the corps leader Asano Ryōzō ordered his entire corps to leap into the river and then ordered people to throw hand grenades among those struggling in the stream. Then he ordered that any survivors be killed by sword. Twelve hundred died. Six surviving children were raised by Chinese families. One of the children saved that day became Mme Ma Yun, vice chairman of the People's Congress of Tongliao City, Inner Mongolian Autonomous Region.

On 16 August 1945, at the Japanese development corps in Inner Mongolia, with their retreat blocked, the corps leader Yamazaki ordered that everyone commit suicide. The corps members began killing one another in a frenzy, some with bayonets, others with poison, strangling the children. Five hundred died. The few children who survived were adopted by Chinese families.

In Hanjia district, Qing'an county, Heilongjiang province, the leader of the development corps, whose name was Ōhashi Munemitsu, ordered everyone to commit suicide; 160 died there.

The acting corps leader at the Yazhou development corps in Fuyu county, Heilongjiang province, locked 356 people inside a school house and set the building afire. The few surviving orphans were raised by local Chinese.

At Jiangmouhe, in Heilongjiang, the head of the development corps threw more than ten people down a well.

Enough. There is no need to write more. There is a detailed table of information on this on page 94 of Liu Guoqiang's book *Japan's Orphans*.

In their great evacuation, the Japanese did not support one another or care for one another. Instead, they struggled to the death against one another. On the evacuation trains, if Japanese officers found the cars too crowded, they took pregnant, screaming women and kicked them off the trains. If the officers heard too many children crying on the evacuation boats and feared that the Soviet army would pursue them and attack, they ordered the women to throw all the children overboard into the river. When 20 women refused to obey, the officers ordered that they be blown up with hand grenades, with any survivors to be dispatched by the sword. Many women watched their children cut down by the army officers.

The worst of the worst was that some women killed their own children.

Liu Guoqiang's book *Japan's Orphans* contains this passage:

> When they reached the Little Luolemi river, some of the young mothers saw at a glance that the worst possible tragedy was unfolding. They pointed to the opposite bank and said to their children: "We will cross. Get into the river." The water did not cover their feet, or their ankles, or their knees. But as the water deepened, the mothers let their own children drink some water. The mothers said: "We have a long way to go: drink quickly, to save time when we reach land." Then, as the children bent to drink, the mothers wildly forced their children's heads under the water. The children struggled, struck and pinched their mothers, but the mothers did not let go of them. In a flash, twenty children were drowned alive.[41]

These were not isolated events. Mothers killing their children and children killing their mothers became commonplace during the great evacuation.

There is a saying: "Tigers do not eat their young." But still...

In the book *Japan's Orphans*, there is the story of one Japanese person on the Great Evacuation who recalled many horrific sights:

> In a tree hung six emaciated bodies. One of them, a male child, was not yet dead. He was taken down by the Chinese, and later became an engineer on a farm. On a hillside lay 30 small bundles – these were 30 little lives, abandoned by their mothers. On the corpse of each child lay the final gift left by its mother:

a knife wound in the belly or strangulations marks on the neck. One fleeing mother's last words to her child were overheard: "Why haven't you died yet?"[42]

The story that hit me the hardest in *Japan's Orphans* was this one:

At the development corps in a Heilongjiang village named Jinggang, an eight-year-old named Mariko was knocked senseless by a gigantic explosion. When she regained consciousness, she found that her father, sister and brother had all been killed. Only her mother, Ōshima Tamiko, sat by the bodies, her hands drenched with blood. When the mother saw that Mariko was not dead, she attacked her, wildly shrieking: "Why didn't you die? You bold little devil! Why didn't you go with them to your death? Why are you still alive?"

The mother threw the child roughly to the ground and left. Trembling with fear, the child bravely hobbled along behind her mother on her tiny feet, keeping a distance and afraid to come close. She begged for food, and when she found a morsel she quietly placed it in front of her mother, then hurried to get out of the way. The mother ate the food her daughter gave her, but still wanted to kill her. The child ran behind a large rock to escape her mother's blows. That night, while sleeping next to a haystack, the child felt a heavy object crushing her and was unable to breathe. She saw a heavy sack lying on her and could hear her mother's familiar whisper not far away. When morning came, Mariko could find no trace of her mother. Later, she was adopted and raised by a charitable Chinese woman.

By the summer of 1981, Tian Ling, formerly known as Mariko, went to Japan to find her mother. After many twists and turns, she finally located Ōshima Tamiko. But she had never been the object of her mother's love, much less received any sort of penance from her mother; they only had a brief and frigid conversation. That struck terribly at Mariko's already wounded heart. "You are Mariko! I recognise you! But I can't recognise you! You don't speak Japanese. You haven't been to college. How will you live if you come back here? It is still a battlefield here. You can't live here. Go back to China!"

Still later, when Ōshima was destitute, she sought out Mariko, whom she had abandoned and harmed so badly, and asked her for funds to protect her in her old age. Mariko did not understand, and asked her Chinese mother what to do. Her Chinese mother told her: "She is your mother no matter what. Child, whether she acknowledges you or not, you must acknowledge her. Whether she raised you all these years or not, now you must support her. I say to you: if you do not now support your mother, I myself will no longer recognise in you the same girl."[43]

One, a Chinese mother. The other, a Japanese mother. A world of difference.

In his diary of the invasion of China, Azuma Shirō writes of 31 August, the day of his departure. As he bade farewell to his mother, she said this to him:

> This battle is more valuable than anything you could buy. Go with joy! If you have the misfortune to be taken by the Chinese troops, commit hara-kiri. I have three sons. Losing one will make no difference.
>
> Then she gave me an inscribed dagger. My mother's words filled me with joy. I thought my mother was magnificent. I swore before her that I would be glad to die.
>
> My nurse and I parted tearfully. She hoped I would return alive, and implored me to come back alive. My birth mother said farewell with a smile and spoke calmly. She encouraged me to die unhesitatingly. My nurse was from the countryside, while my birth mother was from the city. I think the two women's feelings were vastly different.[44]

Here are two completely different mothers, one encouraging her son to die, and the other hoping that he might come home alive.

In wartime, the worst and most bestial parts of man's nature torture all mothers everywhere.

In the great evacuation at the end of the war, 4,500 Japanese children were left behind by their parents.

As a mother myself, I cannot believe that they could do something so completely without conscience. The principles of Heaven itself do not allow explanatory interpretations or sympathetic understanding of mothers abandoning their children.

We do not hear reports of mothers killing their children to save themselves in China under Japanese invasion, or of husbands killing their wives and children. We hear many, many moving stories of husbands aiding wives, of mothers saving children, of children taking bullets to save their fathers, of mothers giving their children a chance to live at the cost of their own lives. We don't hear of mothers who threw away their children to save themselves. A Chinese mother would prefer to die herself in order to protect her child. They would give their last bite of food, their last drop of water, their last lifeline of hope to their children, to succeeding generations, to the roots and seedlings of generations to come. Never would they trade abandoning their children for their own chances of living. Even less would a Chinese mother kill her own child in order to live herself.

As Chinese people see it, abandoning one's child is the most selfish, the most unforgiveable evil and the mother's ultimate disgrace. And even in life or death situations, Chinese men would never cut down their wives or children in order to save their own miserable lives.

This contrast made me ponder deeply and soberly.

After the surrender, there were countless scenes of the strong killing the weak or of mutual slaughter among the Japanese.

And the Japanese government? How did it treat these subjects who had no place to turn?

The Japanese in the Great Evacuation could not imagine that their own government's Supreme War Council would put out a series of directives after the Japanese surrender, abandoning them to their fate.

The commander of the Kwantung Army proclaimed: "For the resurrection of the empire, even more Japanese people must remain in China."

On 19 August, four days after Emperor Hirohito had announced Japan's unconditional surrender, the government sent the following order to the Kwantung Army in northeast China: "Japanese soldiers and civilians remaining in China may change their nationality if they wish."

On 26 August, the government sent a message to diplomatic posts abroad: "Japanese citizens abroad should not rush to return to Japan, but should remain calm and stay where they are."

At the end of August, the government again addressed Japanese emigrants: "Emphasising the achievements of our rule in the past, Japanese abroad should make every effort to remain where they are, with the main aim of a harmonious and prosperous existence. For the sake of that lofty goal, they must be patient and suffer adversity."

It is not hard to see the underlying message in these orders from the Japanese government: "In our hearts, we have not lost China. Leaving a million Japanese to hide in China for the long term will enable the Rising Sun to rise again from the dead, and the Eastern Mountains to rise again!"

Obviously, the Japanese government still entertained the fond dream of invading China.

Japan surrendered. The Chinese people should have taught them a lesson, out of resentment at what had been done to the Chinese people – the deaths and injuries, the suffering. They ought to have killed some of the Japanese. But the Chinese people were too generous – generous to the point of foolishness, generous as lambs. Not only did they not exact revenge on the Japanese; they adopted and raised the many abandoned Japanese children – the 'wolf cubs'.

In my lifetime in Heilongjiang, many of these orphans remained. On the dock at the port of Huludao in Liaoning province, a fellow named Liu Xiuye, who managed the office in the city of Shenyang that handled Japanese prisoners and other Japanese, facing the frigid wind, offered some words to all on board a ship leaving for Japan filled with the last batch of Japanese soldiers and civilians that he repatriated (altogether, 1.05 million were repatriated); they cause us to ponder deeply:

> After you return to Japan, you need to think very carefully, step-by-step about how you were treated by the Chinese, and how you treated the Chinese yourselves. I hope in the end that you will carry with you only friendship, not swords. Goodbye.[45]

But do the Japanese know how to reassess?

Of the 4,000 Chinese households raising Japanese orphans, how many had suffered from Japanese arrogant mistreatment? In some, men had been shot. In others, women had been raped. How many had seen their lands seized? How many had had to flee their homes? How many had become destitute?

It is safe to say that not a single household among those 4,000 had escaped some kind of mistreatment and harm at the hands of the Japanese. But our Chinese compatriots repeated this saying: "The children are innocent. What do they have to do with the crimes of the Little Devils [the Japanese – tr.]? These children have lost their mamas. They are so pitiable!"

But our kindly Chinese brothers and sisters took these tiny lives, shivering and gasping for breath, into their bosoms and brought them to their homes. They put food to the lips of babies howling in hunger. Mothers put their dry nipples to the mouths of these baby animals. They had no milk to give, and the wolf cubs wailed hungrily. The mothers bent over and placed the Japanese babies on their backs, looking for women in other houses who could give them milk. Some of the abandoned children grew up on milk from many homes. The Chinese mothers of some of these children had to beg for food. How many Chinese mothers sacrificed their own flesh and blood to raise children abandoned by their Japanese parents? In Ulanhot, a Chinese man named Wu Fengqi devoted himself to raising three Japanese orphans, and in the end never married.

Our kind-hearted Chinese mothers not only overcame poverty and the terrible difficulties the war imposed on them; they also conquered the indifference and hostility bequeathed by racial hatred. They used their own frail arms to save the abandoned Japanese children from all the catastrophes that surrounded them. They took those children to their own bosoms until the children grew to adulthood. Once friendly contacts between China and Japan were restored, the Chinese mothers unhesitatingly allowed these children to fly from the nest and return to Japan to search for their relatives. Out of all this, how many heartbreaking stories of the separation of flesh and blood might there be?

But these wartime sacrificial articles, these Japanese orphans abandoned in the Great Evacuation, were not received as normal Japanese citizens when they returned to Japan. They became second-class citizens in Japan. The returned orphans went to court to demand that the government provide them with war compensation. The media reported that they brought cases to lower-level courts in Tōkyō, Ōsaka, Sendai, Nagano, Kyōto, Nagoya, Okayama, Fukuoka and Kagoshima, and to higher courts in Tōkyō, Sapporo, Ōsaka, Nagoya, Hiroshima and Takamatsu. But their suits all failed. The judges turned down the original suits on the grounds that "any violations of regulations or illegal actions were committed by a government that no longer exists".

Writing this, I have again fallen into deep thought.

I make comparisons: Japanese mothers abandoned their own flesh and blood, while Chinese mothers who had suffered so much from Japanese military invasion gathered these children up. Japanese mothers allowed their children to perish, while Chinese mothers raised those children at any cost, and then, when the children had grown, released them to return to Japan in search of their birth parents.

The contrast helped me to realise for the first time that our Chinese sisters, even though they might not have had much education, and in some cases could not even read their own names, were nevertheless the most beautiful and greatest mothers in the world. Those so-called elegant ladies were insignificant in front of our Chinese sisters. They could not begin to equal the magnanimity of our Chinese sisters. In their simplicity and generosity, the Chinese mothers composed an anthem of human love.

But did the Japanese appreciate this kindness?

(12)

I felt deeply moved by these Chinese mothers who saved and raised the abandoned Japanese children.

And another foreign woman moved me as well and led me to deep admiration.

As Nanjing descended into hell, a tall foreign woman in a long dress, wearing big eyeglasses, her eyes deep and resolute, fearlessly faced the Japanese troops. Her head held high and her chest thrust forward, she shepherded several hundred young Chinese women through the bloody streets lined with corpses into the refugee reception centre that she led – the Nanjing Women's College.

Four times she had refused the US embassy's offers of assistance. At the embassy, she had stated that she would remain in Nanjing, shoulder to shoulder with the Chinese people. She signed her name: Minnie Vautrin.

Though she had never married and had never enjoyed the taste of motherhood, she bequeathed to the entire world a brilliant image of motherhood.

When the Japanese entered Nanjing, she said: "I cannot leave. I personally feel that I cannot leave. Men are not asked to leave their ships when they are in danger and women are not asked to leave their children. At this time I cannot abandon China."

Vautrin's words should be inscribed on the souls of the Chinese. Let her words forever rouse the souls of our people and inspire our sense of responsibility.

The ordinary person holds responsibility for the life or death of the state. When the nation's life is on the line, the question is: Leave or stay? Be loyal or be a traitor?

This question tormented the soul of every young Chinese woman, but it did not include foreigners. Vautrin was not Chinese, but she had the heart of a Chinese. At 51, she had devoted her entire energies and all her love to humanity – more precisely, to China.

Month after month, like a mother caring for her offspring or a chicken guarding her chicks, she protected young Chinese women and guarded Chinese refugees.

In her capacity as head of the International Committee's Refugee Reception Centre at Ginling Women's College, though she was not young herself, she threw herself into the work of refugee protection. Thousands of women and children with no place to go entered into her college's campus, flocking together under the wings of this woman who had herself never been a mother.

Further, at great risk, she took in wounded Chinese soldiers, letting them stay there as ordinary refugees, after taking and burning their uniforms and any other military items.

In her diary for 17 December, Vautrin wrote:[46]

> More women are arriving, exhausted and terrified. They tell me they have passed a night of terror. The Japanese soldiers have continually come to their homes, raping 12-year-old girls and 60-year-old women alike. The husbands were driven away. The soldiers ripped open the bellies of pregnant women.

Night after night, Vautrin slept in her clothes so as to be able to run out and meet any sudden emergency. She was like a spinning top, never stopping day or night, busy from morning 'til night, taking in thousands of refugees, finding food for them, setting up patrols of the campus, asking foreigners from the International Committee to take turns on night patrol duty, stopping marauding Japanese soldiers from assaulting the women, confronting lust-crazed Japanese troops, surrounded by soldiers, slapping their faces with her fan.

She was an educated woman, but unrivalled in strength.

She said: "Ginling Women's College is my home. I will not leave it."

She spotted a young Chinese man wearing an armband with the Japanese flag, bringing some food to a Chinese woman in the refuge. She said to him: "You are Chinese. You don't need to wear the Rising Sun flag. Your China is not lost! You had better remember this day, when you put on that plaything. Never, ever forget this."

She encouraged the hopeless refugees, saying: "The Japanese are doomed to defeat!"

In her diary, she wrote:

> We feel that war is the people's crime. It violates the most profound feelings in the depths of the souls of all creatures. But we can give of our energies to assist those who are suffering and help those families that have been burned or shot, and people

who have been blasted by cannon fire or aerial bombings, to recover.

People in Nanjing called her the 'Female Bodhisattva'.

In 1938, the national government bestowed its highest honour for a foreigner: a jade medallion with the three colours – blue, white and red. Later, the government also presented her with a silver medal, in recognition of her extraordinary contributions in China.

But she was too exhausted.

The battering of her spirit was more than she could bear.

She noted many times in her diary the pain she was feeling in her heart:

> Ah, Dear God, please control the bestiality of the Japanese soldiers in the city tonight!
>
> How ashamed Japanese women would be if they knew all the atrocities of the Japanese armies!
>
> Too tired! I am too fatigued to write a word or even to think.[47]

She collapsed from exhaustion, and fell into a profound depression.

But the straw that broke the camel's back was not her grave illness; it was an article.

Not long after the puppet government of Wang Jingwei was established, in April 1940, the Nanjing newspaper *Purple Mountain Evening News* published a famous article entitled 'The Real Criminals'.

The article read: "Let us have a look at the so-called 'compassionate woman bodhisattva'! Minnie Vautrin is actually a swindler, a rebel who sold China out. We must expose her. We must put on her head the price she received for giving Chinese women and girls to the Japanese soldiers." The article said that the so-called

Ginling Women's University had become a brothel. On Christmas Eve 1937, a Japanese officer had demanded: "We require a hundred prostitutes be selected from a thousand refugees." Vautrin had asked the Japanese to agree "not to take women from good homes, and to let the girls volunteer".

Other sources confirm that this event did happen, but not in the way that article reported.

On the night of 24 December, a Japanese officer, accompanied by a Chinese interpreter, came to Vautrin's office and demanded that 100 prostitutes be selected from among a thousand refugees. They said that they wanted to start a brothel for the soldiers, and that if they had access to the brothel the soldiers would no longer abuse women from good homes.

Rabe's diary told it this way:

> As the Japanese atrocities intensified, I saw her at the front of a line of a hundred female refugees, leading them to the reception centre at her college. Then a Japanese officer had the weird idea of setting up a brothel for the troops. Minnie wrung her hands, casting her eyes toward the great hall where hundreds of the women had been forced to seek shelter. Faced with the demand to produce 100 women, she would die before turning over a single one.
>
> But then something unexpected happened. A Red Cross worker whom we knew well and respected – who could imagine that he was this sort of person – turned to the great hall and said a few words. With that, a fair number of young women (note: all were prostitutes) came out. They went willingly to the new brothel without regret. Minnie Vautrin said not a word.[48]

On that day, the Japanese officer left with 21 of the refugees. He was very dissatisfied, and claimed that many more prostitutes were inside the safety zone.

Vautrin recorded in her diary that day:

> A huge mob of young girls came to me to ask whether the Japanese were going to come and take 79 more of them. I could only say to them that if I had the power to block them, I would not allow them to do that.

A person can stand to pay an enormous price, but it is harder to stand an immense and unjust distortion. Reading the newspaper article, no one understood how Vautrin's heart bore such a wrong. Several days later, she handed in her resignation. A month later, on 14 May, despondent, Vautrin left Nanjing, retracing the steps that had brought her to China 28 years before. On the ship taking her to the US, she tried repeatedly to kill herself. A year later, on 14 May 1941, the anniversary of her departure from China, this woman of peerless strength and goodness turned on the gas oven in an ordinary apartment in the state of Indiana and ended her life at the age of 55.

In her will, she wrote: "I have failed as a missionary in China. The grieving spirit I share with her is worse than death." Clearly, she departed this world burdened by enormous spiritual agony.

At the end, she wrote: "If I could live my life again, I would want to serve China. China is my home."

This great and lonely woman had no parents, no family home. Her brother sent her body to the little Michigan village of Shepherd for a simple burial. A map of the Ginling Women's University campus was etched on her headstone, with the words: "Minnie Vautrin, the Goddess Guanyin, China missionary." And then there were four Chinese characters, meaning "Eternal Life for Nanjing".[49]

News of Vautrin's death reached China, and on the day of her funeral the teachers and students of Ginling Women's University in Chengdu held a sombre memorial service in her honour.

A great and lonely soul departed, with the final words to the world: "Eternal Life for Nanjing."

The glory of man's nature that she spread, like a star never to be extinguished, will eternally light this world of unending mutual slaughter and war.

If we go today to the Ginling Women's College of Nanjing University, we will find a bust of a foreign woman, resting in a quiet grove of trees. She gazes at China with her deep-set eyes, and at the destiny of China's women...

(13)

At 9am on 23 February 1938, Rabe departed.

Accompanied by his secretary Han Xianglin and members of his staff, he boarded the British gunboat HMS Bee and sailed to Shanghai. There, he rejoined his wife and child for the long trip home to Germany. On board the ship, Rabe's eyes filled with tears as he turned to look again at all the people on shore who had come to bid him farewell, to say goodbye to the city where he had spent ten years of his life, and to part from the nation where he had lived for three decades.

He departed bearing the profound gratitude of hundreds of thousands of people in Nanjing.

Actually, for the Japanese, the international safety zone was a burning irritation, and Rabe was a thorn in their flesh. They repeatedly demanded that the zone be shut down and that the refugees be sent home. The Japanese secret police posted diplomatic notes to the zone: "All refugees must leave the refugee sites by 4 April. All property and structures belonging to those refugees who do not leave by the deadline will be sealed."

On 18 February 1938, the Nanjing Safety Zone International Committee disbanded, and changed its name to the Nanking International Aid Committee. The safety zone could no longer exist, and the refugees there were forced out. Many had no homes, and were left to the streets.

Around this time, Rabe received a recall order, a message sent from Siemens via the American embassy on 1 December 1937 in answer to Rabe's request for instructions. He had reported to Siemens: "I am remaining in Nanjing to take charge of the work of the International Committee, and am building a refugee zone to protect 200,000 civilians."

Siemens's reply had read: "Not approved. Move to Hankow to protect the company's interests."

This message took two months to arrive. So many Chinese lives were saved in the meantime.

Rabe's health was not strong. His diabetes was severe. He only slept two or three hours each night. Whether it was the message from his company in Germany or his own precarious health, he could wait no longer. On 9 February, before he left, the Japanese embassy invited the foreigners of the International Safety Committee to come to the embassy to enjoy a concert arranged by the army. Among the numbers on the programme were the *Blue Danube Waltz, Mongolian Long Songs* and Schumann's *Träumerei*.

Rabe sat in the concert hall, filled with disgust. That morning, he had seen Chinese corpses murdered by the Japanese everywhere. In the afternoon, he was invited to a concert. In all the world, there had never been a concert this hypocritical and vicious. It was like sitting through a musical performance in front of a heap of corpses. When the concert was over, the foreigners had to endure having their pictures taken by the *Yomiuri Shimbun* photographers, to be used for Japanese propaganda worldwide.

Rabe departed. But he left behind in the hearts of the people of Nanjing unforgettable gratitude.

On this first day of the new year in the lunar calendar, the refugees gave Rabe a length of red silk, three meters long and two meters wide, and a letter of thanks.

In his diary for 31 January 1938, Rabe wrote:[50]

The Chinese New Year. My servants and employees have come with New Year wishes. The refugees in the courtyard have lined up carefully to come and bow three times to me. All are grateful to me for protecting and saving them. But sadly this is not a permanent solution. They have presented me with a red banner, three meters by two, with Chinese characters on it... I asked one person to translate it into English:

You have the heart of a Bodhisattva,

Your nature is chivalrous,

You have saved millions of unfortunates,

And aided those in the direst of danger.

May the blessings of Heaven be upon you,

And Good Fortune accompany you

And may God bless you.

– The refugees of your Refugee Reception Centre.

What did they take me for? I haven't even stepped down from my role as 'mayor' yet, and already they are calling me the 'Living Buddha Who Saved A Million Souls!'[51]

When they learned that Rabe had been recalled to Germany, three thousand women and girls from the Ginling Women's University campus ran out to surround him and kneel before him, imploring him with flowing tears not to leave Nanjing but to stay and continue working as head of the International Committee.

As the time of his departure neared, the International Committee organised a large farewell gathering at which the missionary James McCallum and all the members of the committee heartily sang Rabe's praises.

From its creation on 22 November 1937 to its dissolution on 18 February 1938, Rabe and the more than twenty foreign members of the International Committee, at lethal risk to themselves, joined their fates to their Chinese compatriots, living or dying together, through the cruellest and most terrifying months mankind has known, and thus saved the lives of 250,000 people. Under the hardest imaginable conditions, the International Committee thought of every conceivable way of assuring food supplies for a quarter of a million refugees, making possible their survival. This could only be a miracle, created by the International Committee.

Among the saved were not only Chinese common folk but many Chinese military officers.

Sun Yuanliang, commander of the 77th Army, was concealed among Minnie Vautrin's female refugees at the Ginling Women's College. The chief of staff of the Central Military Academy's faculty, Qiu Qingguan, was hidden by Miner Searle Bates in a secret room in the attic of the Ginling University administration building. The head of Tang Shengzhi's guard unit, Long Yingqin, and a Major Zhou, hid on the second floor of Rabe's residence. Another person with the pseudonym Luo Fuyang lay recovering from his wounds in Rabe's house. This man, who was named Huang Guanghan (others discovered his real name to be Wang Zhigang), was a pilot in the Chinese air force who had shot down several Japanese planes. When the Japanese attacked Nanjing, he was ill. He hoped to get away across the Yangtze, but because he was so weakened, he floated into a smaller rivulet and could move no further. Finally, with all his remaining strength, he managed to reach the international safety zone, where Rabe concealed him in his house, pretending that the pilot was a household servant. Now, as Rabe prepared to depart, he took the pilot on board HMS Bee as his servant, thus managing to get him out of Nanjing and on to Hong Kong.

Rabe was gone. He left behind him sounds of sad remembrance, scenes of people kneeling, the words of the poor, none of which could express the gratitude of 250,000 people.

Rabe's heroism earned not only the praises of the Chinese people but also the praise of Dr Trautmann, Germany's ambassador to China. Trautmann's letter read:

> During the period from November 1937 to February 1938 in which you voluntarily served as chairman of the International Safety Committee and the International Aid Committee, at great risk to yourself and out of a spirit of humanitarianism, you achieved much and made many sacrifices. I express to you my appreciation. Your conduct has brought honour to our Fatherland. Permit me to inform you that, in recognition of your work in Nanjing, I have asked our Foreign Ministry to ask the German Red Cross to award you a medal.

The mission of the International Committee was over.

But the mission of calling for justice was not. Righteous people used their pens, their cameras and their motion picture cameras to record what they saw during the Nanjing Massacre. They published their materials in newspapers and magazines around the world, offering precious proof to mankind, and using that irrefutable proof to reveal the slaughter of the Chinese by the Japanese armed forces. Furthermore, the missionary John Magee and Dr Robert Wilson appeared as witnesses for the prosecution at the International War Crimes Tribunal of the Far East. Louis Smythe and Miner Searle Bates also offered testimony at the Chinese military trials of Japanese war criminals.

(14)

The Nanjing Safety Zone International Committee rescued 250,000 Chinese compatriots and made a gigantic contribution to the people of China. Many of them suffered serious psychological injuries from their experiences. After their return home, some faced different forms of further injustice: arrest, interrogation or imprisonment. They too became victims of the Nanjing Massacre.

Minnie Vautrin committed suicide. The surgeon Robert Smythe was suddenly stricken with epilepsy in 1940 and came close to a nervous breakdown; he had no choice but to return to the US, suffering ever after from epileptic seizures and nightmares of war. The missionary John Magee had his fill of contact with the Japanese; he died in 1953 at the age of 69. George Fitch, while addressing an audience about the Nanjing Massacre, was suddenly stricken with amnesia.

Rabe's ending was even more wretched.

On 15 April 1938, Rabe and his wife returned to Berlin, the city they had left so many years before. At first, they were welcomed as heroes. The German state secretary commended him for his distinguished work in China, and awarded him a Red Cross medal. Later he received Germany's Silver Service Medal. The Chinese government awarded him the Blue Jade Medal.

At that time, Rabe was not fully aware of conditions in Germany. He travelled widely, lecturing and showing Magee's films, appealing on behalf of the Chinese people. He was furious and impassioned, filled with righteous indignation and obsessed with exposing the crimes of the Japanese in the Nanjing Massacre. He sought to call Germany's attention to the crimes the Japanese were committing in their invasion, and hoped that Germany would stop the Japanese crimes against China. He raced to the cinema hall at the Siemensstadt, in Berlin; the Policy Bureau of the Foreign Ministry; the East Asia Society; the Defence Ministry and elsewhere, presenting reports and making speeches.

But what he discovered was that people were not particularly interested in what he had to say. Instead, the Gestapo sent him a warning, forbidding him to speak about Japan's crimes.[52]

Rabe was at a loss: "What has happened to my German countrymen?"

He remembered a song he sang as a child, when the church bell chimed:

> From beginning to end, always loyal, honest and upright,
>
> Straight to your grave.
>
> Never deviate from God's Way,
>
> Not even a finger's width!

The sound of the church chime had admonished the goodhearted, honest, courageous and upright German John Rabe. But now, when the Chinese people encountered such horrific Japanese behaviour, his German countrymen listened with indifference. "What has happened? How could my compatriots have become so coldhearted? How can they lack all feelings of rectitude like this? How can they have no empathy?"

Rabe had been away from Germany for too long – 30 years.

He had no comprehension of the popular mood in the Germany he saw before him. He did not realise that his recall to Germany by Siemens had a national background to it. Not only he, but the head of the German military advisory group to Chiang Kai-shek, General von Falkenhausen, had received a telegram from Hitler at the same moment, ordering him back to Germany immediately or else to face the consequences.

At that point, the moral and kind Rabe could only make one last effort to place his hopes on Hitler personally. He knew that Hitler, the savage deceiver of the German people, had long since allied with Italy and Japan, and that Hitler's Nazi Germany was feverishly planning Blitzkrieg against Czechoslovakia and Poland with the ultimate goal of conquering all of Europe.

Rabe hoped to tell Hitler personally of Japan's crimes in Nanjing, but he failed to gain a meeting, and could only write Hitler a letter:

Respected Chancellor:

My many friends in China believe that you have not received a detailed report of the true situation in Nanjing. For this reason, I am sending you with this letter a set of my privately-delivered speeches. I do this to fulfil my pledge to my friends still in China, to tell you of the sufferings of the Chinese people. If I may trouble you to receive the aforementioned body of material, my mission will be complete.

I have recently received a notice that I am to cease making speeches like these or showing photographs. I will obey all orders, since I do not intend to oppose German policies or the German authorities.

I guarantee to you my vow of loyalty and of obedience to you.

– John Rabe, 8 June 1938, written at Siemensstadt, Berlin[53]

A few days later, what came for Rabe was not a summons from Hitler, but two cold-eyed Gestapo agents wearing black. Rabe was arrested. All his diaries, his speech drafts and John Magee's films were confiscated.

He was interrogated for hours at Gestapo headquarters. Finding nothing anti-German in his activities, they finally let him go.

But the Gestapo warned him: "Shut your mouth. No speeches. No publications. No words against Japanese interests. No showing of the Magee films."

He ultimately recovered his diaries, but the films were confiscated for good.

To cover him, Siemens sent him to Afghanistan on an eight-week assignment. After that, he returned. From that moment on, Rabe was silent.

He could not fathom his nation's behaviour. But, "Right or wrong, this is my fatherland." This was a constant thread throughout his life. And so he obeyed the Gestapo's orders rigorously, as silent as a mountain peak in the Alps, bearing the sadness that he had no way of extending righteousness and no way of telling the world about the crimes Japan had committed in China.

Dr Robert Wilson wrote this in a letter to his family:

> Rabe was an outstanding figure in Nazi circles. Through those weeks of working so closely with him, we discovered that he was honest and kind-hearted, truly outstanding. I have a hard time connecting his estimable qualities with his reverence for the Fuehrer.[54]

Over the next several years, Rabe, like many other Germans, suffered the costs of war. His home was bombed, and he moved his residence several times, living for a time at his son-in-law's home. Hungry, he survived on acorn flour and mustard leaves. He used the furniture and utensils he had sent home from China to barter for potatoes. His wife shrank to only 44 kilos. Out of money and without work, he often had to depend on the generosity of his friends. He suffered from diabetes, high blood pressure and heart problems, as well as troubles with his stomach.

In his diary for 3 September 1945, Rabe wrote:

> I managed to bring home two potatoes that had fallen from a Soviet truck. How precious these hunting trophies are these days. Everyone struggles to grab them in the streets; without them there is nothing to eat. It is true; we have reached this point of desperate hunger. Hunger is painful, but crying out in pain doesn't fill the belly. The question is, how much longer can we go on like this?[55]

In those bitterest of most unendurable of times, Rabe continued to work. In 1941 and 1942 he had condensed the original six parts and eight separate volumes of his Nanjing diaries into two volumes, and between 1943 and 1945 he finished other works including 'A Record of a Million Things Never to be Forgotten'. In his early days in Beijing, he had composed 'Things I Have Seen in Beijing', in which he offered detailed descriptions of every kind of human and natural landscape: old Chinese customs, marriage and funeral customs, foods, architecture, laws, temples and streets. When this Chinese writer opens these volumes, I gasp with surprise at the level of detail in his introductions to China.

At the end of the second world war, Rabe's perilous journey still was not over. First, he was arrested by the Soviet Union and interrogated for three days. Then the British detained him, subjecting him to day-long sessions of harsh questioning.

Finally, he was fingered by his German countrymen and accused of belonging to the Nazi Party and of being the deputy chief of the Nazi Party organisation in Nanjing. His letters to Hitler, and his fawning verbiage towards Hitler, were adduced as proof of the accusations.

In the so-called 'denazification' movement, one fixed rule was that former members of the Nazi Party could not hold public office and were not permitted to work in companies.

Rabe wrote an appeal to the headquarters of the denazification authority, requesting that his criminal label be removed. He explained that he had joined the Nazi Party so that he could receive funding to start a German language school in Nanjing.

In fact, the only time he held responsibility for the Nazi organisation in Nanjing was when the leader of the group was on holiday.

Rabe wrote in his diary for 18 April 1946:

> Yesterday my appeal for release from denazification was rejected. Even though I saved 250,000 people as head of the

International Committee of the Nanjing Safety Zone, my request was turned down. That was because for a short while I served as the deputy head of the local Nazi organisation in Nanjing. There, I was the 'living Buddha to several hundred thousand'; here, I am an 'Untouchable', a person deprived of all rights, abandoned. 'Untouchable' – a person abandoned by society. Ah! How I long to cure my nostalgia!

Did the 'nostalgia' Rabe mentioned refer to Germany or Beijing?

On 3 June 1946, the Denazification Commission finally threw out Rabe's 'Nazified' label, on the grounds that he had committed successful acts of charity in China. But the Rabes still had no employment, and assuaged their hunger by eating wild vegetation.

In early 1947 (some say early 1948), news of Rabe's travails reached distant Nanjing. The Chinese people are a gracious people; "a drop of kindness is returned from the well". All the more when the kindness saved lives! And so an effort by survivors of the massacre

John Rabe and his wife Dora, 1947.

to raise funds quickly began. In a matter of days, they raised a million *yuan* in the Chinese currency of those days, about two thousand US dollars. That was no small amount at that time. In March, the mayor of Nanjing went to Switzerland, where he purchased milk powder, sausages, coffee, tea and meat which were sent to Rabe in four large packages. After that, the city of Nanjing sent Rabe a monthly food packet. These gifts of food went far towards alleviating the Rabes' hardships, and saved the lives of Rabe's entire family.[56]

The Chinese government also announced that if Rabe wished to return to China, it would provide him with housing and a stipend. But Rabe did not return to China.[57] On 5 January 1950, Rabe passed away at his daughter's home. The cause of death was a stroke. A great man passed quietly, accompanied only by his wife and child.

The 250,000 lives he saved, and the 2,000 pages of his diary were his most precious bequests to humanity – true records of the crimes of the Japanese military.

(15)

In Berlin, with the help of Miss Li Wen from the Chinese embassy and carrying some yellow and white chrysanthemums, I went to find John Rabe's grave in a quiet tree-lined cemetery laced with fragrant grasses. I could not help thinking of the poem by Zang Kejia: "People live, but he is gone; some have already died, but he still lives."

Rabe died, but he will live forever in the hearts of the Chinese people.

Under a vast and limpid blue sky, a great man rests beneath a simple black and white tombstone. The tombstone was designed by Professor Wu Weishan, the renowned Chinese sculptor and dean of the Nanjing University Research Institute of the Arts. The design is unique and unusually imposing, a rectangle in black and white. The dates of birth and death of Rabe and his wife are inscribed on the black surface. In the centre lies an image of Rabe's head. The black portions seem to be a gesture of respect to the dead. The white constitutes a prayer for the living and for peace in the future. Pebbles surround the headstone, while a slab of white marble in front of the headstone reads, in Chinese:

In Gratitude

Eternally Remembering Rabe's Internationalist Generosity

Nanjing, China

2013

I lingered for a long time before this grave, grieving, with tears in my eyes, because I knew the story behind this tombstone.

In late December 1996, Rabe's granddaughter Ursula Reinhardt and her husband Otto drove to the Kaiser Wilhelm Cemetery at Fürstenfeldbrück in Berlin to view John Rabe's grave. They wanted to arrange for a small marker to commemorate Rabe's rescue of a quarter of a million people in Nanjing, but they had no funds. The cemetery manager told them that the term for rental of the grave site had expired, and that they would need to arrange for a new grave. His granddaughter was to remove Rabe's gravestone. She had no choice but to remove the stone and store it in her garage.

Reinhardt wrote to the Chinese embassy in Germany and explained her predicament. She proposed to donate the headstone to China.

China's ambassador to Germany, Shi Mingde, explained to me what happened next. At the time, as a political counsellor in the embassy, he went to Reinhardt's home to speak with her. He asked her to donate the headstone to China for transfer to China, so that the people of Nanjing could forever commemorate Rabe. Reinhardt agreed. And so the gravestone made the long journey to Nanjing, to its resting place in the Memorial Hall for the Compatriots Murdered in the Nanjing Massacre by the Japanese Invaders.

At that time, Shi Mingde learned that Reinhardt had in her possession a great quantity of Rabe's diaries, and asked Reinhardt if she felt she could donate those to China as well. Reinhardt concurred, but when the German ambassador to China learned of this, he declared that the diaries were cultural properties, and that, while copies of the diaries could be donated to China, the original diaries could not be donated. The Chinese embassy in Berlin acquired copies of the diaries rather than the originals.

On the morning of 11 December 2013, the commemorative stele in honour of John Rabe, created by contributions from the people of Nanjing, travelled to Berlin, where it was installed in the cemetery of the Gedachtniskirche, amid a solemn ceremony. The Nanjing municipal government donated funds to cover rental of the site for forty years.

The tombs of John Rabe and his wife Dora, Berlin.

Now, a great soul rests in peace for eternity in this tranquil graveyard.

As my visit came to an end, Young Rabe told me that he had hoped to build a monument in Berlin and in Nanjing to commemorate John Rabe's great contribution in saving the lives of 250,000 people. But while the Berlin government approved such a memorial for Oskar Schindler, it did not approve a memorial for Rabe.

I did not understand. Was that solely because Rabe was a Nazi Party member? But so was Schindler.

Young Rabe shrugged his shoulders and shook his head.

In my view, not only should the Berlin government have agreed to the memorial, but John Rabe deserves a place of honour in the history of humanity's struggle against fascism.

PART 2 NOTES

(1) 托马斯.拉贝（德）编著《约翰.拉贝画传》8-15页，江苏人民出版社2009年版 ed. Thomas Rabe, The *Illustrated Biography of John Rabe*, Jiangsu Renmin Chubanshe, 2009, pp. 8-15 (Hereafter HZ)

(2) Ibid., pp. 35-37

(3) Ibid., p. 49

(4) (约翰.拉贝著《拉贝日记》19页，翻译组译，江苏人民出版社,江苏教育出版社2009年版) John Rabe, The *Diary of John Rabe*, Jiangsu Renmin Chubanshe, Jiangsu Jiaoyu Chubanshe, 2009, p. 19 (Hereafter RJ)

(5) (约翰.拉贝（德）著，埃尔文.维克特,选编，朱刘华译《拉贝日记》.金城出版社2009年版，18页) John Rabe, ed. Erwin Rickert, tr. Zhu Lihua, The *Diary of John Rabe*, Jincheng Chubanshe, 2009, p. 18 (Hereafter JLER)

(6) Ibid., p. 4

(7) HZ, pp. 77-80

(8) RJ, p. 26

(9) (张纯如（美）著《南京大屠杀》第106页，谭春霞、焦国林译，中信出版社2013年版) Zhang Chunru (Iris Chang), The *Nanking Massacre*, tr. Tan Chunxia and Jiao Guolin, Zhongxin Chubanshe, 2013, p. 106 (Hereafter Iris Zhang)

(10) RJ, p. 48

(11) HZ, p. 69

(12) Name in French: La Zone Jacquinot

(13) HZ, p. 69

(14) Ibid, p. 70

(15) (何建明著《拉贝先生》第92页,作家出版社2015年版) He Jianming, *Mr. Rabe*, Authors Publishing House, 2015. p. 92

(16) JLER, pp. 41-42

(17) RJ, pp. 80-81

(18) JLER, p. 45

(19) RJ, p. 95

(20) (朱成山主编:江苏古籍出版社2002年版《南京大屠杀与国际大救援图集》第38页) ed. Zhu Chengshan, *An Illustrated Collection on the Nanjing Massacre and International Assistance*, Jiangsu Guji Chubanshe, 2002, p. 38 (Hereafter NMIA)

(21) HZ, p. 79

(22) RJ, p. 136

(23) Ibid., pp. 147-149

(24) Ibid., p. 169

(25) HZ, p. 79

(26) NMIA, p. 136

(27) Ibid., p. 137

(28) Ibid., p. 108

(29) Ibid., p. 113

(30) Ibid., p. 126

(31) Theodore Roosevelt, *The Strenuous Life*, 10 April 1899 http://www.bartleby.com/58/1.html Translator note: The text here displays Roosevelt's original wording. The author, in the Chinese version of this book, uses a widely-used translation of the same passage, as found, for example, at https://sanwen8.cn/p/796cLbV.html

(32) HZ, p. 77

(33) (孙震编辑《暴行——侵华日军罪恶实录》，三环出版社1991年出版，全篇记载) ed. Sun Zhen, *Atrocities: A Record of the Crimes of the Japanese Army Invading China*, Sanhuan Chubanshe, 1991 (Hereafter SZ)

(34) (Various media reports)

(35) JLER, pp. 76-77

(36) RJ, p. 216

(37) HZ, p. 136

(38) Iris Zhang, p. 146

(39) (胡平著《一百个理由》200-201页，长江文艺出版社2005年版) Hu Ping, *One Hundred Reasons*, Changjiang Wenyi Chubanshe, 2005, pp. 200-201

(40) (关亚新、张志坤著《日本遗孤调查研究》第2页，社会科学文献出版社2005年版) Guan Yaxin, Zhang Zhikun, *Researches On Japanese Abandoned Orphans*, Shehui Kexue Wenxian Chubanshe, 2005, p. 2

(41) (刘国强著《日本遗孤》102页，辽宁人民出版社2011年版) Liu Guoqiang, *Japanese Abandoned Orphans*, Liaoning Renmin Chubanshe, 2011, p. 102 (Hereafter RBYG)

(42) RBYG, pp. 94-102

(43) Ibid., pp. 294-296

(44) (东史郎（日）著《东史郎日记》第5页，江苏教育出版社1999年版) Azuma Shirō, *The Diary of Azuma Shirō*, Jiangsu Jiaoyu Chubanshe, 1999, p. 5

(45) RBYG, p. 167

(46) RJ, p. 231

(47) Translator note: All quotations from the Vautrin diary are here

translated into English from a Chinese rendering of Vautrin's original text

(48) Translator note: Vautrin's original words are: "Oh, God, control the cruel beastliness of the soldiers in Nanking tonight, comfort the heartbroken mothers and fathers whose innocent sons have been shot today, and guard the young women and girls through the long agonizing hours of this night. Speed the day when wars shall be no more. When thy Kingdom will come, Thy will be done on earth as it is in heaven."

(49) NMIA, p. 131

(50) Translator note: The following quotations from the Rabe Diary are translations from a Chinese version of the original text, and faithfulness to the original German cannot be guaranteed

(51) HZ, p. 81

(52) Ibid., pp. 87-88

(53) Ibid., p. 88

(54) Translator note: Translated from a Chinese version of Wilson's original text

(55) HZ, p. 93

(56) Ibid., p. 97

(57) Ibid

PART 3

Paradise in Hell

The Inextinguishable Sounds of Mankind's Harmony

Humanity always seems to be dressed in western clothes and leather shoes. Its soul is somehow embodied in skin and flesh, without distinguishing between good and bad, virtue and evil. Only when war is near, and killing and torture put each person's conscience to the test, may the soul appear clearly to the world, like an egg whose shell has been peeled away. Only then might we discover that the nature of man and beast, which, we had thought, were so close to one another, are actually utterly removed from one another.

Berndard Arp Sindberg in the refugee camp at the Nanjing Jiangnan Cement Works.

(1)

Why would the Queen of Denmark place a yellow rose at the Tree of Peace in Nanjing? Why would a young fellow from the Land of Fairy Tales write an extraordinary life story in Chinese? I entered that Land of Fairly Tales with murky questions like this in mind.

Writing about Denmark, the mind calls up ideas of a distant northern Europe, with long, cloudy days, plenty of snow and little fairy-tale cabins. The people, settled comfortably by the fire, with Hans Christian Andersen's fairy tales in their hands, chat about the stories of mermaids, or about the ideas of philosopher Nikolai Grundtvig or the great novel *Madame D'Ora* by the winner of the Nobel Prize for Literature, Johannes Vilhelm Jensen. A tranquil and beautiful fairy kingdom, with a graceful and imperturbable people.

In August 2014, I arrived at a seaside cottage in the harbour city of Aarhus, on the Jutland Peninsula, my mind full of warm and beautiful expectations of such a fairy kingdom. A wild sight greeted my eyes. The gale howled from the sea, while white waves seemed to touch the sky. The smell of the sea hit me in the face, washing away all the pollution that had for so long been accumulating in the bottom of my heart.

I could not help thinking of Bernhard Arp Sindberg, who wrote these words in his *Quick Jottings from a Sailor's Life*:

> His life was bound up with the blue ocean, swaying palms, the sounds of the east and the racket of gunfire. He was like every ordinary wandering mariner, who found his pleasure and grief in war, defeat and victory.
>
> Now, the vessel of his life lies moored at the RHF Retirement Apartments. But his eyes still burn with the old distant gaze. One never knows when he might feel the call of the sea again.

A lover of the sea, he was someone who drifted across the oceans of the world. Now, in the autumn of his life, his eyes, still gleaming, peer into the distance. Aroused by the winds, his soul still hears the call of the sea, as a pilot hears the call of the sky and an athlete the call of the playing field.

The lines of the poet Cao Mengde came to me: "The ancient thoroughbred rests in his stall, dreaming of the great distances…"

I thought of General Patton's loneliness after he left the field, because the battlefield was his soul's home, the refuge of his spirit.

On this day, a 70-year-old author, full of hope, arrived in this harbour city on the Jutland Peninsula to search for the footprints left on humanity's shore by a Danish man, to hunt for a Danish life both ordinary and magnificent. As I stood by the pounding sea, though my misted eyes did not burn with his gaze into the far distance, they did burn with the desire to follow a man's life. Deep in my soul, I still felt the urgency of paying homage to the noblest spirits of mankind.

And so I arrived.

I had come from the distant East, pursuing a dream, even though I had passed the age of dreams. But dreams are for me what the sea is for the sailor, or the open grasslands are for a fine horse.

I had asked Li Jinsheng, cultural counsellor of the Chinese embassy in Denmark, for his assistance, and had managed to make contact with Marianne, the daughter of Sindberg's sister. Before coming to Denmark, I had gone to Nanjing to visit the old Jiangnan Cement Company factory area, searching for traces left behind by history, looking for any droplets of remembrance there. I stood for a long time in the cold and bleak factory, calling up in my mind that slice of blood-soaked history when the Chinese people were so humiliated.

In the doorway of that seaside cottage, in addition to the wind, I was greeted by Sindberg's two grand-nieces, Marianne and Linda, with their husbands. All four were in their fifties or sixties – not so young. My granddaughter Zhang Runqiao served as my interpreter. In the cottage, as the ocean gale hammered at the windows, Sindberg's descendants and I began our happy conversation.

Seated in the tiny living room, I felt the special warmth of the Danes, over green tea, coffee and a modest luncheon. Marianne talked steadily, painting pictures with her words: piled books of images, heaped masses of interesting stories, past event after past event leapt before my eyes. We talked for six and a half hours, from ten in the morning to half past four in the afternoon. When Marianne was a student in the US, she had often visited the Sindberg home, going out with her uncle for a meal at a restaurant and enjoying his warm feelings.

When Runqiao and I said goodbye to Sindberg's relatives that evening, we left with a rich harvest.

Thus, a trove of yellowing papers, holding the remembrances from that terrible time and the unique qualities of that living, breathing Dane, came before me and flowed into my pen.

(2)

Perhaps the exact time of Sindberg's birth foretold a life of wandering.

In 1911, far from his own northern Europe, in a distant Oriental nation, the Xinhai Revolution was successful in overthrowing a feudal dynasty and bringing to an end thousands of years of imperial dynastic rule. Japan, after the Meiji Restoration of 1868 and the rapid increase in its national wealth and strength, defeated two huge states – China in the war of 1894 and Russia in the war of 1905 – to become the great power of Asia. With that, Japan's ambition to dominate the world inflated like a giant soap bubble.

On 19 February 1911, the squalling of a newborn baby punctuated the stillness on the Jutland Peninsula. A new little life had come to the household of a cheese manufacturer in the city of Aarhus. The little one looked much like most other Danish infants – golden hair, a pair of amber eyes. He was the second oldest of five boys in a family that ultimately enjoyed seven children, and the liveliest and most mischievous of all them.

The baby's parents, Johannes Sindberg and Karen Marie Sindberg, married in 1903. They divorced years later, but there is no clear record of the date of their divorce.

The father had strong feelings about politics, and at one point founded a 'Fairness Party' which advocated for freedom and fairness for all mankind. He also ran unsuccessfully in a legislative election. In 1938, he edited a weekly magazine.

Sindberg's mother ran the cheese factory. A nanny took care of the children. The children's happiest moments came when their mother took them out in the family car for a visit to the clothing store, where she bought new outfits for them. When they emerged from the store, they looked like gorgeous little gentlefolk and princesses. In Marianne's cottage, I saw snapshots of the five boys in their new suits, looking much like movie stars.

Although the patriarch did not win his election, his ideals of freedom and fairness had a major influence on his entire family. The thinker who exercised the greatest influence over this family and over the Danish nation was the philosopher Nikolai Grundtvig.

Grundtvig's conception of the life of the individual derived from his conception of humanity. To Grundtvig, each individual possessed a dual nature, and a destiny that was greater than nation or nationality. To him, each individual arriving in the world was at one and the same time a member of a nation or race and a member of humanity as a whole. In human existence, membership of the human race occupied pride of place, superior to one's nationality or racial identity. Regardless of religion or skin colour or nation state, one is above all a human being, and thereby distinct from all other animals. One might ardently love one's nation, but it was never to be forgotten that there is an even higher love and loyalty, and that is loyalty to mankind and reverence for mankind's destiny.

Such thoughts were too deep for the young Sindberg, who found them as obscure as a dark and dense forest. He never really did understand them very clearly. But the father taught his children that, as human beings, their lives should be governed by human warmth and uprightness; if someone needed help, the children were taught, they should offer that help. The thinking of the adult had a subtle influence on the young Sindberg; as spring rain that silently nourishes the slender shoots, or the cool and languid rays of the northern European sun, the ideas of the father little by little left a lasting mark on Sindberg's young soul. He grew into a man whose life bore qualities that never faded: human warmth, and satisfaction in helping others.

Growing up in this economically comfortable household, amid such ideals of freedom and fairness, Sindberg was of a carefree disposition. The little fellow with the amber eyes was always inquisitive and forever thinking up naughty tricks. As a toddler, he ran away into the woods to find the secrets of the forest. His frightened family went looking for him and found him deep in the woods. His mother discovered that any time a chicken flew away or a dog ran away, it was because the young boy had been doing the animal a good deed. So the boy acquired names like 'Always Curious Baby' and 'Naughty Little Devil' – the family always had a good laugh about him over tea or at the dinner table.

The first risky trick the child thought up came when he was seven years old.

His uncle on his mother's side lived in the US. On a visit home to see family, he put an idea in young Sindberg's head, saying: "Little Sindberg, if you want to visit America when you are grown, be sure to look me up."

The child raised his head and said with happy surprise: "Really?"

"Of course, really!"

"Ah – great!"

This one exchange opened a new window on the world for the wild young boy's soul. At the age of only seven, the dream of leaving home to see the world germinated in young Sindberg's head. Like a newly hatched chick, in his youthful brain he piled up the materials he needed to build his nest, awaiting the day when he could spread his wings and take flight.

At 14, a restless youth whose feathers still had not filled out, he and two schoolmates made their way to Hamburg, Germany and prepared to ship out for California. But his mother tracked him down after he had boarded the ship, and his father took him home 'in custody', with a tongue-lashing. After he finished middle school, he had no interest in studying, and he hated the stink of the cheese factory. He found work as a painter, but that left him exhausted. He yearned for the sea and for freedom, and longed to travel the world.

At 17, the young man's feathers were full-grown.

One day, when the air was filled with the fragrance of trees and plants, the young man's seven-year-old secret plan finally became a reality.

Standing on a ship's deck, bound for America and listening to the raising of the ship's anchor, the eyes of this ingenuous young man were filled with happiness and regret. From the top deck, he bade his parents a silent farewell: "Dearest Papa, Mama, brothers and sisters, goodbye. Please forgive me for leaving without saying farewell. Don't be angry with me. I will write to you…"

And with that, an inexperienced youth bent on setting off into the world and full of happy anticipation, began a life of wandering that took him to the US, Russia, Greenland, China and Canada, among other places. He worked as a navy sailor and a civilian sailor, a hotel reception clerk and a dairy factory worker, among other jobs.

Filled with romantic wanderlust, he went to Algeria on a five-year 'life or death contract' with the French Foreign Legion. But the hardships of life in military camps, the extremely strenuous training regimen, the monotonous patrols and the ferocious dogs quickly destroyed his illusions. So, he stole a bicycle and deserted, which put him on a wanted criminal list for ten years.

He was young and full-blooded. He loved to battle injustice. In fact, he just loved to fight.

Once, when he was a sailor, he saw a fellow sailor sadistically mistreated, and came to blows with his superior officer; that got him locked in the brig. He got into a row with fellow employees while working as a reception clerk in a Shanghai hotel, and was fired. Working in a Danish dairy products company in Shanghai, he was sacked for quarrelling with his German co-workers.

In short, by the time the young man was 20, he had been fired and fined over and over again for quarrelling and brawling.

The Danish consul in Shanghai warned him: "No more brawling with other Danes, or you will be expelled from China."

Thus, it came about that a young Dane who loved to fight for the underdog, loved risk and loved to see the world, came to perform some earth-shaking deeds when, in August 1937, the Japanese army invaded Shanghai and then Nanjing.

(3)

We cannot write about the Danish Sindberg's experiences in Nanjing without writing as well about the German Karl Günther.

On my visit to Germany, I had hoped to meet Karl Günther's descendants, but with my funds running low and the path full of twists and turns, I did not find a way of making contact with them. Just when I was giving up in despair, I received a private message on my blog site, pointing out some typing errors in my blog articles. I sent a note of thanks.

Little did I know that an important clue very close at hand could be dug up from thousands of miles away through my blog.

The writer knew that I had interviewed Sindberg's family in Denmark. He told me that he was acquainted with the Chen family, descendants of one of the founders of the Jiangnan Cement Works. He said that not only had the Chen family known Karl Günther but that they had had very close ties to both Günther and his son. It was on the elder Chen's recommendation to the Jiangnan Cement board of directors that Karl Günther was appointed acting factory manager in Nanjing.

A gift from Heaven! I wrote back at once, asking my email partner whether he could introduce me to the Chen family when I returned to Beijing. He readily agreed.

So, on the very night I returned to Beijing from Europe, I made a date to meet this stranger at the Jinsong metro station the next morning at nine-thirty. The next day, right on time, at the south entrance to the metro station, a grey-haired elderly fellow of dignified bearing appeared: Xu Zuzhe, a retired postal system cadre. He was an educated man who was preparing to publish a book on telecommunications that he had worked on for a decade; the book was likely to be of considerable historical research value.

My instinct, after so many years of globe-trotting and looking into the eyes of so many people, was that this was someone to be trusted.

I went with Mr Xu, this complete stranger, to an older building and entered a sixth-floor apartment. The apartment was small and simple. In one of the two rooms, an old man of 87, slightly hunchbacked, appeared before me.

This was Chen Kekuan, a retired postal worker who enjoyed stamp collecting. He was the second son of Chen Fanyou, one of the founders of the Jiangnan Cement Company.

Truly, Heaven must have been watching out for me and paying me back for my good heart!

My long talks with Mr Chen opened surprising new doors for me, and almost turned my original plans upside down.

My original plan was to do interviews about Sindberg and Günther, and then write about how these two foreigners rescued Chinese compatriots during the Nanjing Massacre. But I had my internal doubts. What brought these two together? How could they manage to save thousands of people with their bare hands?

When I finished hearing what Mr Chen had to tell me about the history of the Jiangnan Cement Company and examining the stack of materials, and particularly when I heard the beseeching tone of his remarks, I got the feeling that he was concealing some topics that were not easy to mention.

He said to me: "Mme Zhang, as a descendant of the Chen family, I hope you will write about that period of history in a spirit of 'seeking truth from facts', and that you will write the story of the Jiangnan Cement Company's refugee camp truthfully."

I said to him: "Don't worry. I most definitely respect history and I respect my materials. I will write truthfully." But I felt uneasy. I asked him: "Why do you raise that?" But I could not really ask more.

That evening, I received a phone call from Shanghai. It was from Chen Kekuan's third brother, Chen Kejian, who invited me to Shanghai for a visit. He said he had even fuller and more accurate materials.

I headed to Shanghai. When I reached the Chen residence, two elderly and well-educated ladies received me warmly.

Chen Kejian was 83, a retired cadre from the Shanghai municipal government. His mind was crystal clear, his thinking nimble.

After hearing this elderly gentleman talk for several hours, and having reviewed the many materials he offered to me, I came to the conclusion that my original work plan was too simple and too subjective. I needed to change my approach, reorganise my materials and start anew with a much more penetrating thought process.

He said to me: "Mme Zhang, I sincerely hope that you will write about this period in a spirit of seeking truth from facts, and truthfully convey the situation of the Jiangnan Cement Company's refugee camp. We deeply thank the two foreign friends, Mr Günther and Mr Sindberg, for rescuing so many Chinese compatriots. But I hope you will not exaggerate the role these foreigners played by minimising the role we Chinese played. We have to be respectful of history. After the Japanese invaded Shanghai, what did the board of directors of the Jiangnan Cement Company do? Was it as some rumours said, that the entire board fled, leaving Jiangnan Cement in the hands of two foreigners? Please consider very carefully the materials I am giving you. I spent ten years, after my retirement, going to archives and reading vast amounts of historical material before writing this. After you read it, I think you will come to a clear assessment."

Then he talked about a number of things that were difficult to speak of. He spoke with high emotion and then bowed his head and sat silent for half a day. I watched his grey hair trembling slightly in the sun's rays.

My mind was troubled. Why was he like that?

The two old white-haired women put the same solemn question to me. They were descendants of the founder of Jiangnan Cement; I could only treat them with the greatest seriousness.

Finally, Mr Chen made a comment that made me pay close attention. "After the Japanese invaded," he said, "they put every possible pressure on my father to get him to restart production at the cement works. My father was not afraid of their violent treatment – to him, death was preferable to dishonour. He resolutely refused to cooperate with the Japanese, and found one excuse after another to avoid resuming production. He held out for six years. At the time of Japan's surrender, Jiangnan Cement had not produced a single bag of cement! The Japanese knew Jiangnan Cement could produce a high-quality product at great speed. The cement could be used by the Japanese forces, and they wanted the production for themselves."

Playing Chess with the Devil

I was startled. "Was it really so?" I asked.

"Absolutely. Many people in Nanjing knew all that. If you don't believe me, go to Nanjing yourself and enquire of the old folks in the area around Jiangnan Cement. Just look into the history!" He spoke with complete certainty.

I decided to go back to back to Jiangnan Cement in Nanjing, and I asked the elder Mr Chen to help me get in touch with Mme Xu Erxin.

Xu Erxin was the daughter of Jiangnan Cement's main financial officer, Xu Shennong. When she was young, she had gone often to Karl Günther's office, and gained a clear understanding of both Günther and the situation at Jiangnan Cement.

The next afternoon, I met Xu Erxin at a little hotel in Nanjing. She was a cultivated elderly woman of 83, retired from a career as a doctor at the Drum Tower Hospital. Her sister, Xu Erwei, had been the first person assigned by China to work at the United Nations. Her father, Xu Shennong, had been a schoolmate of Chen Fanyou at Beiyang University. Chen knew how trustworthy Xu Shennong was, and had assigned the financial affairs of Jiangnan Cement to him.

According to Mme Xu, on the eve of the Japanese invasion, Günther had not yet arrived as acting general manager. Her father was worried that the Japanese would sack the company's assets, so he put a number of gold ingots, a quantity of silver coins and a mass of paper money into cotton sacks, belted them around his waist, put on a long cotton gown and took several workers with him on a dash to the north bank of the river where they could hide. After Günther arrived as acting general manager, several weeks later, her father and the other workers returned to the plant and turned all the money they had secreted on their own persons over to Günther. This was the money that the plant later dispensed to the workers and staff to serve as the funds for rescuing the refugees.

I had heard rumours that Xu Shennong had been made a scapegoat, amid accusations that he had absconded with the company's funds. In reality, he had gone to great risk to protect large sums of money.

Mme Xu told me that when the Japanese arrived she was only five or six years old and her family was living in a dormitory on the grounds of Jiangnan Cement. There was no school on the grounds, so her father taught her mathematics, Chinese and English every day in his office. She frequently watched Günther call on her father for a conversation. Günther was a man of middling build and cold manner, unsmiling and without much small talk. Her father let her call Günther 'Uncle', and Günther would stroke her hair to be friendly. Günther spoke Chinese fluently, but he and Chen spoke English in their meetings, in very low voices. They seemed to be afraid that others would hear them.

Mme Xu's impressions of Günther were that he was stiffly old-fashioned and honest. He approached his work very responsibly. He enjoyed hunting, and the young girl often saw him in his giant leather boots, accompanied by his hunting dogs, with his hunting gun on his back. His grey-haired wife was very beautiful and resembled her husband.

The next afternoon, I braved a heavy rain for another visit to Jiangnan Cement. After an hour's bus trip, I came to the deserted plant. I made my way to the frigid and empty administrative office of the old factory. Chen Kejian had notified the plant's management by phone. A woman from the plant's management greeted me in a waiting room, and presented me with a history of the factory. What I found in it concurred with what the elderly Mr Chen had told me.

As I left, I could only see the deathly stillness of the factory area. I saw not a single person, only utter bleakness. A few rows of 70-year-old Chinese parasol trees, apparently healthy, grew on the factory grounds. They had seen a lot of history; they had seen the Nanjing Massacre by the Japanese military. They had watched Günther and Sindberg and all the factory's personnel who stayed behind as they worked to protect the refugees. And, of course, they had seen the Japanese forces' wild plunder of Jiangnan Cement.

Near the administration office, I could see the factory's chimney belching smoke into the ash-grey air, casting the sky into darkness. To tell the truth, I had a great desire to get inside the chimney, to get inside the plant, to see the cement it produced. What was it like? What was it about this plant that so gained the good graces of the Japanese?

(4)

Next, I concentrated on reading the large body of material I had acquired. I read the first part of Chen Kejian's first article in the 2014 publication *Wind and Rain on Mount Zhong*, whose subtitle was 'What I Know About the Jiangnan Cement Company's Camp for Refugees'. In his article, Chen Kejian wrote:

> As the son of Chen Fanyou, the founder of Jiangnan Cement Works, I have always been very interested in the company. In my published biography of 'Cement Chen', I used primary materials in my possession to talk about the refugee camp at the Jiangnan Cement Works. Needless to say, the contributions made by the two foreign friends, Günther and Sindberg, were outstanding. But it is regrettable that for unknown reasons some people wrote inaccurately, or lost sight of history, or exaggerated reality in such a way as to suggest that the two foreigners all by themselves created the camp that rescued 30,000 refugees. This historical distortion has spread falsehoods and hurt the feelings of our nation's people, and is disrespectful of history. How was the board of directors of Jiangnan Cement supposed to respond to the sudden invasion of the Japanese? Did the plant manager and senior management leave in an orderly manner, or did they run off in panic? What brought the two foreigners to the plant? Who were the refugees? How did the band of Chinese and foreigners who stayed behind work together to run the refugee camp in such a way that there was not a single fatality?

After I read this article, I pondered deeply.

The questions raised in the article were the very questions I wanted to understand. But I reminded myself not to be so swayed by my first impressions that I let go of historical facts.

Days later, as I emerged from the mountain of materials, rubbing my tired old eyes, my mind's confusion had faded into a feeling of deep respect – the respect I had been longing for.

In the person of the elder Chen, I seemed to be able to touch the souls of knowledgeable and experienced Chinese people, and see their precious spirit of a race taking on its own heavy responsibilities. I could see why the two Chen brothers of the next generation, already in their eighties, decided to raise their voices so loudly. I knew I had to revise and refresh my own way of thinking; if I did not, my own articles would be biased and would fail to do justice to history. That would be so unfair to a pioneering Chinese national industrial company.

Thus, a Chinese industrialist of an older generation, Chen Fanyou or 'Cement Chen', entered into my field of vision.

To understand the Chen family, I must first go farther back in time.

In the chaos at the end of the Qing dynasty, the court was corrupt. At a time when hordes of corrupt petty officials schemed and plotted to become high-ranked officials so that they could soak the people and ascend to honour and wealth, there was one educated fellow, whose official garb boasted important symbols of his stature and who had held high posts such as candidate daotai of Jiangsu and superintendent of the Northern Coast Defence and Customs, who wanted to escape from all the plotting and scheming and bloodletting.

He was the founding figure in China's cement industry, the grandfather of Chen Kekuan and his brothers. His name was Chen Yifu.

With his own eyes, Chen Yifu witnessed the great and magnificent China being divided up like a melon by the western Great Powers. One by one the Unequal Treaties strengthened their hold on the heads of the Chinese people. The imperial treasury went bankrupt, perpetually paying the indemnities exacted by the Powers.

He could not stifle a groan: "I take no interest in being an official. All I really care about is industry. The fundamental strategy for dealing with China's poverty is this – if we do not stimulate industry, we can never succeed."

Chen Yifu was strongly influenced by the 'Self-Strengthening Movement' of the great statesmen Zeng Guofan and Li Hongzhang. He was sent to Japan by the government to study the machinery-building industry. Soon after, China's first machinery-building factory was established at Tianjin. Later, he gained recognition by the renowned industrialist Zhou Xuxi and participated in the creation of China's first cement-production facility, the Tangshan Qixin Cement Plant, becoming the dominant shareholder in the company.

The Qixin Company was headquartered in Tianjin. In the 1920s and 1930s, Chen Yifu held a succession of responsible positions, first as head of the general affairs office and then as managing director. At the same time, he was chairman of the board of the Kailuan Mining Bureau, north China's biggest enterprise. Not only did Chen Yifu not wish to be a government official; he ordered his sons and grandsons not to become government officials, too.

His oldest son, Chen Fanyou, was noticed by the high-ranking Nationalist government leader Chen Lifu and by the minister of railways, Zeng Yangfu. They made plans to put him in high government jobs, but Chen Fanyou received two cables from his father, Chen Yifu, calling him as eldest son to return in order to succeed his father.

Chen Fanyou entered Qixin as an engineer but rose quickly to become the second generation 'Mr Cement Chen'.

Chen Fanyou was born in Tianjin in 1898. He graduated from Nankai University in Tianjin, one year ahead of Zhou Enlai, and then passed the examinations to enter the Northern University's department of civil engineering, where he roomed with Chen Lifu, who was studying in the department of mining. The deep friendship between the two started from this time.

When Chen Fanyou graduated from Northern University in 1922, the first duty his father assigned to him was to return to the ancestral home, Shidai county in Anhui province, to raise $200,000 and take on the job of designing, supervising and building a major concrete bridge. Working for three years, he created a bridge 180 metres in length, with eleven apertures, capable of handling four automobiles abreast. This was China's first reinforced concrete highway auto roadway bridge.

This bridge brought prosperity to the people of the area for decades, until the Japanese invasion when the Chinese army blew the bridge up in an effort to slow the Japanese advance as they tried to cross the river. Although the bridge was later restored, in

Chen Fanyou, general manager of the Nanjing Jiangnan Cement Works.

1970 it was submerged beneath the lake that filled behind the newly constructed Chencun Reservoir Dam.

In addition, the Chens, father and son, provided financial support to the local schools in their native region for 90 years. Today, the high school administration building located in the Congshi Upper Middle School in Qili village, Shidai county is known as the 'Fanyou Instruction Building', bearing the name of Chen Fanyou. The middle school in the same village, for its part, built the 'Fanyou Library'.

Chen Fanyou was a prominent design figure of his generation. In Tianjin today, there remain a number of buildings in the style of the Republican era that he designed. In Tangshan, the China Cement Industry Museum displays the Number 8 Kiln, which ran for 60 years and was unshaken by the Great Tangshan Earthquake. Its design was from the pen of Chen Fanyou.

Under his father's strict supervision, Chen Fanyou – bright, young and educated about both China and the west – travelled to the US, Italy, France, England and Denmark to study the cement industry. He set his sights on taking the best elements of western industry and breaking the trail for the cement industry in China. Just as he rose to leadership of Qixin, filled with high aspirations for his country and for his family, Japan seized northeast China in the Incident of 18 September 1931. The cement industry in the northeast fell into the realm of the Japanese, while the industry in the Tangshan area itself fell within the shadow of Japanese power. In order to prevent the Qixin Cement Company from being swallowed up by Japan, Chen Fanyou recommended to the board of directors that the company select a location farther to the south and build a brand-new plant with a 200,000-ton capacity. The board approved, and responsibility for selecting the new location fell to Chen Fanyou, who had both Chinese and western expertise.

Chen Fanyou led a team on a year-long exploration. In Nanjing, at the base of Qixia mountain on the east side, he discovered limestone and clay mines with rich reserves suitable for the production of high-quality cement. So, he decided to purchase 2,400 *mu* (400 acres) of land there on which to build a modern cement plant. In October 1935, after many ups and downs and much cost, he received approval from the Nanjing municipal government's social affairs bureau to build the facility.

The Qixin board, in setting up the Jiangnan Cement Company, decided that the company's interests would be well served by installing as board chairman Yan Huiqing, (known in the west as WW Yan), a Qixin Company board member, diplomat and statesman who had served on five occasions as premier and once as acting president in the national government in Beijing, before the Chinese Nationalist Party's establishment of the Nanjing National Government. Yuan Xinwu, the sixth son of Yuan Shikai, (the first president of the newborn Republic of China in 1912, who fell from power after a failed attempt at imperial restoration in 1916), along with Chen Fanyou and Wang Zhongliu, formed the executive committee of the board. Chen Fanyou became general manager in charge of building the Jiangnan Cement Company's facilities.

(5)

In November 1937, after two years of urgent work, the first modern cement works utilising equipment at international standards and advanced technology was completed at the base of the eastern side of Qixia mountain in Nanjing.

The plant had purchased more than 3,000 tons' worth of rotary kilns and other key equipment from the Danish firm F.L.Smidth & Co., using special ships and boats to transport the materials from Denmark to Nanjing. Two production lines with annual capacity of 100,000 tons were fully installed. Electrical equipment came from the German firm Siemssen & Krohn and the British firm Jardine Matheson. Excavators, large cranes and maintenance equipment were all installed in good order. Around the periphery, a moat twenty metres wide was dug to protect the plant. Pilings were installed along the outer side of the moat, and cement blocks were stacked to build a barrier. Outside of that, a hedge of thorny bushes, two metres wide and a metre tall, was installed. Finally, on the outside of everything else, the facility was ringed by barbed wire. These multiple layers of defence would make it hard for thieves or hoodlums to barge in. Inside the compound were several hundred plane trees, forty residences, dormitories for workers, an amusement club, a dining hall, a primary school and plots for growing food. Everything needed to support the lives of the employees at the plant was put in place.

On 4 November 1937, tests of both production lines went successfully. Furthermore, the plant had accumulated more than 2,000 tons of limestone and 7,000 tons of Huainan coal.

All was in readiness; only one thing was missing.

But no one would have imagined that in the eight years from its completion to the Japanese surrender at the end of the war, this plant – the first built in Asia by its 415 shareholders and their 4.5 million *yuan* investment to include the highest levels of production equipment and technology – would produce not a single grain of cement.

In the week following the successful test run, Shanghai fell on 12 November, and the national government announced its plans to relocate to Chongqing on 22 November.

In the days that followed, Chen Fanyou and members of his board hardly slept. The board hurriedly put out its recommendations:

First, to prevent Japanese seizure of the plant, "personnel and machinery shall move out separately". Engineering and technical personnel and their families, and vital documents, were to evacuate to Hankou. Non-technical personnel and their families left behind in Nanjing were to move to Chen Fanyou's ancestral home area of Shidai county in Anhui province.

Second, a group of 43 employees led by the top financial

officers Xu Xinnong and Shen Jihua were to form a team to handle disposition of the plant's equipment. Important machinery was to be dismantled and buried, submerged in the factory moat or stored in secret locations.

Third, the familiar strategy of "using the barbarians to control the barbarians" would be employed. Since Jiangnan Cement had not yet fully paid for the equipment it had acquired from F.L.Smidth & Co. of Denmark and Siemssen & Co. of Germany, Jiangnan would ask the two companies, as creditors, to send representatives into the Jiangnan Cement Works. Moreover, Jiangnan would hire Karl Günther, representing Siemssen & Co., as plant manager at a high salary. Günther, upon taking up the position, was to order that the flags of Germany and Denmark be displayed over the plant.[1]

This strategy of "using the barbarians to control the barbarians" reflected lessons learned from the Eight Nation Allied Army's occupation of Beijing. At that time, any business flying the flag or displaying other symbols of a foreign country was spared from looting. Thus, the Jiangnan Cement directors decided to put a foreigner in as acting plant manager in order to withstand the Japanese invasion.

Reality soon showed the wisdom of this decision, which not only protected the plant but also protected thousands of refugees.

There was a history behind the board's decision to select Karl Günther as acting plant manager.

Karl Günther's father, Hans Günther, a geological engineer, arrived in China in 1900 and went to work as a technician at Qixin Cement in Tangshan. In 1906, he was appointed chief technician. He contributed much to the development of market channels for Horse brand cement. Before the Eight Nation Allied Army invasion, Qixin Cement turned over a set of valuable materials to Hans Günther for safekeeping. The English tried over and over to obtain the materials from Günther, but he refused to turn them over, saying: "This is a Chinese enterprise. I cannot give them to you." Thus, Günther managed to preserve Qixin Cement's assets.

At the end of the first world war, the elder Günther was forced to return to Germany because he was a national of the defeated country. For years, he was not able to find work there, and in 1924 he returned to Tangshan. Out of solicitude for Günther and his family, Qixin Cement handed over to him, at no cost, a magnet-manufacturing plant. On 27 February 1936, Hans Günther shot himself to death, apparently because of family quarrels and money problems that left him mentally unbalanced. His son Otto Günther became the head of the magnet factory.

Hans Günther had two sons in China. Karl, the elder, was born on 11 August 1903 in Tangshan. He returned to Germany for study, and in November 1933 received a doctorate in Materials Science from the Berlin Technical University. Altogether, he lived for 30 years in China, finally returning to Germany in 1950.

Yang Yuanxin, one of the Qixin Cement Company board's executive committee members, sought out Günther and said to him: "If you stand with me now as we try to preserve the Nanjing plant, into which we have put so much investment but which has yet to go into production, you won't have to worry about your future – you will be a great man!" Günther, receiving his orders in the face of critical danger, happily accepted this vital mission.

(6)

The old adage, 'individual personality shapes destiny', is not a bad one.

How the Danish fellow Sindberg managed to wind up at Jiangnan Cement was purely the product of his own personality.

Before he went to Jiangnan Cement, Sindberg went through a phase that can only be called unusual. During that phase, he saw with his own eyes how the Japanese army, aroused by militarism, collectively lost both its reason and all individual humanity, and descended into a viciousness unknown in historical experience. Sindberg returned to Shanghai from a holiday in the US on 19 August 1937. The Battle of Shanghai was in full swing, and the company Sindberg was working for was shuttered. Unemployed, Sindberg spent a month as a 'soldier' in the 'International Commercial Militia' squad recruited by the governing International Council within Shanghai's foreign concessions. His duties consisted of gathering up corpses and body parts scattered everywhere and depositing them at a designated location for final disposition.

In the middle of September, Sindberg read an employment notice in the newspapers. Philip Pembroke Stevens, a reporter for the *London Daily Telegraph*, had just returned to Shanghai from Spain, and was advertising for a driver. Sindberg promptly responded and got the job.

So, over the next couple of months, as the Shanghai battle raged, people often saw Stevens's large and brand-new Chrysler sedan, painted an eye-catching white and flying a large British flag, shuttling back and forth night and day amid the gunfire along the front line.

Sindberg served not only as Stevens's driver but as his assistant and photographer. His many photographs became valuable historical materials later.

With Stevens and a Chinese interpreter, Sindberg took part in interviews along many of the roads at the front line. As he drove, he often saw the unbearable sight of large groups of Chinese who had been injured in Japanese gas attacks. He and his team did their utmost to load the wounded into their car and transport them to the Red Cross or to hospitals. But there were too many injured. They lay under the scorching sun, crying out in their suffering and waiting for someone to take them to hospital. Often, they found crowds of injured Chinese in an overloaded car or truck, imploring the driver to move them to hospitals. Sindberg and Stevens were in agony when they had to refuse those appeals because they were trying to reach the front to continue their reporting. When they returned from their front-line reporting mission, their car was usually filled with the wounded.

Sindberg was sincere in his praise for the Chinese soldiers. "The Chinese troops fill me with admiration," he wrote. "They sing happy songs as they march to the battlefront. Their uniforms are ragged, and they carry their equipment on bamboo poles. When reinforcement troops see their wounded comrades by the roadside, not only are they not intimidated, but these wrenching scenes seem to motivate them to continue their advance."

Every day, through the most severe stage of the Battle of Shanghai, Sindberg the driver and Stevens the reporter were constantly on the move amid the din of artillery, dodging their way through bomb craters, through countless brushes with death. They ate their meals and slept every day amid the clatter of guns and the sounds of aerial bombing.

They built a quiet partnership. Stevens affectionately called him 'Bad Boy Sindberg'. He said that Sindberg was smart, cunning and full of tricks – fully able to keep out of danger.

Hearing such praise, Sindberg's face broke out in a grin: "I've been a devil since I was small, and a lot of children obeyed me!"

During this stage of the Battle of Shanghai, Stevens's dispatches to the *Daily Telegraph* provided the entire world with the most up-to-date news of the war. His life exemplifies the sacred mission of the war reporter.

The eleventh of November 1937 was a day accursed by the gods. After days of bitter fighting, that morning saw a quiet lull. The sky was cloudy, and the air was filled with the stench of gunpowder. Sindberg and Stevens were standing on the cement platform of the power plant in the French Concession, about fifty feet above ground, watching the withdrawal of the Chinese forces and the advance of the Japanese, and taking photos.[2]

Stevens had climbed behind a concrete beam. Sindberg first concealed himself behind a concrete pillar, and then climbed up to the observation platform inside a water tower.

Around noon, heavy gunfire erupted from both sides. The Japanese raked the area with machine gun fire, and a bullet suddenly felled Stevens. Sindberg had no way to climb down to the concrete beam where Stevens lay. He shouted "Are you all right?" time and again. At first, he could hear his comrade's faint voice, but after a time there was only silence. Blood streamed from Stevens's forehead and down his arms.

When the Japanese gunfire stopped, Sindberg rushed to Stevens's side. His face covered with blood, Stevens had stopped breathing.

And so, a vile Japanese bullet took the life of a great war reporter.

On the afternoon of 14 November, Sindberg was filled with gloom. He had gone to Stevens's funeral, where a crush of reporters asked him for interviews.

Then Sindberg went to the spot where his comrade had died, to take some photographs. In his pictures, the bullet holes are clearly visible. I can only see him frowning, with the wind ruffling his curly hair.

With the loss of his comrade, Sindberg was in trouble. He knew he was in the most meaningful phase of his life. He had seen too much death, too much violence and evil. He had seen the bowing 'modest gentlemen' turn into fiends who killed without blinking an eye or into bestial rapists after one glance at a woman. He had seen thousands upon thousands of Chinese people dying under the bombs and swords of the Japanese troops, their bodies stacked in piles two and three metres high.

Sindberg was not highly educated. He could not place the violence he was seeing in a more elevated and deeper theoretical framework. But from his childhood he still retained the influence of the Danish philosopher Grundtvig: a man loves and is loyal to his country, but there is a higher love of humanity and of human destiny. This was the pure conviction that determined his later actions.

The reporter was dead, and the Danish fellow was out of work.

He could not count how many times he had been jobless. He could not leave China; neither his partner's death nor the violence of war caused him any doubt. The baptism of death only made him stronger and more fearless.

He went to the Danish consulate in Shanghai to see if they could help him find a job.

As it happened, the Jiangnan Cement Company had just sent a telegram to the Danish consulate in Shanghai, asking that the Danish company F.L.Smidth & Co. send someone to Jiangnan Cement as a representative of Jiangnan's creditor. The company's message asked the Danish consulate to send its own representative to Jiangnan Cement in Nanjing.

Just at that moment, Sindberg arrived at the consulate looking for work.

The consulate asked Sindberg if he would be willing to go to Jiangnan Cement, within the war zone. Money would not be an object.

Sindberg agreed at once. The company promptly provided Sindberg with proper identification. It also asked Sindberg to provide the consulate with a statement.

The statement read:

> To the Danish consulate in Shanghai:
>
> I have, of my own volition, volunteered to go to the Jiangnan Cement Company premises at Qixia mountain in Shanghai, whose production has been interrupted by war. I accept the

dangers involved. If I am injured, crippled or killed, except for reasonable medical costs, I will not seek compensation from F.L.Smidth & Co. or any other related entity.

Until I complete this assignment and return to Shanghai, I shall receive compensation in the amount of £100 per month. If I die, these funds shall be sent through the Danish consulate, to be divided equally for the support of my mother and father. Their addresses are attached. Parents: Mrs Karen Marie Sindberg, Sct.pauls plads 11, Aarhus. Father: Mr Johannes Sindberg, Holsteinsgade, Odder Kommune, Jylland.[3]

This 'living will' was signed on 1 December 1937, the very day on which the Japanese military in China issued Orders 7 and 8 for the assault on Nanjing. The military high command's words were: "The Central China Command shall join with the Navy to attack and occupy the enemy capital, Nanjing."

I could not help wondering why Sindberg would risk life and limb to go to the Jiangnan Cement Works at that moment. He had not been in China for very long, and did not have deep-seated emotional ties to the Chinese people. What would he do when he got there? Was it only the high pay that motivated him, or was he simply in love with danger?

The pay that the plant's board of directors authorised for Günther and Sindberg was undoubtedly very high – two and a half times the compensation of Chen Fanyou from the executive committee of the board, more than 14 times the pay of senior staff, 50 times the pay of ordinary technical workers and 100 times the pay of ordinary workers.[4]

But after reading Sindberg's letters to his family and friends, I came to the conclusion that money alone was not what motivated him to go to Jiangnan Cement.

In one of his letters to his family in Denmark, Sindberg wrote:

Playing Chess with the Devil

A cement plant that imported Danish machinery is now in the middle of the war zone, and I have already been sent there to raise the Danish flag. This is very dangerous, but, if I succeed, it will have been worth the risk.

In a letter to a boyhood friend in his home town, he wrote:

You wouldn't believe this place. Blood is flowing in rivers. All the farm villages have been razed to the ground. All farm animals and poultry have been seized. All I can see in every direction are the corpses of Chinese farmers and soldiers, and the dogs and wild beasts that are feasting on them. Occasionally I encounter an old person or a woman, lucky to survive. They struggle to find anything at all to assuage their hunger, wandering aimlessly.[5]

Since August, each day I have been unable to get away from personally experiencing the terrors of war. Blood! Blood! Blood is everywhere!

Six thousand peasants are now inside the Cement Works compound, including women and children. They have lost everything – they are as though naked. Some are huddled under the eaves of the plant itself. Others are in the thatched huts they have built beside their own farm plots. Our national flag protects them. But we do not have enough food. God only knows how these pitiful people will suffer as the days go by. Spring planting is going to be impossible, because all their animals have been seized and eaten by the Japanese. There is no seed to plant this spring. Virtually all food and poultry has been seized by the Japanese...

Reading through these letters, it was easy to see a warmly compassionate and righteous young man, speaking from the heart. I was touching a soul at once ordinary and great.

(7)

On 27 November 1937, four days before Sindberg signed his living will, Karl Günther and a Japanese language interpreter, with Qixin Cement's chief technician Wang Tao, made the dangerous journey from Tangshan to Shanghai. At the German consulate, Günther received the document granting him full powers:

> Authorisation of Passage:
>
> Günther, a citizen of Germany, has been assigned to enter the Jiangnan Cement Works in the suburbs of Nanjing and take charge of it, in order to protect the legitimate rights of the German creditor. All legitimate rights shall be accorded him as licensee.
>
> German consulate, 12 December 1937[6]

In early December, on the eve of the fall of Nanjing, with Japanese bombing incessant and the population trying to escape by every route, Günther and Sindberg, with their Chinese interpreter Li Yulin and their Japanese interpreter Yen Jinghe, arrived at the Jiangnan Cement Works at Qijia mountain after risking all dangers, and bearing the heavy mandate entrusted to them by the company.

Günther and Sindberg, two foreigners from two different countries, were 34 and 26, respectively. One was a stiff, cold PhD holder, well accustomed to management. The other was a young extrovert, with a yen to defend the underdog and a fondness for getting into brawls. With their utterly different personalities, they strode into that bloody and vicious phase of history.

By that time, most of the personnel and workers from the plant had departed, on orders of the board of directors, leaving behind only a small cohort to guard the plant. Once Günther and Sindberg arrived, they got active immediately, commanding that enormous Danish and German flags be sewn and flown all around the grounds.

At the gate, they posted a sign reading: "Jiangnan Cement Works, Under Joint Management of Denmark and Germany." They spread lime and charcoal to display the image of a huge German flag on the ground. Sindberg had people use paints to create a Danish flag, of 1,350 square metres, on the roof of the main factory building. And they organised those personnel carrying arms into teams for patrolling night and day.

These systematic measures were indeed effective. Thenceforth, as the Japanese bombers appeared, only one misdirected bomb landed near the main kiln, but it caused no damage. Sindberg, in a letter to his childhood friend, said with unmistakable pride:

> I raised the biggest Danish flag in all of China inside the plant. And I had people paint a gigantic Danish flag, 1,350 square metres in area. On the roofs of our buildings. The flag was clearly visible from the sky. I think this is without doubt the biggest Danish flag in the history of the world!

On 6 March 1938, the main newspaper of Eastern Jutland, the Aarhus *Stiftstidende,* printed a letter from Sindberg, entitled, 'An Aarhus Man in the Orient: The Largest Danish Flag Flies Over Nanjing, China'. When I visited Sindberg's niece in Denmark, she showed me the relevant newspaper.

Qixia mountain fell to the Japanese on 9 December.

On the 13th, the Japanese forces occupied the city of Nanjing and began their six-week 'great massacre'. Nanjing became a hell of corpses piled high amid rivers of blood.

From early December, a flood of refugees fleeing along the Shanghai-Ningbo line or escaping from Nanjing poured into Qixia mountain and the Nanjing Cement Works. The refugees included many Kuomintang military officers and officials. The Kuomintang general Liao Yaoxiang was hidden among them. After his defeat, on 13 December, Liao Yaoxiang shed his uniform and concealed himself in a family's pile of rice straw. When he heard that the Qixia Temple had set up a refugee centre, he raced there. The abbot of the temple was a wise and courageous patriot who protected many of the refugees; he helped a number of officers and officials escape from danger. After a week, Liao Yaoxiang boarded a boat by night, quietly made his way to the far bank of the river and thus escaped from Nanjing.

At that time, everyone, including Günther and Sindberg as well as the Chinese leaders and ordinary employees remaining at Jiangnan Cement, provided great assistance to the refugees. They set up housing for them in the plant's employee dormitories or in work sheds. They had military officers abandon their uniforms for the clothes of ordinary civilians and commingled the officers with the mass of refugees to prevent their discovery by the Japanese.

At 2,400 *mu* (about 400 acres) the grounds of the Jiangnan Cement Company were expansive. The actual production areas were not large, and since they were surrounded by the moat, neither

Karl Günther (with his hands in his pockets) at the Nanjing Jiangnan Cement Works refugee camp.

the refugees nor anyone else could enter. The remaining areas could accommodate a great many people, and in fact constituted the largest refugee reception zone in Nanjing. But as the numbers of refugees grew, available housing in buildings and work sheds became insufficient. There was no alternative but to allow the refugees to build their own shacks from reeds, rice straw and tar paper. A great many refugees found their only shelter in these frigid and damp straw huts, suffering through the long days of cold and rain.

The leadership team that remained in place agreed that the refugees were too numerous and too jumbled together. In order to prevent fires or other emergencies, they decided to break the refugees into smaller groups, and chose twelve representatives to be responsible for sanitation, conduct coordinated management of the camp and send out night-time patrols. Furthermore, those responsible personnel from the plant conducted observations throughout the day and night to head off any untoward events, and dispensed emergency food supplies to the refugees in accordance with actual, observed conditions.

Through this period, the Japanese soldiers came repeatedly to cause a commotion. Sometimes they showed up many times in the same day, seeking to lay their hands on Chinese officers and soldiers, or to plunder, or to seize Chinese women.

Every time the Japanese troops showed up to cause trouble, the men standing lookout rushed to Günther and Sindberg to report. The two men would race out, display their identification to the Japanese troops, and say: "This plant is jointly managed by German and Danish investors. It does not belong to Chinese. We hope your senior officers are very clear about this!"

Seeing the foreigners, the Japanese had to leave in disappointment.

One day, a worker ran to report to Günther: "Bad news! One of our personnel named Xia Liuhua has been seized outside and taken away by the Japanese. The Japanese have forced him to do coolie labour. Please, Mr Günther, try to save him!"

Günther got in his car and drove to parlay with the Japanese. He told them that four men in Japanese custody were his employees, and asked for their immediate release. The Japanese officer stood squarely in front of the German and refused. In reality, of the four men he had seized, some were not employees of the plant but were country people from the nearby hills.

On another occasion, several Japanese troops managed to enter the refugee camp, looking for women. Sindberg grabbed two hunting guns and ran out. When the Japanese soldiers saw a foreigner coming towards them with hunting guns, they turned tail and escaped.

To protect the refugees from harm, the company personnel remaining behind had no choice but to treat the Japanese well, with good food and good drinks, so that they could leave an aura of good feeling after the Japanese had eaten and drunk their fill.

Günther and Sindberg divided up their tasks.

Günther was responsible for everything inside the factory itself. Sindberg was more familiar with the Nanjing area, and besides he was fearless. He was responsible for going into the city, and for direct contact with the head of the International Committee, John Rabe. In his diary, Rabe spoke well of Sindberg many times. He also lent Sindberg a Ford car.

Sindberg gave Rabe a document confirming his borrowing of the car: "I guarantee that I will not damage this car, and take responsibility for returning it safely." That was on 21 December 1937.[7]

With the Ford at his disposal, going into Nanjing was much more convenient. Sindberg did many things for the Nanjing International Committee and for the refugees.

He used the Ford to transport the injured to hospitals, and to bring desperately needed grain, vegetables and poultry to the International Committee. Every time Rabe encountered Sindberg bringing some chickens or a pig or a hundred eggs, he embraced Sindberg, called him 'God' and told him that he had brought life-saving supplies to the International Committee.

Sindberg also used the Ford to take the American missionary John Magee, head of the Red Cross, out to Qixia mountain for an inspection, so that Magee could secretly shoot films of the violent misdeeds of the Japanese forces. Those films were unique records of the Japanese military's atrocities in China, and became treasured visual materials for the entire world.[8]

From the mass of materials, I also learned this story:

On 23 December 1937, Sindberg heard news on his portable radio: Japanese bombers might attack British ships. He was concerned that HMS Bee, tied up at Xiaguan in Nanjing, might be struck. Only ten days before, the American gunboat Panay, with American diplomatic and social service agency personnel aboard, had been bombed by the Japanese, with several people killed or wounded. Sindberg was very anxious, and wanted to contact HMS Bee, but he had no communications equipment. So, he had someone get behind him carrying a large Danish flag, and he jumped into the icy river, aiming to swim to HMS Bee with the news so that the ship could leave Xiaguan in a hurry. Thus, the story went, he averted a disaster that would have seen many lose their lives.

I cannot tell whether this story was true or not. But, given Sindberg's personality, it certainly could have been true.

(8)

In the refugee encampment at Jiangnan Cement were people who had lost limbs in the Japanese bombing. There were no doctors or drugs. There was nothing for them; they could only moan as they awaited death. Everyone was upset, but people were powerless to do anything.

Sindberg, on many occasions, hauled sufferers towards hospitals in the city. But when he reached the city gates, Japanese sentries would block his way. Try as he might, Sindberg could not get into the city, and he would return to the refugee camp, unsuccessful. To get into town, he had no choice but to cultivate some kind of warmer connections to the Japanese troops.

On one occasion, Sindberg strapped a wounded boy of six or seven on his back and tried to take him by motorcycle to a hospital inside the city. A Japanese soldier had broken into the boy's house to try to grab some chickens, and when he failed he detonated a hand grenade, injuring the boy's eyes. The wound was infected, and the child's life was at stake. When they reached the city gates, the Japanese sentry absolutely refused to let them enter. Sindberg could only plead with the sentry to play God and allow him to take the dying child to the hospital, but the sentry rudely refused. Sindberg felt the sentry had no humanity, and he knew that the boy would die if he did not get to the hospital. He drove his motorcycle to another one of the city gates. When he got there, he gunned his engine and smashed into the guard house, finally delivering the boy to the hospital and saving the lad's life.

Faced with the unending flow of refugees and the constant appeals for help from Chinese outside the wall who were up against the encircling Japanese forces, Sindberg, Günther and the remaining plant personnel held a discussion and decided to set up a clinic.

Thus, with Yan Jinghe's report to the Jiangnan Cement Company and Sindberg's request inside the city to Nanjing Red Cross head Father Magee, the Red Cross provided major assistance. Sindberg guaranteed the lives and the safety of two nurses, whom the Red Cross assigned to him. Sindberg further obtained substantial quantities of drugs, bandages and medical supplies from the Red Cross. Thanks to the assistance of the Red Cross, Jiangnan Cement was able to open a temporary clinic in a two-storey administration building at the plant.

With a temporary clinic finally set up in the refugee encampment at the cement works, the helter-skelter rush of sick and wounded people from every direction was put in order. At its busiest, the little hospital was receiving and dealing with seventy to eighty people each day.

When I visited Jiangnan Cement, I found the little former clinic, obscured behind some large trees. It was a small two-floor building of mixed brick construction. But though the old building was still there, everything had changed. The staircase to the second floor was filled with junk, and the second floor was clearly abandoned. Only on the first floor were there signs that some company had used the building. I stood in front of this nondescript old building, which by then had gone through historic changes and had become a Protected Cultural Building under the Nanjing municipal government. For a long time, my thoughts were jumbled.

I wondered to myself how many lives were saved here.

I have no way of knowing. But I do know that two foreign friends, and the plant personnel who remained behind, managed to deal with the Japanese military by every means at their disposal – both soft and hard – to achieve those results. And because of that, the Jiangnan Cement Works did not experience the wholesale massacres and repeated waves of rape that took place in other areas. Jiangnan Cement, in the Qijia district of Nanjing, was the only refugee centre in which no refugee died or was hurt.

(9)

The Qijia Temple, only five Chinese *li* from Jiangnan Cement, fared differently. Japanese soldiers broke in to the temple repeatedly, killing, looting and raping.

One Japanese invader later admitted that he had raced into the temple repeatedly and raped between fifty and sixty women. When he could not find more women, he opened fire and killed people.

According to the records in my research materials, the thousand-year-old Qixia Temple, led by Abbot Jiran representing several hundred monks, managed through their righteousness and bravery to protect more than 24,000 Chinese refugees.[9] But still, the monks directly witnessed the rape of two women in the courtyard of the Great Hall, "under the very eyes of the Buddha".

The records reveal that in the space of 15 days, from 4 January to 19 January 1938, Japanese soldiers burst into the temple 11 times, killing, burning, looting and raping.

One of the monks recalled a most appalling incident on 15 January:

> Japanese soldiers flooded in. They gathered all the young women together in a group and selected some, whom they wantonly violated in the Great Hall of the temple. One drunken soldier arrived late and demanded liquor and women. When he found neither, he became enraged. He wanted to rape a girl of twelve of thirteen. An elderly monk intervened to protect the girl, and angrily denounced the soldier for his lack of humanity. The soldier, humiliated, exploded with anger and cut the monk down with his sword. At the sight of this, two younger monks boldly surrounded the soldier and disarmed him. Then the monks beat and kicked the soldier. One of the monks attacked the soldier's head with the butt of his gun. It was not long before the soldier was dead.

In order to protect a child, the followers of the Buddha, whose hearts were filled with mercy, had to violate their deepest prohibition against killing.

Temples are Buddhist holy places, like western churches. Since ancient times, even the most vicious casual murderer and bandit stood in awe of the temple. To treat the temple with contempt might bring retribution down upon him. Holding to the principle of "laying down the butcher's blade and becoming a Buddha" could offer a path to redemption. But the Japanese soldiers in this temple, in the sight of the great Buddha, openly slaughtered, raped and plundered. There was nothing vile that they would not do. The temple's shrines became couches for the satisfaction of these bestial soldiers' lusts.

In an attempt to draw the attention of the international community to the crisis at the Qijia Temple, a group of about twenty better-known refugees at the temple signed a letter drafted by the Abbot Shuran. An urgent appeal to the world, the letter was titled: 'A Message to All Who Care, in the Name of Humanity.'

> Whoever you are, please help us to prevent the recurrence of this inhuman and abominable cruelty.[10]

The letter from the Qijia Temple went to the Jiangnan Cement Works. From there, Günther and Sindberg brought the letter into Nanjing city by car.

The date was 2 February 1938, the fourth day of the new year in the lunar calendar. Nanjing lay under a rare and heavy snowfall. Sindberg braved the snow and made his way into the city, to hand the letter to John Rabe, head of the International Committee. Rabe passed the letter to the hands of other foreigners.

Meanwhile, the refugees' representatives passed similar messages to Günther and Sindberg, describing the Japanese atrocities in detail, attaching correct figures and providing name lists of those murdered:[11]

> Besides killing people in battle, looting, and burning many innocent people to death, in our mountain villages and market towns the Japanese are burning, killing and raping. Because of your [Günther's and Sindberg's – tr.] grace, ten thousand of our lives are under your protection. We implore you to tell all this to the embassies. The foreign embassies are principled and humane. They will share all of this with the allied peoples of all nations, in order to block the terrorist behaviour of the

Japanese and rescue the refugees from their travails. If, with that assistance, we can return to our homes soon, we will be profoundly grateful. The Japanese have slaughtered 2,000 water buffalo. From Longtan to Taipingmen in Nanjing, a distance of 50 Chinese li, every structure belonging to all two thousand farm families have been burned. All structures belonging to the ten thousand families in the thirty-kilometre stretch from Yangzhen to Zhongshanmen in Nanjing have been burned to ashes...

Attached to this letter were name lists of those killed or wounded and of women and girls seized by the Japanese. Many of the female captives were between the ages of 9 and 15.

But all the letters of appeal or resistance, all the lists of signatures, disappeared like Nanjing's snowflakes into a torrent of muddy water, murder, rape and looting. All of it went on, with even greater intensity and brutality.

The monks of the Qijia Temple wept, and the women huddled inside the temple wept as well.

Between heaven and earth, no place was safe.

The refugees fled towards Jiangnan Cement. At the height of the exodus, Jiangnan Cement Works took in as many as ten thousand people in a single day.

All in all, how many refugees did Jiangnan Cement save? In the research materials, some say 20,000, others 30,000. An accurate count is difficult, because the refugees flowed in and out.

To protect this vast number of refugees, the two foreign friends Günther and Sindberg made the most extreme efforts.

One of the fortunate survivors of the Nanjing Massacre, Su Guobao, recorded that when he was twelve, the Japanese threw his three-year-old brother into a river and decapitated his aunt and uncle. His home was burned. Günther and Sindberg came to the reed hut where he was sheltering. Each gave him a silver dollar and 36 catties of rice for his family. He performed the kowtow before them out of gratitude. That rice, and those two coins, preserved the lives of his entire family.

On 4 February 1938, the Japanese army issued a military order dissolving all refugee camps.

Hearing that order, the refugees in the Jiangnan Cement camp tearfully refused to leave. It was May before they were finally forced to disperse.

Everyone knows that two foreign friends made huge contributions to the protection of the refugees at the Jiangnan Cement camp. But fewer people know that behind them stood a group of solid and wise Chinese industrialists. From the start, they chose to use the strategy of "using barbarians to manage barbarians". They arranged a planned evacuation, and hired the two foreigners at high rates of pay to oversee the small team remaining on the site, with the goal of protecting the company's assets and responding to any contingency that might occur. The plant's manager Chen Fanyou and others exercised leadership from a distance, communicating by letters, and so contributed hugely to the protection of the refugees. Thanks to firm support from afar, coupled with the preservation of the Jiangnan Cement workforce and the close cooperation with the foreigners, it was possible to save a great many refugees at Jiangnan Cement. In the saga of the War of Resistance and the struggle against fascism, this stood as a glorious anthem celebrating the cooperation of Chinese and foreign friends in assisting China's refugees.

(10)

On 20 March 1938, Sindberg had no choice but to leave the Jiangnan Cement Works.

The reason for his departure was that he and Günther had come into conflict. Both the men treated the Chinese refugees responsibly and with great friendliness. But Günther was employed as the acting manager of the plant. He was responsible to the board of directors of the Tianjin Jiangnan Cement Company. Sindberg was at Jiangnan as representative of the Danish company F.L.Smidth & Co.; he reported to that company. The division of responsibilities between the two men was not entirely clear, and disagreements were inevitable. In addition, both men had strong personalities that did not admit of compromise.

Karl Günther was a man of few words, cold of bearing, blunt of speech. His personality exhibited the finer aspects of the German nationality. Moreover, he had full authority over the plant as acting plant manager. His behaviour was arrogant, and he was filled with pride for his nation, Germany. On the wall of his office hung a map of the world. When, on 14 March 1938, he heard the broadcast news of Germany's absorption of Austria, he posted a small red banner over Austria on the map. After that, his red banners precisely followed the footsteps of the Nazi armies until it covered almost all of Europe. But later, after Germany's defeat, he still did not take the flags down, leaving them fluttering over the lands that, by then, were free of German occupation.

Sindberg, also a European, was of a completely different nature. His nature was ardent. He revelled in fighting for the underdog, brawling and joking. Once, he shouted to the refugees: "Danger! The Japanese are coming again!" and then laughed heartily.

Once the clinic was established, the tide of sick and injured rose daily. The vast jumble of people made for disorder throughout the entire factory area. Günther was very unhappy with Sindberg, who was in charge of the clinic. The two men were never close, and at times had come to blows. This incident was even more intense; the only thing they did not do was take up guns. Günther reported to the board of directors that he could no longer work with Sindberg. And so, the board of directors contacted Sindberg's Danish employer to dismiss Sindberg. They asked the Danish embassy to dispatch someone to the plant, and sent Sindberg more than a month's pay as severance.

Although Günther and Sindberg both had strong personalities and personal drawbacks, no one is perfect. Neither of them was concerned with his own safety. In a time of extreme crisis, both worked at protecting the factory and at saving a large number of Chinese refugees. This great spirit of humanitarianism is precious, and it should be kept in the forefront. Later, the German Red Cross presented Günther with the Red Cross Second Class Honour, in recognition of his extraordinary achievements.

The refugees, when they learned that Sindberg was leaving, were sorry to see him go. They presented him with a silken banner with the words "Seeing the Right, Acting with Courage" and the names of 11 of the refugees.[12]

"Seeing the Right, Acting with Courage" was a true portrait of Sindberg. It was the highest praise that the people of China could bestow on this young Dane.

A letter from Jiangnan Cement to the company's board of directors in Tianjin said of Sindberg:

> He was a brave young man. We understand that he had good relations with the foreigners in Nanjing during his time at the Nanjing Cement plant; that he was faithful in performing his guardianship duties. Only 28 years old, his record is still rather thin.

Sindberg left Jiangnan Cement on 20 March 1938, after 107 days.

One hundred and seven days is a short stretch in a person's life, like the flower *tanhua*, which blooms briefly and is gone. But in that brief moment, its flower is the most gorgeous, the most brilliant. Like a match, the brief moment of flame lightens the darkness and illumines the world.

In 107 days, the spirit of this ordinary young Dane rose to glory. Because of those 107 days, his name has entered into the annals of humanity's struggle against fascism. His deeds will be forever remembered by the Chinese people.

When Sindberg reached Shanghai, he went to his company's offices and collected his salary of £400, his bonus of £100 and travel money for his return home.

Then he took a bundle of important letters that he had saved and went to the American consulate in Shanghai, where he delivered the appeals from the refugees. The letters themselves were from Harold John Timperley, special correspondent of the *Manchester Guardian* and editorial adviser at the magazine *Asia*. Timperley had been a friend of the war correspondent Philip Pembroke Stevens, and a worthy journalist. His book, *What is the Meaning of War: Japanese Atrocities in China*, appeared in print in London and New York in 1938. In his letters, Timperley spoke warmly of Sindberg's humanitarian spirit, and sought to testify to his character.

(11)

On 25 April 1938, Sindberg picked up his US visa and set out from Shanghai to Hong Kong on a passenger boat. Standing on the deck, gazing at a sea the same colour as the sky above, gazing into the distance, watching the coastline receding from view, seeing as well the land of blood and tears, a thousand thoughts filled his mind and his sympathies. But he knew that he had to leave.

Originally, just after Sindberg departed, the Japanese took over everything that Sindberg had done. What they never imagined, however, was that as soon as Sindberg – a young fellow from a neutral country – got a look at the Japanese slaughtering Chinese civilians and raping Chinese women, he could never again maintain neutrality. Not only did he do his utmost to save Chinese refugees and support the International Committee of the Nanjing Safety Zone; he also took a great many photographs of the Japanese atrocities. He brought with him all his rolls of film on the trip back to Europe, as well as the moving pictures taken by the American missionary John Magee. The Japanese had wanted to search him as he left, but because he was from a neutral country they had to behave with caution, so they only issued him an ultimatum to leave immediately. Otherwise, they warned the Danish consulate, they would make it difficult to send any more Danes to Jiangnan Cement.

On 7 May, Sindberg sent an air letter to his father: "I am carrying out an important mission for the Chinese government..."

No one had any idea what Sindberg's 'mission' might be. The research materials offer no clues. They only show that during the time he was in Hong Kong, he made a trip to Hankou, which had not yet fallen to the Japanese. Soon after that, he received a letter from the Chinese delegation in Geneva inviting him to come to Geneva on 2 June.

On 2 June 1938, the International Labour Conference convened in the League of Nations Palace of Nations in Geneva. The Chinese delegation intended to use the occasion to expose to the world Japan's atrocities during its invasion of China, so that its War of Resistance could incur the international community's sympathies and so that it could struggle for the support of the international labour movement. They invited Sindberg, as a citizen of a neutral country, to come to Geneva to bear witness to what he had seen during the Nanjing Massacre and show the visual record of Japan's offences to the League of Nations delegations and the media, and screen films of the Japanese invasion of China.[13]

This is probably what Sindberg meant by his reference to an "important mission for the Chinese government". While he was in Hong Kong, the Japanese sent him another ultimatum, warning him to leave Hong Kong at once.

On 17 May 1938, Sindberg hurriedly sailed from Hong Kong en route to Europe. He left so suddenly that he was unable to withdraw the funds he had banked in Hong Kong, and he had to write to his father to ask for financial help. He cabled his father from the ship, and they agreed to meet when the ship made port at Brindisi, Italy on 29 May. Worried that he might run completely out of money if his father did not show up on time, he sent a telegram to his father, asking him to cable 500 Danish kroner to the Lloyd's Shipping office in Brindisi for his retrieval. His father, when that message arrived, was suspicious, having no idea what his son was up to. Why would he want so much money? At that time, 500 Danish kroner was no small sum. Knowing that Sindberg had money in his pocket, the father wondered why he was asking for such a big sum to be wired to him.

At the port of Brindisi, father and son finally met face-to-face after many years. They embraced, and talked for a long time. Sindberg told his father all that he had seen and heard in China.

Sindberg's father saw that his trick-playing, risk-loving boy, who loved to fight for the underdog and had fled the family nest, had grown to manhood. His eyes overflowing with hot tears, he said over and over again to his son: "Sindberg! Your father is proud of you! Your father is proud of you!"

His father realised that Sindberg had acted in the truest spirit of the great philosopher Nikolai Grundtvig: a man must love and be loyal to his country, but he must also be faithful to humanity and concern himself with the destiny of mankind.

The father told Sindberg that he planned to write an article based on Sindberg's letters from China to his friends and family, putting on paper the dangers and risks his son faced there, for publication in the *Aarhus Weekly*. When I visited Sindberg's niece Marianne in Denmark, I read that newspaper.

Sindberg was very happy, and said: "Thank you, Father, thank you!" over and over.

This frisky child turned grown man, like children everywhere, had longed for his father's approval. He had yearned to be the pride of his parents and his whole family. Now he had finally gained a special distinction – a pride that came from China.

Father and son arrived in Geneva on 2 June. They were warmly received by the head of the Chinese delegation to Geneva, Zhu Xuefan, and others, who had been waiting expectantly for his arrival. On the evening of 3 June, in the great hall of the Chinese Library created by Li Shizeng, amid glittering lamps, more than 100 people from League of Nations member states and from the media arrived at the invitation of the Chinese delegation, attired in their elegant western clothing, chatting and laughing amiably. They came to see a film.[14]

Before the screening, the head of the Chinese delegation, the distinguished patriotic personage Zhu Xuefan, spoke to the crowd in his sonorous and deep voice, introducing a very special guest.

A travel-worn young Dane named Sindberg, his face deeply serious, stood to face the guests.

Zhu Xuefan introduced Sindberg to the assembled guests. During the great Japanese military slaughter of Chinese compatriots at Nanjing, Sindberg, disregarding mortal danger, had saved a great many Chinese. He went on: the film that the guests were about to watch had been smuggled out of China by Sindberg, at the risk of his own life. Then, Zhu Xuefan said this to the reporters present: "Do not print news of this film in your newspapers, for fear of causing great trouble for Sindberg and the foreign friends in China."

Before showing the film, Sindberg spoke at some length to the audience, warning them of its cruel and bloody content. "Women and children should not watch this," he said. "Please take them out of the room."

Although almost all those remaining were men, and although Sindberg had warned in advance of its vicious and bloody content, as the film showed the dwellings of the Chinese burned to ashes, and Japanese soldiers lopping off the heads of Chinese victims as though they were cutting the tops off radishes, and Japanese soldiers ramming pieces of wood into the vaginas of the women they had just raped, and a young girl screaming in despair as she tried to run from a pile of bodies lying in pools of blood, the entire room burst out in sobs and angry expostulations.

These films of Japanese atrocities shook the viewers beyond their imaginations.

This was the first time that the media of the League of Nations had seen the staggering atrocities that Japanese fascism had committed in Nanjing.

By the time the film ended, night had fallen. The Chinese delegation invited Sindberg and his father to a restaurant for a meal. In Sindberg's passport, the delegation's leader, Zhu Xuefan, inscribed the words: "Mr Sindberg. A Friend of China. Zhu Xuefan, June 1938, Geneva."

Three other members of the Chinese delegation – Pan Jinan, Zhu Baohua and Liu Xuancui – added their commemorative inscriptions to Sindberg's passport. The delegation asked Sindberg to lend them his films so that two copies could be made. One copy would be sent to the League of Nations, and the other copy to the US. Sindberg agreed. Zhu Xuefan wrote letters to the Chinese consulates in Denmark and the US, introducing the Sindberg story. The Chinese delegation also sent a Chinese carpet to Sindberg's father as an expression of gratitude.

Then Sindberg went with his father back to the family home in Aarhus. A month later, he left for America.

(12)

Now, I need to talk about the Jiangnan Cement Works.

Wherever the Japanese went in their invasion of China, besides killing, burning and raping, they plundered in every imaginable way. They plundered small things like chickens, ducks and geese, foodstuffs like rice and wheat, or clothing. But they also plundered big things like railroads, mines, factories, antiquities, and works of art like calligraphy and paintings. The small-scale looting satisfied the hunger and the venality of troops themselves. The large-scale plundering was driven by Japan's national avarice.

To take one example, after Nanjing fell to the Japanese, Mitsui Bussan Kaisha forcibly took over the large Nanjing Yongli Ammonium Factory. They changed the name of the facility to Bōrei Chemical Company, Pukou Industrial Installation, and turned it to the production of war materiel. In 1942, all the equipment used to produce nitric acid at this plant was shipped to Japan and installed in the Ōmuta Tōyō High Pressure Company's Yokosuka plant in Kyushu. After Japan's defeat, the Chinese government conducted repeated negotiations for the return of the equipment. The machinery was finally returned to Nanjing in 1948.

After they took Shanghai and Nanjing, the Japanese seized several large-scale domestic cement production facilities, including the Shanghai Cement Works and the Nanjing Longtan Cement Works. Naturally, they were reluctant to leave the Nanjing Jiangnan Cement Works – with its top-of-the-line equipment and superior mineral resources – alone. From the moment the Japanese occupied Nanjing on 13 December 1938, the Jiangnan Cement Company and Japan waged a marathon struggle that went on for years.

After Nanjing fell, the Japanese racked their brains to find a way to seize Jiangnan Cement. For the members of the Jiangnan Cement board of directors, as they saw their country's fall and the enemy's massive looting, the question was whether to stand firm or to appease the Japanese and fall beneath the boots of the enemy. This was the agonising choice confronting every member of the board.

When I learned that Yuan Xinwu, a member of the board's standing committee, was the sixth son of Yuan Shikai, I thought to myself that Yuan Shikai had signed Japan's infamous '21 Demands', and had been denounced as a traitor. Did his son harbour any special feelings for Japan, as his father had? What I learned from my interviews was that Yuan Xinwu had stood four-square with the rest of the board and had done nothing to sell out the interests of his nation or his company.

By telephone, telegram and postal mail, Yuan Xinwu and Chen Fanyou sent their instructions to the company leaders remaining at the plant, including Geng Zonggui, Zhao Qingjie and Sun Baiguan, and conveyed the board's decision to Karl Günther with respect to receiving the refugees, dealing with the Japanese and protecting the plant's assets. At the same time, they pondered how to use their knowledge to resist the Japanese army's and Japanese companies' forcible occupation and acquisition of their factory.

The board's guiding motto was "a broken jade is more precious than an unbroken tile". They had to adopt every possible means of contending with the Japanese.

The Japanese knew that the raw materials used at Jiangnan Cement were very good, and that the plant produced a very high-grade product, suitable for military use. When Nanjing fell, Japan's Mitsui Yōkō and Onoda Cement Company immediately sent personnel to Jiangnan Cement and ordered the plant personnel who remained there to resume production at once.

But the plant personnel dodged the order by replying: "The cement company board of directors is in Tianjin. This is a matter of great magnitude. We are not authorised to respond."

With that, Mitsui Yōkō and Onoda Cement commenced a systematic assault.

They began by sending a memorandum to the board of directors of Jiangnan Cement in Tianjin, demanding that Jiangnan Cement immediately resume production. They went on: "We demand that Jiangnan Cement, under a Military Trusteeship, sign an agreement to specify products for sale and marketing." Then they engaged in talks with the Danish firm F.L.Smidth & Co. in an attempt to assume direct control of the Jiangnan Works. With this met with refusal, Onoda sent one of the members of its board of directors standing committee, Asaeda Shintarō, and the deputy director of the cement department of Mitsui, Nishida Miyaage, to meet with Yuan Xinwu and Chen Fanyou and deliver a stark message: "The military is very unhappy that Jiangnan Cement has not resumed production. Please tell them to be careful."[15]

From 13 December 1937 to 14 July 1943, a period of five and a half years, the Japanese tried by every means – threats, bribes, financial incentives – but never gained control of Jiangnan Cement.

The Jiangnan Cement Company unbendingly stuck to its principle of "no aid to the enemy, no compromise", and produced not a grain of cement. They found various reasons to refuse, and were firmly uncooperative with the Japanese. This was extremely irritating to the Japanese, and the two sides remained locked in a perpetual conflict of wills that neither was willing to relinquish.

It is deeply distressing to examine the eight-year struggle between Jiangnan Cement and the Japanese.

With the start of the Pacific War in December 1941 following the Japanese attack on Pearl Harbor, Japan urgently required vast quantities of military materiel. Seeing that Jiangnan Cement was still unwilling to go back into production, the Japanese resorted to uglier methods. On 14 July 1943, a representative of the Japanese embassy in Beiping sent a stern demand to Yuan Xinwu of Jiangnan Cement's board standing committee: because Jiangnan Cement had continued to postpone production, its machinery and equipment were now useless junk. Since the aluminium production facility at Zhangdian in Shandong province urgently needed equipment, Jiangnan Cement's machinery was to be dismantled. The Japanese message also ordered Jiangnan Cement to sign without delay a cooperation and leasing agreement with the Nippon Keikinzoku Company [Japan Light Industrial Company – tr.]. Jiangnan Cement's board members were furious when they received this message, and tried to find people who could mediate the dispute, but they were not successful.

On 6 September 1943, the head of the economic department of the Japanese consulate general in Shanghai, Ōta, met with the chairman of the board of Qixin Cement, Gu Huiqing, and presented him with a six-part document ordering the 'loan' of cement production equipment.

For his part, Gu Huiqing made use of the Chinese Company Law to decline the arrangement, saying that because the matter was so significant he had to discuss it in a full meeting of the company's shareholders; as board chair, he lacked the authority to advocate for it. He called a quick meeting of the shareholders and held a vote. The vast majority of the votes opposed the deal, and raised a separate proposal to "die honourably, rather than live with dishonour".

As soon as the shareholder meeting ended, a representative of the Japanese embassy in Beiping sought out Yuan Xinwu and asked for a heart-to-heart meeting with the shareholders in order to get them to change their position. Yuan answered with indignation: "I truly feel that is beyond my power. As a last resort, my only recourse it to step down and let someone wiser step in." With that, he turned and left, leaving the Japanese consular official in a rage.[16]

On 14 September 1943 the minister plenipotentiary at the Japanese consulate general in Shanghai, Tajiri Akiyoshi, again sent a message to Gu Huiqing adding a new item to the list of six demands presented to Gu earlier: "The removal and reinstallation of all machinery is to be regarded as a military necessity." And he declared that the dismantling and removal of Jiangnan Cement's machinery was to commence before the end of the month.

On 15 September, Jiangnan Cement's entire board and supervisory personnel went to Wang Jingwei's puppet government in Nanjing, asking it to reject the 'loan' of Jiangnan's machinery. The regime not only failed to stand by the side of the cement company – one of

From Left: Xu Shennong, Wang Tao, Chen Fanyou, and Geng Zonggui on the grounds of the Nanjing Jinagnan Cement Works.

its own nation's enterprises – but stood completely by the side of the Japanese, in the words of a familiar Chinese saying, "taking the thief as the father, and helping the villain". This compelled Jiangnan Cement to turn over all its production equipment.

The Wang Jingwei pseudo-government issued an order over the signature of its Ministry of Industry on 22 October:

> On this matter we have sought the views of the Supreme National Defence Council. Because this matter is closely connected to the Greater East Asia War, we must provide assistance. On the question of the machinery at the Qijiashan plant, the Japanese

side urgently requires its dismantling and removal. Time is pressing. This must be speedily negotiated and handled.[17]

Reading this, my nationalistic spirit was aroused. What enraged me was not so much the Japanese but my traitorous Chinese countrymen.

"Because this matter is closely connected to the Greater East Asia War, we must provide assistance." Such words flowed smoothly from Wang Jingwei's lips. It was as though the invaded was not his own China, and the slaughtered were not his fellow Chinese, but rather were foreigners with whom he had no connection. Was "assist in the Greater East Asia War" nothing more than assisting the Japanese in their slaughter of Chinese and other Asian peoples as they ordained themselves the hegemons of Asia? Do not forget: 300,000 Chinese bodies massacred by the Japanese were buried beneath the feet of the Wang Jingwei regime. If we counted out those 300,000 bodies in detail, they would amount to half the population of Nanjing.

But even when the Wang Jingwei regime issued its order, Jiangnan Cement still would not comply. The company's shareholders took another vote, and again rejected dismantling and removing the company's machinery.

Japan's schemes to remove the machinery failed time after time.

The Japanese resorted to their most vicious trick, declaring that Jiangnan's refusal to agree to removal of the machinery smelled of anti-Japanese activity. The Japanese military policy ordered preparations for the arrest of Chen Fanyou, of the company board's standing committee. The Japanese embassy put a stop to that, however.[18]

That tactic did not work, and the Japanese once more had to put pressure on Wang Jingwei's 'Nanjing government'. Once again, in the name of the government's Ministry of Industry, the government applied pressure to Jiangnan with their Work Order 0301: "Time is pressing, and there can be no further delay. Jiangnan Cement is ordered to turn over all machinery designated for use in aluminium production." Once more, the Jiangnan board voted, and refused to obey the government's command.

The officials in the Ministry of Industry of the Wang government were vexed. After four days, on 17 December, they sent another command to Jiangnan, this one Work Order 0025, together with a detailed list of the items in question and requiring Jiangnan Cement to hand over the listed items: two 131-metre revolving kilns and four milling machines valued at US$1.32m.[19]

Gu Huiqing, chairman of Jiangnan's board, answered irately: "To this very day, Jiangnan's board has not agreed to the dismantling and removal of the company's machines. We have received the Ministry of Industry's directive. The Ministry can decide whatever it wants."

Two days later, on 19 December, Japanese officials, escorted by representatives of the Wang Jingwei government and under the protection of the Japanese army, entered the Jiangnan Cement Works.

On the 21st, a secretary from the Japanese embassy, accompanied by officials of the Wang Jingwei government's Ministry of Industry, called acting plant director Karl Günther to a meeting and demanded that he coordinate the dismantling and removal of the plant's machinery. Günther refused: "Our company has not yet received the full satisfaction of our financial demands on Jiangnan Cement. The machinery has still not been fully installed. No trials have been run. The formal transfer of our machines to Jiangnan Cement has not taken place. Our company is unable to write off these debts. You must act with prudence." His final remark was: "I will make a report on this to the German embassy."

The twenty-third of December 1943 was a day for weeping.

On that day, everyone, from the chairman and members of the Jiangnan board to acting plant director Karl Günther and all the Jiangnan personnel who had remained at the plant, wept quietly.

They watched as their child, which they had watchfully nurtured for eight years with their hearts' blood, was dismantled by the thieves into eight pieces and carted away.

From the site selection of 1935 to the completion of the plant in 1937 to the final confiscation in 1943, hundreds of people, high and low, had struggled for eight years and resisted the Japanese for six of those years. Ultimately, they could not escape their fate at the hands of the plunderers.

On 26 December 1943, a train, heavily laden with the crime and fury, and carrying the first batch of Jiangnan Cement equipment created by the sweat and blood of the Chinese people, sounded its whistle and departed, bound for Zhangdian in Shandong province.

That marked the end of the prologue in this drama of forcible seizures.

The next act of the drama was even more violent and still more shameless.

On 27 December, the day after the first train departed with its load of machinery, the Ministry of Industry of the Nanjing government, in great haste, issued its next Industry Work Order, Number 403, with an added Administrative Order, requiring that Jiangnan Cement turn over all machinery shown on the itemised list it attached.

The first batch of equipment had not yet been fully taken away when, on 23 April 1944, the Japanese sent up their demands for a second batch of machinery, again with a detailed itemised list. But this order once again ran into the Jiangnan Cement board's stout rejection.

On 8 May 1944, the Wang government's Ministry of Industry shamelessly handed the Jiangnan board demands for the dismantling and removal not only of the second batch of machinery but of a third batch as well. Yet again, they ran into the vigorous opposition of the Jiangnan board.

So, on 27 May, the Wang government sent yet another order to Jiangnan, commanding the company to hand over all machinery and equipment demanded by the Japanese.

On the 29th, the company sent Geng Zonggui as its representative to a negotiation with the Japanese and the Wang government. Geng said gravely that the Japanese and Wang Jingwei 'authorities' had to provide Jiangnan Cement with a very clear statement of its views, on paper, stating that the so-called 'borrowing' of the second set of machinery and equipment would be the last, and demanding that the Japanese firms involved accept full responsibility for compensating Jiangnan Cement for these so-called 'loans'.

That stern attitude aroused the ire of the Japanese.

On 6 June, the Japanese dispatched Lieutenant Colonel Tanabe Shinji, a military investigator, in uniform and with a murderous look on his face, to confront Geng Zonggui across the desk. Without sitting down, he emitted an explosive exclamation, slammed his pistol down on the negotiating table, bristled with the arrogance of the Japanese army, and said sternly: "You have to turn over all the equipment. Do not try to talk price – this is not a business deal." He went on: "I have already discovered that you have hidden some of your equipment in the mud at the bottom of your factory's pond. Jiangnan Cement must turn everything over to the Japanese side. Do not protect any of it. Your actions are those of enemies of Japan."

Under those circumstances, Geng Zonggui had to feign friendliness. "Brother Tanabe," he said, "I have studied abroad. I have seen how the white man looks down on the yellow races. I harbour great resentment in my heart. It is my hope that the Chinese and the Japanese, as brothers sharing the same parentage and the same race, can act as allies, helping each other with equal generosity, cooperating loyally with one another, to build east Asia and elevate Brother Tanabe's views to an even higher level. I trust that Brother Tanabe will agree with me."[20]

Geng Zonggui's words numbed his opposite number. Tanabe rose and shook Geng's hand and put away his pistol. Then Geng Zonggui went through the motions of nailing shut a secret chamber with wooden planks. What he stored inside, however, was not important equipment, but merely some electrical cables. Tanabe was fooled. Thus, at least a small portion of Jiangnan Cement's important equipment was protected, and the plant's machinery was never fully handed over to the Japanese.

On 3 July 1944, the Wang government's Ministry of Industry lowered yet another order on Jiangnan, this one numbered 925, commanding Jiangnan to provide the additional machinery grouped in the second and third batches, in accordance with Japanese demands.

The final shipment of Jiangnan's machinery was dismantled and taken away on 4 September. Japan had stripped the Jiangnan Cement Works clean.

Thus, in that period, the Wang Jingwei government fully satisfied Japan's demands, in total disregard of the fierce opposition from Jiangnan Cement's shareholders and board of directors, and in utter disregard for the rights and dignity of their Chinese compatriots. They imposed six separate orders on Jiangnan Cement, in the name of the Ministry of Industry of the Nanjing government, each one more severe and pressing than the one before. In the end, the Wang government called in the Japanese military to occupy the Jiangnan Cement Works, and under the watchful eyes of the Japanese armed forces the process of dismantling and removing Jiangnan Cement's machinery got underway.

As I write these words, my hands at my keyboard again fall still.

I am compelled to turn my thoughts from Jiangnan Cement to Wang Jingwei and his ilk.

As a Chinese, and the descendant of a northeast China family subjected to Japanese domination for 14 years, I have to pause my scribbling for a while and turn my glance backward in time. I must use my aged and clouded vision to try to penetrate through the mists of 70 years in order to examine closely the unprecedented phenomenon, known to the entire world, of treason among members of our own Chinese race.

This treason meant the following: in the face of the enemy, neither holding to a common hatred of the enemy nor a shared resistance to the enemy, but instead selling out our fellows with not a trace of national identification; coercing our fellows even to the point of killing them; and insanely aiding and abetting the doers of evil. Moreover, this was not an isolated case.

During Japan's occupation of China, from Aisingoro Puyi and Wang Jingwei at the top, to the countless small puppet regimes they set up everywhere, all the way down to the heads of the traditional mutual-responsibility groups known as the *bao* and the chiefs of countless rural villages, 'bought souls' were everywhere. Diligent traitors were everywhere as well. Knowledgeable people referred to this as the 'culture of treason'. Moreover, this 'culture of treason' did not arise only after Japan invaded; it was also present in the late Qing and even in earlier dynasties. These people, who sold out their nation and the interests of their people without hesitation, traded their own miserable existence for glory and wealth.

When, on 29 August 1842, the high Qing dynasty official Qiying sat on the British warship HMS Cornwallis to sign the first of the humiliating Unequal Treaties in China's modern history, the Treaty of Nanjing, he unexpectedly got himself drunk, and then sang a few Manchu songs. The next year, when he went to Hong Kong to exchange the formal instruments of ratification of the Treaty of Nanjing with the British invader Pottinger, he got drunk again. But this time, he took Pottinger's son as his own adopted son, and presented to the British the gold goblets and paintings and elegant fans that he had brought with him for the occasion. As his departure neared, he embraced Pottinger with tears in his eyes.

This disgraceful performance by the aged Qiying, including his drunkenness, was never recorded in the history books of the Chinese; it was recorded by English people on the scene at the time. It made its way into English history books, where it turned the Chinese into objects of derision. This kind of awful behaviour made later generations blush with shame.

Against this background, we can see that the behaviour of the Jiangnan Cement Company's directors, acting on the principle of refusing to ingratiate or bend before the enemy, was truly admirable.

On 3 February 1944, an article appeared in the *Liberation Daily* in Yan'an, under the title, 'A Confiscated Factory in the Occupation Zone', blasting the Japanese for their forcible seizure of Jiangnan Cement's machinery and equipment.[21]

(13)

No one felt greater pain or agitation, watching the tragic forcible stripping of the Nanjing Cement Works, than Chen Fanyou. Ten years of blood and sweat had been wasted. The investments of hundreds of people had come to naught.

This man, who had been a company director and then the factory director through the whole process of site selection, design and construction, stood in the disordered and desolate grounds of the cement works, and sighed: "All the major machinery and accessories of our Jiangnan Cement Works have been stolen, leaving nothing. This plant, which I managed through ten years of hardship, is now destroyed."

Chen Fanyou, who had made speeches on the streets in the May Fourth Movement of 1919 with the proletarian revolutionary Zhang Tailei as a patriotic young person trying to arouse the Chinese people to their nation's humiliations over the preceding half-century, came early to recognise a fundamental truth: it was a law of life and death in the natural world, the law of survival of the fittest. So, he and his father pursued the path of building China's industries to save the nation.

But ten years of total commitment were swept away with the Japanese confiscation of Jiangnan Cement.

In his grief, he could not help but cry out: "My country, my country, when will you finally arise, great and strong?"

He remembered the words of Yue Fei's famous collection of poems *The River, Full and Red:*

> My wrath bristles through my helmet,
>
> The rain stops as I stand by the rail
>
> I look up towards the sky and let loose a passionate roar
>
> At the age of thirty, my deeds are nothing but dust,
>
> My journey has taken me over eight thousand li
>
> So do not sit by idly, for young men will grow old in regret
>
> The Humiliation of Jinkang still lingers
>
> When will the pain of the Emperor's subjects ever end?

But grief alone can only beat down the weak and make the strong still stronger.

In Chen Fanyou's heart was this: "No reconciliation! No Peace! No Obedience!"

He held firmly that China would not allow Japan to run rampant forever. He believed that the Chinese people would certainly drive Japan away from China's gates and would, sooner or later, stand proud and joyful.

So, on the very evening that he left the abandoned and desolate Jiangnan Cement Works, he made a resolution: he would provide rewards to the people who had protected the plant so successfully for such a long time.

He spoke with Yuan Xinwu, the company director, and arranged for bonuses for all those who had protected the plant. The highest bonus was 25,000 Chinese yuan. He presented the bonuses as a way of acknowledging what these people had done in protecting the facility, resisting Japan and protecting the refugees. He also calculated that these people were loyal and dependable, and could become the nucleus of the workforce that would resurrect Jiangnan Cement in the future.

Not long after the Japanese stripped Jiangnan Cement of its machinery, in mid-September 1944, a surprising message arrived from Xuzhou, in northern Jiangsu. An anti-Japanese guerrilla band had annihilated 23 Japanese. These 23 Japanese were from the Nippon Keikinzoku Company, and were on their way to dismantle the Jiangnan Cement Works. One of the Japanese was named Terazaka. When they heard this news, the staff and workers at the cement works demanded just retribution. What's more, the Japanese had spent years trying to figure out how to dismantle all of Jiangnan Cement's machinery and move it to Zhangdian in Shandong province, but the fate of the Shandong plant was the same as Jiangnan Cement's – not a single ingot of aluminium was produced before the Japanese surrender on 15 August 1945, just as Jiangnan Cement had never produced a granule of cement. After the end of the war, Jiangnan Cement, which had been the place of safety for tens of thousands of Chinese refugees, became the detention centre for more than ten thousand Japanese prisoners of war.

As to the fate of Karl Günther, that presented another case of cause and effect. The Japanese emperor announced Japan's unconditional surrender on 15 August. While the Chinese were singing and dancing in the streets in celebration, the German Günther was running into colossal problems. A newspaper carried an order that all nationals of defeated nations were to be sent to designated concentration points to await repatriation to their home countries. This order left Günther completely sleepless. He remembered that when his father had returned to Germany after the first world war he was without income, without employment, nearly without food and almost left to wander the streets. After that, his father had brought the whole family back to China.

Günther hurriedly wrote an appeal to Chen Fanyou and the Jiangnan Cement directors. He wrote:

> For the past eight years, I have faced mortal danger on countless occasions in service to the company. I have borne heavy risks, and suffered many humiliations. I have served the company conscientiously, but not for the money. I have done my best for the sake of the company's future. Now my life has encountered its worst difficulties. All of my hopes lie in China. I have lived in China continuously for 25 years. In reality, all my work has been for the Chinese. Sending me back to Germany now is a death sentence. I will have no chance of working there. I ask you to support me wholeheartedly. Please explain my activities to the Chinese government. If some people are fortunate enough to be exempted from this order and are not sent back, I believe that I deserve to be one of them.[22]

With Günther's contributions in preserving the cement works and rescuing the refugees in mind, Chen and Yuan sent a company representative to the Nanjing municipal government with a paper entitled, 'An Appeal by the Jiangnan Cement Company that Karl Günther Be Retained and Not Repatriated', for presentation to the city's mayor. The mayor made a special exception and agreed that Günther and his entire family were not to be marshalled to the detention centre for repatriation. Günther's habitually stolid demeanour gave way to tears of gratitude. Dr Günther was later promoted to be an engineer in the company's chemistry laboratory. He worked there until his departure with his wife and son for Germany in December 1950.

(14)

In 1945, after the war ended, Chen Fanyou earned the praise of Dr Weng Wenhao, minister of economics and vice chairman of the Executive Yuan in the Chinese national government, in recognition of his outstanding skills and personal qualities. Weng was preparing to have Chen named as a member of the government's Resources Commission, but Chen tactfully declined that honour. As in earlier years, Chen had little ambition to become a government official; his hopes lay with his cement plants. He felt he could not turn away from the company's internal organisational problems. From the company's founding in 1935 to the end of the war, its shareholders had received not a penny of dividends. He felt a deep debt to the shareholders, to his colleagues and to the workers who had laboured with him. Determined to bring Jiangnan Cement back to life, he threw himself wholeheartedly into that task.

In the years that followed, he and his colleagues encountered almost unimaginable hardships and difficulties.

Unable to recover the company's machinery and equipment through three years of civil war, he sought to raise capital from countless sources, using patient persuasion to raise additional funds from several hundred shareholders in order to purchase once again the necessary cement production equipment from foreign firms and reinstall it all in the plant. It was like trying to cross a mountain range by leaping from mountaintop to mountaintop. But in the end, Chen Fanyou managed to crash his way through.

After the founding of new China, Chen Fanyou became the chairman of the Association of Allied Companies for the Advancement of the Cement Industry. On 17 September 1950, after 16 years of turmoil, Japanese expropriation and later reconstruction, the Jiangnan Cement Works finally began production. Chen Fanyou saw his reborn son as a 'Golden Wheel', and hoped that 'Golden Wheel' brand cement, like gold itself, would surge onward in the future.

Many eyes were moist with tears at the sight of the first production run of cement emerging from the kilns.

How many lengths of sixteen years does a person's life hold? A factory is held up for sixteen years.

Whose sin is all this?

Chen Fanyou saw more than simply the formal start of production at his factory. Through the dust, he discerned a people, bullied and humiliated by Great Powers for more than a century, finally rising strongly to its feet. He knew that, whether it be a person's or a business's destiny, it was linked tightly to the fate of the state and the nation, as a child is linked to its mother.

In the month that it started production, September 1950, Jiangnan Cement turned out 15,000 tons from its single kiln.

By 30 September of the following year, with two kilns in operation, production rose to 152,000 tons.

Jiangnan Cement's high quality and standards, as well as its low cost, endeared its product to its customers. Soviet experts dubbed it "the best cement in the Orient". Speciality cement products from Jiangnan Cement were put to use in the Yumen oilfield project in Gansu province. Until then, China had completely lacked the type of cement used in oil drilling; Jiangnan Cement filled the gap. This was of exceptional significance during the War to Resist America and Aid Korea and during the Struggle to Resist Imperialism's Blockade of China.

Chen Fanyou saw that the brand-new Chinese nation was 'poor and blank', and that every sector needed to be modernised. He donated his properties in Beijing, Tianjin, Shanghai, Nanjing and Beidaihe to the local governments, without compensation. At Lane 1547, Yan'an West Road, Shanghai alone, he transferred eleven connected foreign-style garden homes. When the War to Resist America and Aid Korea broke out, in June 1951, Chen Fanyou answered the nation's call for financial donations by having Jiangnan Cement contribute 95 million yuan. He also arranged for Jiangnan Cement to join with China Cement Company in a sizeable donation for the purchase of five airplanes to serve on the war front.

Such sincerity of heart shines through, even under the moon's beams.

But only half a year later, on 31 March 1952, a pioneer of China's cement industry, a renowned national industrialist, departed. The nation was then consumed with the Three Antis/Five Antis movement. A mentally unbalanced individual who had been criticised for some accounting error by Chen Fanyou was locked in an unresolvable conflict with Chen. This man saw the Three Antis/Five Antis movement as his opportunity, and accused Chen of absconding with national tax funds. When Chen Fanyou tried to speak with the man, the fellow turned his back on him.

For Chen Fanyou, an honourable reputation was life itself. He held to the idea that "a gentleman may kill, but he may not humiliate". Unable to clear away the lies the other party had forced upon him, he concluded that only by ending his life could he prove his innocence.

In a farewell letter to a young woman who was a member of the Jiangnan Cement Workers Union, he said: "Do not cease this great Three Antis/Five Antis movement on my account or disrupt our production."

The night of 31 March 1952 was an ordinary one. In the residence at Number 3, Lane 580, Fahua Road (now Xinhua Road), a distinguished entrepreneur wrote three valedictory letters, swallowed a large quantity of sleeping pills and ended his life at the age of 55.

In his letter to his wife and seven children, he wrote: "You are all active, forward-looking elements. I know you can all work hard to serve the nation. Except for a small portion of my assets that I set aside for your mother's maintenance, all my assets shall return to the people. I hope that you will convey my wishes to the people's government." Furthermore, he wrote his wishes for his funeral: "I want a simple cremation. Do not notify all our relatives and friends." He attached a detailed listing of his assets and a loose-leaf account book to his farewell letter.[23]

Thus departed a pioneer of China's cement industry, a master of architecture and design, a patriotic businessman, filled with love for his family, sadness over Jiangnan Cement's incomplete fulfilment, and resentment and hatred for those who slandered him. His departure was a huge loss; not only for Jiangnan Cement, but for China's entire cement industry. The slanderer gained nothing from Chen Fanyou's departure. The cement works fired him, and when he refused to leave, the two sides got into a legal conflict in court.

A noble figure in the Chinese people's industrial world was thus brought carelessly down by an insignificant and petty individual. The heavy burdens of 16 years, including all the problems brought by the Japanese menace, the chronic shortage of funds and the challenges of building his factory not once but twice, failed to crush this pioneer of China's cement industry. But in the end, he was crushed by a few slanderous words, light as a bird's feather. So strong a man was yet so frail.

On 24 January 1953, Chen Fanyou's widow, Wei Xuntong, sent a message to the people's government regarding the donation of Chen Fanyou's assets, in accordance with his will. At that time, the government had no policy regarding acceptance of donations. It was not until 1958 that Chen's children succeeded in donating all of Chen's assets to the people's government. The assets included shares and fixed-interest securities valued at 1.45 *million yuan*, as well as homes in Shanghai and Tianjin. Wei Xuntong not only donated her husband's assets to the state; she also, from her modest means, sought to realise her husband's unfulfilled charitable intentions by continuing to provide financial assistance to schools. In 1956, Wei Xuntong was invited to participate in a Congress of Representatives of the Family Members of Industrialists and Business People from the Entire Nation, and was received by Chairman Mao Zedong and other state leaders.

On a visit to the Tangshan Cement Works in 1955, Premier Zhou Enlai learned of Chen Fanyou's suicide and the injustice that led to it. He murmured: "What a pity! What a pity!"

(15)

Today, 70 years after the victorious end of the war, the two Chens, father and son, known as 'The Cement Chens' have stepped from obscurity out of the pages of history to stand before me and to pass into my pen.

Their spirit of love of country, of refusal to bend before the powerful foe, of building their enterprise in the face of immense hardship and of always struggling ahead no matter what the obstacle, deeply affected me. I think China really needs more of this kind of rock-solid, aspiring entrepreneur. The Chinese race needs more of this nationalistic spirit of taking on whatever needs doing, and never trying to be ingratiating with foreign aggressors.

Chen Fanyou departed before he should have left us. But people have not forgotten him, and they remember him in many different ways.

Today, in the Memorial Hall for the Compatriots Murdered in the Nanjing Massacre by the Japanese Invaders many photographs of the Jiangnan Cement Works are on display. Chen Fanyou is described as a 'Historical Personage'. The China Cement Industry Museum in Tangshan has preserved the Number 8 kiln that Chen Fanyou designed and whose construction Chen Fanyou had supervised in 1941. Manuscripts from the elder and younger Chens are preserved in the Shanghai Library's Collection of Manuscripts from Renowned Individuals.

During my project, my great regret was that I did not spend time with the family of Karl Günther. I could only do what I could with the written materials that I had acquired in forming my concluding remarks. After Günther took his whole family back to Germany in

1950, he held jobs in a mining or an oil company. He travelled to the Philippines, South Africa, Indonesia and Zimbabwe, working at training or management jobs. He died at the age of 84 in 1987, and his ashes were scattered at sea; there is no grave. In 2002, Günther's widow and son travelled to Nanjing for a visit at the invitation of the Nanjing Municipal Chinese People's Association for Friendship with Foreign Countries.

And what of Sindberg?

In 1938, he settled in the US, and worked as a sailor, a ship's mate and a captain. During the second world war he joined the US Merchant Marine, providing support and logistics services to the US Navy, sailing his ship through dangerous seas under enemy air attacks, amid hidden mines and submarines. For his bravery, he was honoured by US President Truman.

Sindberg's niece Marianne told me that, while he was in Nanjing, Sindberg had been in love with a Chinese girl, but that her parents opposed the relationship and they had to go their separate ways. In Marianne's seaside cottage, I looked at a loving photo of Sindberg and that young Chinese woman, with the delicate eyes and eyebrows of a southern girl. Marianne told me that Sindberg loved the girl deeply, and that she was the love of his life. He married once, when he was sailing on the Canada run in 1950, but the marriage soon ended and he never remarried. By April 1984, Sindberg had settled quietly into a retirement apartment in California, his eyes misted with age but gleaming with their familiar gaze into the far distance. He was planning to write what he called 'A Quickly Written Life of a Sailor', but he had only written a little bit of it when death took him away, aged 73. An ordinary and yet magnificent Dane thus quietly departed. His ashes were scattered at sea on 1 May 1985. A man who spent his life wandering the oceans will forever be joined with them.

When Sindberg's sister Bitten Andersen received her late

brother's effects, she found many photographs and written items and saved them. And so, a man like Schindler remained buried by the dust of history. No one knew of his great deeds; not even his sister and his niece. Sindberg had never spoken to them about what he experienced in Nanjing. His sister was only twelve when Sindberg arrived in China, and she knew nothing of what he did there.

Marianne told me that Sindberg was never publicised in the US because after the war ended the Americans supported the Japanese right wing and distanced itself from China. Sindberg lived as a visitor in the US. Given the political climate there at that time, it was better to keep quiet about what he had done in Nanjing. But history does not remain silent forever.

At Nanjing University in China, a professor named Gao Xingzu was researching the history of the War of Resistance, publishing his work entitled Researches on the War of Resistance Against Japan. He and Dai Yuanzhi, the Jiangsu province reporter for the national China Youth News, discovered the clues leading to Günther and Sindberg while investigating the Nanjing Massacre, and finally brought them to light.

In the year 2000, the first travelling exhibition from China on the Nanjing Massacre came to Aarhus in Denmark. China created this traveling exhibition because the Nanjing Massacre was a part of the history of all mankind, a gigantic catastrophe, unprecedented in the world, that bestially murdered humanity and strangled civilisation. But the impact of this catastrophe, in which the Japanese military took the lives of 300,000 Chinese compatriots, was far smaller than the impact of the atomic bombs dropped on Hiroshima and Nagasaki. All the world knew about the American atomic bombings of those cities, but precious few knew about the monstrous crimes of the Japanese forces in the Nanjing Massacre. On the Japanese political stage in particular, controlled by rightist elements, the crimes committed in Nanjing were strenuously denied. China therefore decided to tell the whole story to the world by organising the travelling exhibition on the Nanjing Massacre in an attempt to awaken and warn all mankind never to forget the immense blows that the invaders had inflicted on mankind itself. During the tour of the travelling exhibition, the Chinese embassy in Denmark published an advertisement in the Danish newspapers seeking Sindberg – a Dane who had witnessed the Nanjing Massacre. Sindberg's sister Bitten read that advertisement, and with that the 'Danish Schindler' emerged from obscurity after half a century and returned to China and the world.

Sindberg's niece Marianne donated the large collection of Sindberg's photographs, materials and the banner inscribed by the refugees that he received prior to his departure, to the Memorial Hall for the Compatriots Murdered in the Nanjing Massacre by the Japanese Invaders. Sindberg had finally returned to his Chinese 'home'.

On 17 April 2014, the memorial hall welcomed a distinguished visitor to pay her respects: Denmark's Queen Margrethe II. Accompanying the queen on her visit to China, in addition to Prince Hendrik, was Sindberg's niece Marianne. This was Marianne's sixth visit to China.

In April 2006, Marianne had brought a group of 26 friends and relatives to China, following the route that Sindberg had himself followed and matching the very footprints of their loved one. As a way of remembering her uncle, Marianne had spent four years telling the Sindberg story to Denmark's greatest master gardeners, who produced a new variety of yellow rose, symbolic of bravery, that took the name, 'Eternal Nanjing – The Sindberg Rose'.

On that visit, Marianne wanted to bring a yellow rose from Aarhus, and she asked Queen Margrethe II to personally place that rose, so symbolic of bravery and of peace, under the Tree of Peace just outside the wall of the memorial hall. There, the flowers of courage and peace could bloom in the very soil that had seen so many lives lost and so much blood spilled.

On the appointed day, both inside and outside the memorial hall, the sounds of musical instruments and voices could be heard performing *Eternally in Nanjing – Sindberg*. Denmark's Queen Margrethe said: "We cannot change history. But we can study its experiences and learn its lessons. Today as we commemorate him, we want not only to look to the past but to look to the future." The queen noted her country's feelings of pride at the discovery of 'Denmark's Schindler'. She asked Marianne why Denmark had not publicised Sindberg's life and written work.

Marianne smiled and shrugged her shoulders. She said she was preparing to write about her uncle.

Later, Marianne told me: "The reason that Denmark did not make much of my uncle at that time is that he was listed as a military draft-dodger. On his train ride to Geneva, he spotted some police. He hid himself in a hurry, thinking that the police might be about to nab him." She hoped her uncle's story might be made into a movie, like *Schindler's List*, that the whole world would come to know.

Marianne said to me: "When I saw Japanese right-wing politicians using all sorts of slippery words to conceal the realities of the Nanjing Massacre, I realised that the Japanese had not seriously repented for what happened there. Some Japanese politicians had written shallow apologies to the countries Japan had invaded, as a group, while on the other hand they supported visits to the Yasukuni Shrine and tried strenuously to cover up the evidence of the Nanjing Massacre. To speak the truth, I met over and over with Japanese politicians and scholars, introducing them to Sindberg's deeds and showing them those heartbreaking black and white photographs."

Truly, mankind cannot obliterate history. Especially such a ravaged and humiliating history; even less can it be denied. To forget it would be an offence against not only the nation, but against humanity and righteousness themselves.

In South Korea, there are four sculptures of young so-called 'comfort women'. One of them stood for a long time in front of the Japanese embassy in Seoul. The four sculptures represent the hundreds of thousands of women forced into sexual slavery by the Japanese military. They seek from the Japanese government both compensation and apology. They demand that solemn respect be paid to the people and to the women themselves.

In China, at the Memorial Hall for the Compatriots Murdered in the Nanjing Massacre by the Japanese Invaders, three hundred thousand souls cut down by the swords of the Japanese cry out in anger.

All this says to the world: "Mankind refuses to forget! All peoples, regardless of their nationality, have the right to exist. All have the duty to safeguard world peace."

The refugee camp at the Nanjing Jiangnan Cement Works.

PART 3 NOTES

(1) (吴熙祥著《洋灰世家》211页，上海人民出版社2010年版) Wu Xixiang, The Cement Family, Shanghai Renmin Chubanshe, 2010, p. 211 (Hereafter CF)

(2) Ibid., p. 214

(3) (注：戴袁支著《1937-1938：人道与暴行的见证》34页，江苏人民出版社2010年版) Dai Yuanzhi, 1937-1938: Witness to Humanity and Atrocity, Jiangsu Renmin Chubanshe, 2010, p. 34 (Hereafter HA)

(4) CF, p. 214

(5) CF, p. 219

(6) CF, p. 214

(7) HA, p. 120

(8) CF, p. 225

(9) HA, p. 126

(10) CF, p. 225

(11) HA, p. 138

(12) CF, p. 226

(13) HA, p. 180

(14) Ibid

(15) CF, p. 231

(16) Ibid., p. 233

(17) Ibid., p. 234

(18) Ibid., p.235

(19) Ibid., p. 236

(20) Ibid., p. 238
(21) Ibid., p. 237
(22) Ibid., p. 244
(23) Ibid., pp. 286-87